LITERACY

LITERACY

An Overview by Fourteen Experts

EDITED BY

Stephen R. Graubard

WITH AN INTRODUCTION BY

Jerome Bruner

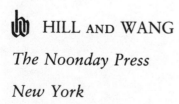 HILL AND WANG

The Noonday Press

New York

Copyright © 1991 by the American Academy of Arts and Sciences
All rights reserved
Published simultaneously in Canada by HarperCollinsCanadaLtd
Printed in the United States of America
This edition first published by The Noonday Press, 1991

Library of Congress Cataloging-in-Publication Data
Literacy: an overview by fourteen experts / edited by Stephen R.
  Graubard; with an introduction by Jerome Bruner.
      p.   cm.
    Articles originally published in the spring 1990 issue of
Dædalus, from the proceedings of the American Academy of Arts and
Sciences.
    Includes index.
    1. Literacy—United States—Congresses.   I. Graubard, Stephen
Richards.
LC151.L478   1991   302.2'244—dc20   91-3355   CIP

These articles originally appeared in the Spring 1990 issue of
Dædalus, Volume 119, Number 2, from the Proceedings of the
American Academy of Arts and Sciences.

Contents

Introduction

Jerome Bruner

W HEN AND UNDER what circumstances does illiteracy become a social, indeed, a political "problem"? Answers
to such questions will surely depend upon what we take
"literacy" to be. Is it simply being able ritually to sign your name
(as it was through so many years of American voting history), or
should we require that a literate person not only decipher but
comprehend what a piece of written text is about—grasp not simply
what is *written* but what is *meant*? If we insist upon the latter
criterion, then at what level of comprehension should we set the
line? A commonsense, pragmatic approach to all issues of this order
must obviously start with "It depends."

The first "depend" will surely be related to our national aims—
bread-and-butter objectives like America's economic competitiveness in world markets, or more idealistic ones like our sense of
what constitutes a decent and responsible life for a citizen of a
compassionate democracy. It soon becomes abundantly plain that
"literacy" is an issue that far transcends the mere mastery of reading
and writing, one that has deep roots in our national history. After
all, as the reader will soon discover in the essays that follow,
America has *always* had a "high" level of illiteracy—often considerably higher than at present. But this is the first time in our two
centuries of nationhood that it has become a political storm signal.
Raise it in just the right way and in just the right context and
elections can be won or lost, political reputations made or broken.
For there is some deep sense in which we all recognize that our
national future, even our identity, hangs on the issue of getting our
citizens to read and write better than they are now doing—and
using their literacy skills to become better informed, more educated,
and somehow more "useful" in effecting the national purpose.

Viewed historically and from a distance, the present turmoil of
debate is rather surprising. After all, less than a century and a half
ago it was even illegal in most slaveholding states to teach a slave
to read, and less than two generations ago *Brown v. Board of
Education* was hailed as a landmark decision of the Supreme Court.
The usual discussions of literacy in the pages of our daily and

weekly press are so intent upon fixing blame for our present troubles that they tend to overlook the complexities of the problems involved. Their targets are by now quite familiar: the failure (or the underfinancing) of public education, television overdosage of the young, the incompetence of teachers or our failure to attract talent into teaching for lack of an economic incentive, our failure as parents (or as a culture) to instill a respect for learning in our children, and so on down the accusatory list.

Or the discussions center on our lack of national foresight, and urge us to reverse history by a few well-directed legislative acts. We have failed, in light of these debates, to recognize our growing need for more skilled manpower and womanpower, or we have been blind in dealing with the multicultural transformation of America produced by an enormous influx of immigrants, or we have been betrayed by university intellectuals who in their vanity disdained the importance of maintaining a "culturally literate" citizenry. All of these doubtlessly reflect real issues, even if they are rhetorically exaggerated. And there are many more.

We have come to recognize that literacy is linked with virtually all aspects of our national life, public and private. It is a passport to employment and a key ingredient to a fulfilling life. And without requisite literacy (a matter still to be defined), we can neither survive as a democratic nation nor prosper as an economic power. We also know, although the recognition is still dim, that literacy is only a first step in the empowerment of *mind*, albeit a crucial one. For what we learn from history, from anthropology, and from studies of human development is that literacy not only provides access to the culture's written record, it also shapes the way in which mind is used. The written record frees mind from the burdens and risks of memory. It provides texts to reflect upon at leisure and outside the hubbub of active dialogue. Simply knowing how to write or how to decipher what has been written does not guarantee that these powers will be developed. But without these first steps, it is incomparably more difficult to achieve them. Not surprising, then, that the specific issue of literacy is so often discussed in the same breath as the more general issue of educational attainment. For of what avail is literacy if it is not used to achieve a fuller measure of mental functioning?

We have just passed through a decade of "reports," beginning with *A Nation at Risk*, the opening gun in a long decade of evaluations and assessments of American education. The level of achievement of students in our schools (as several essays in this book document vividly) is not only poor by abstract standards— fewer than a quarter can perform complex arithmetic tasks or write a comprehensible and persuasive letter of application—but poor by comparison with the performance of students in Western Europe and Japan. The United States, the richest and most educationally boastful country in the developed world, is at or close to the bottom of the league in literacy, numeracy, science, and most of the other curricular topics that can be measured comparatively—like geography.

But these reports—including the recently published *The Educational Reform Decade*, prepared by the Educational Testing Service in late 1990 in an effort to sum up what was found during the preceding decade—bring to the fore one other matter that is at least as disturbing as the overall literacy crisis itself. We are not only falling short educationally as a nation, but we are doing so in a way that threatens to create an undereducated underclass, one that falls ever farther behind, where unemployment runs impermissibly high among the less-privileged young (some four in ten African Americans between eighteen and thirty are without jobs), and where projected illiteracy levels among them foretell the likelihood of future unemployability. Our performance in regard to the rising generation of Hispanic Americans is not much better. By now, a new demographic question has arisen: are we locking an emergent underclass into urban ghettos so gripped by crime, drugs, and destructive street culture that even our best efforts at education might not prevail, even if we had the will to improve presently substandard ghetto schools, a will that seems to weaken as middle-class America moves to the suburbs?

Yet, as this excellent volume makes abundantly clear, problems of illiteracy exist at *all* levels of American society, problems that impinge upon our future as a nation, even if they are unjustly concentrated among the poor and the less privileged. It is not just minimal literacy that is at stake. If we are threatened by the emergence of an unemployable and politically alienated underclass, we are also endangered by the disappearance of what one author in this volume describes as an "amateur or lay audience of any size that writes, philosophizes, or actively engages in politics, culture, and the arts . . . not . . . for a living." Is our "leadership pool" being dried up in the shielded suburbs? And in a more general but equally compelling way, are we being smothered by our ancient and anachronistic traditions of pedagogy? Many of them arose in response to educational objectives that can only be called "archaeological." Rote methods of teaching reading, for example, stem principally from a time when the aim of instruction was to help the child recite and memorize catechism. Uniformity of instruction in each grade or class reflects an era wedded to the concept of the "melting pot," a concept whose concealment from critical scrutiny and public debate has created a vehement countermovement of ego-enhancing "ethnic education" that some fear might have the effect of leaving the relevant ethnic minorities with more short-term pride but even fewer of the intellectual skills necessary for employment. And our very method of testing the young "objectively," from whatever social class or ethnic group they may come, has tended to push American teachers toward teaching in a manner that emphasizes "right" answers in a set of multiple choices rather than cultivating thoughtful ones generated by reflection and discussion. Has the technological tail of automated and "objective" testing come to wag the entire body of education?

It is not that the nation is lacking for worthy proposals about how to eliminate illiteracy, both "high" and "low." Indeed, as essays in this volume report, the irony is that we know more about the nature of learning and about ways to improve pedagogy than any generation in the history of mankind. There has, after all, been a major "cognitive revolution" in the developed world specifically directed toward an understanding of how information is grasped and used. The full irony, perhaps, is reflected by our success in building "smart" machines in line with cognitive principles while being unable to follow the same principles in devising instruction for the young. We are being forced, finally, to recognize that tradition and history, institutional rigidities and individual predilections, are as important in the conduct of education as technical insights are into the learning process. The challenge lies not only in technical invention but in social and cultural invention as well.

I know of no single volume that presents so thoughtful, so balanced, and so broad a perspective on these crucial issues as this one. We owe a debt of gratitude to the American Academy of Arts and Sciences for having brought together this superb volume of essays on the ramifications of literacy by fourteen outstanding scholars. In their range of competencies and in their common wisdom, they are virtually unsurpassable. And I find it no small occasion for cheer that this report comes from the same august, meritocratic, and peculiarly American academy that has been performing public services of this kind uninterruptedly and with distinction for over two centuries. Unlike the "reports" of the last decade, this one is not so much a catalog of our shortcomings as a goad to thought and future action.

Jerome Bruner

LITERACY

The Roots of Literacy

David Hawkins

In the nineteenth- and twentieth-century history of childhood schooling, there is a persistent failure to understand the roots of literacy, and thus to leave them unnurtured and disparaged— a neglect which the changing character of our society has exacerbated. I briefly illustrate the kinds of in-school context for children's rich engagement with text: for the growth of literacy. Direct observation best defines the nature of this context and the adult capacities required to create and extend it.

In much of our public discussion it seems taken for granted that the written word is the essential vehicle of education—as though what is a necessary condition were also sufficient. In the dictionaries the word *literacy* itself does just such a glide. Minimally, it means the ability to read and write, to decode and encode. Maximally, it means being well read, learned; hence well educated. We may not intend this exclusive emphasis on the written word, but it is predictably going to continue to be taken that way, whatever the intent. *Literacy* leads a life of its own, especially when it gets tied up in slogans and programs. More especially, this is likely when we are confronting educational systems already committed to the belief that the learning of history, of literature, of mathematics and science is just a sort of printout in the minds of students. Unless we are emphatic in what we advocate to the contrary, I believe we will have another round of failure.

So it is education we should be talking about first, and only then the place within it for kinds and levels of literacy. For my part I wish

David Hawkins is Distinguished Professor of Philosophy, Emeritus, at the University of Colorado at Boulder.

1

to set forth, first, a statement of the aims of a general liberal education. Traditional views of liberal education are so book-centered that they leave too little room for discussing just what part in education the printed word *should* play.

With the industrial and scientific revolution it has come about that to live and work well, to be at home in this new world of ours, we need to have an education which is limited neither to the know-how of our jobs nor to our duties of citizenship. The condition of "being at home" has other dimensions than these, has all the dimensions of experience, and it is a meager and miserly puritanism that fails to recognize their import. Only with a secure home base are children freed for wonder and for exploration and enjoyment of what is around them. As children are well supported in their explorations, those from secure backgrounds are strengthened and those who lack early support and stimulation can be given their first opportunity.

Even adult curiosity flourishes only when in some good measure it has grown from a childhood that has found support for being at home in the world. Neither technical competence nor political judgment can grow, optimally, except from such a base.

This brief statement puts a heavy burden on the phrase "being at home," but the meaning is not hard to find or to expand. The antonyms are *estrangement, alienation.* Usually these words are used for persons cut off from participation, estranged from vital human associations. To be a part of life today, yet to live unacquainted with its newfound powers and the limitations that threaten it, is also to live in alienation and to have, in the end, no voice.

Literacy is, of course, necessary to a good education. But it is surely not sufficient. That denial does not get the analysis very far, however, and I wish to extend it. The sort of literacy which is even a necessary condition of good education is not an independent condition, not a sort of platform on which all else can somehow be built. The roots of literacy are many, not all of them obvious or even understood. But the metaphor of the platform is wrong. Literacy is more like a many-branching tree, one we must climb for some, but surely not all, of the fruits of education. Some of the roots of literacy lie near the surface. The mere transduction, from words written to words spoken, or the reverse, is trivially easy for human beings, though enormously difficult for computers. We make it difficult for many children by trying to program them as we program computers, ignoring their great self-programming capacities.

At a slightly deeper level lie the roots reached by the present-day diagnostic tests. Prevailing low-average scores, center focus in much current discussion, indicate some sort of cultural disability widespread in our society. They show that much of our population lacks acquaintance with many matters sampled across a wide universe, matters familiar to those presumably well educated. I use the word *acquaintance* rather than speak of knowledge or understanding; one can score pretty high without much of the latter. To serve the cause of education, one must dig for still deeper roots.

For my part, therefore, I shall look primarily at our traditions and practices of schooling, early schooling through the age of twelve or so. There is little to come after, whether of joys or miseries, that is not prefigured in these years. The ills of illiteracy may have their infective agents distributed far more widely, but in these early years of schooling they come to a focus. Therefore, we can fix the time scale of needed reform, and even a generation is not enough. To begin and then consolidate any major change, we must try to modify the whole loop, the whole cycle. First, we need to give help to the work of teachers and children today. The latter will grow up learning to become tomorrow's parents and teachers, those who may then reinitiate the cycle, at higher levels of quality and for larger numbers. Indeed, *reform* is the wrong word for the many needed changes, each in the wake of others, many still problematic. *Evolution* is the better word—for a long-term commitment of effort and inquiry. And even such an evolution, however promising at first, can all too easily be reversed. It becomes irreversible only as its consequences permeate the fabric of our institutions.

It is easy, and ungenerous, to forget that this world of schooling, as we now know it, is new. In a period of four or five generations, no more, universal publicly supported education has grown at a rate which is a good multiple of that of our population, hence always calling on the too-thin resources produced by previous efforts. The style and presuppositions of this institution, moreover, have evolved from a still older Euro-American tradition. That was a tradition in which schooling itself was mainly limited to the children of relatively educated upper economic classes. From that tradition there has been no really major change—change measured either by those needs it was once intended to serve, or by the new needs imposed by the political commitment to universal education.

The older institution of schooling, designed for a restricted and economically favored class of children, was no peach of perfection. From the records we have, and from the traditions passed on to later times, those schools were predominantly narrow, rigid, and coercive. Here and there the light did shine through, from some masters and mistresses, for some children. There was tutorial education for many of the wealthy. Here and there were the benefits of persistence for those children who by temperament or parental support could seize even mediocre schooling as their only chance. Benign apprenticeships could sometimes lead well beyond the narrow boundaries of a trade.

Through the nineteenth century and into the twentieth, as schooling gained public support and grew to offer some education for all, its failures drew increasing attention from reformers, exacerbated as these failures were by the increasing diversity of preschool backgrounds among the widening circle of its pupils.[1] This diversity needs to be spelled out. It includes that of radically varied family education and commitment to education. It includes all the conditions of social exclusion, especially—for the United States—the background of slavery. So there have been many efforts to reshape these tradition-bound institutions to some kinds of form and function more appropriate to a growing need. Beginnings of major reforms have dotted our history and have left here and there some marks of their passage, but by the measure of insistent need they are minor.

I mention just one example of an early and still prevalent failure, one surely central to the discussion. In elementary schools there has always been a great emphasis on the rudiments of literacy. But books—other than a few schoolbooks—have been in short supply. Originally, it was apparently assumed they would be available, there in the home, waiting. For children from literate backgrounds the motivation to read was taken for granted. They were presumed to know, even in the dreariest of school hours, what needs and ambitions the routine might serve. And then, as some schooling became nearly universal, those from other sorts of backgrounds were accorded the same narrow agenda. Some were from unremitting poverty, others from backgrounds that for other reasons placed little value on schooling as parents or guardians—sometimes correctly—perceived it.

Because of developmental and experiential diversity, the readiness to engage in reading and writing is always uneven among five- and six-year-olds. Correspondingly, however, there are many pathways toward that engagement, differing in substance as well as tempo, which can lead equally to success. Some children already read when they first enter school. Some almost read, and for them the schools can claim success. But the curriculum traditionally has provided only one pathway and one expected tempo as "normal." In former times the wide distribution of children's acquired skills was simply accepted as such. In more recent times, accepting instead the proposition that all should somehow stay "on track," we have evolved a subculture of specialists to whose guidance and instruction children not on track should be referred. That sort of reference, however, involves some formal procedure of diagnosis, apparently modeled after hospital staffing. This formal certification requires that some euphemistic label be attached to the child, such as "educationally disadvantaged." So far as I know, the school itself is not subject to "staffing."

In the absence of any lasting engagement in reading and writing, outside school or after leaving it, those mere reading "skills" we work so hard at can be as soon lost as acquired. As alleged reforms have come along, there are indeed more books in schools, mainly text-books unloved. Here and there are adequate school libraries, most often in prosperous neighborhoods. Our good public libraries, and teachers who use them well, have been only a very partial substitute for books in school. Imperfectly developed under one set of historical conditions, the institutions of schooling have undergone only minor restructuring through a century of radical change in those conditions and in the demands upon them. The story of books is but one indicator.

Since books themselves represent only necessary conditions of literacy, further conditions are what deeply need attention. For every text that comes alive for a child, there must be a live context—both over and above and down underneath the paper and ink. Those sorts of contexts need to come in part, of course, from his experience before he goes to school, and from beyond it. But optimally for all children, urgently for many, the school itself should provide that context. It is a rich context of material provisions, of relation to the world beyond, but also of atmosphere, association, and self-initiated work that skilled teachers can support. The major deficiency of our schools lies there. The ambiance which confronts children in school as they grow up rarely provides very much of this rich context of challenge, opportunity, and success to match the great qualitative diversity of their strengths. Nor does it readily stir the commitment for learning which, unless already severely damaged, they bring with them from the earliest years. The sense and importance of this deep relation of text and context is evident when confronted, but discussion can slide too easily past it.

The metaphoric origins of the word pair *text* and *context*, along with many other riches of our vocabulary, come from the ancient history of the weaver's trade. The elements of discourse—the words and the phrases, the transparent or translucent vehicles of meaning—are woven together to create *text*. But the text itself is always part of a larger text, a weft already woven, hence *context*. In this sense, still almost literal, each text is embedded in prior text, or at least in prior discourse. I say *discourse*, to include the oral traditions that are inseparably interwoven with the written.[2] How well a text can be assimilated depends on the reader's contextual store. It is the abundance of this store which distinguishes the art of reading, and the commitment to it, from the easy skills of decoding.

But beyond that literal meaning of *context* is another without which the whole discussion gets lost: lost, often, because so taken for granted as to be unavailable for any fresh imaginative guidance. It is of course the context of experience, above and below and beyond *all* text. But this very word *experience* cries out for context: the context that lively teachers of the young can supply; and unless one goes to observe classrooms, one cannot understand it. I choose the elementary years in part because I know them better than the secondary, but also because one can observe there the roots of literacy in nascent, branching form. One can see, above all, that children can learn to read and write with commitment and quality *just* in proportion as they are engaged with matters of importance to them, and about which at some point, they wish to write and read. When such conditions are well satisfied, almost all children can teach themselves to read and to write, big words included, and need little of the baneful "sounding out" of the traditional reading lesson. The atmosphere of lively classrooms is thus charged with all the vehicles of communication.

I select from memory a composite fourth-grade classroom. There are books in a corner, some written, published, and bound by the children. On the wall is a graph of the guinea pig's self-selected diet, posted just above her classroom territory. There is a map of birth-places—children's, their parents', and grandparents'—marked on a large world map. Two children are working on a graph of the numbers and their divisors. Two, bent on painting a potted tomato with the right leaf color, are carefully measuring and mixing pig-ments. The walls are full of children's reports of work completed. There is a computer in the corner for mathematical games and puzzles and other forms of self-help instruction. A traffic survey of children's routes to school is in progress, with a map of the school and its neighborhood, a surveyor's trundle wheel for the children to borrow for mapping and finding distances from home. In the hallway a school play is being rehearsed.

Such schools and classrooms do exist, and obviously in greater numbers than one observer can find. Yet their existence supports rather than negates my criticism of our schools. These good class-rooms are powerful demonstrations of possibility. With commit-ment, they can be evolved. They are not magic—just rare!

It is in such contexts, I think, that we can discern the deepest roots of literacy; they are just those of early education itself—not a platform but a tree, no more a precondition than a consequence. But it is not my part to expand further upon the ways good early education can (among other achievements) reduce the dominance of textbooks and workbooks and the "time on task" they steal from occupations more conducive to literacy. I wish rather to define a broader adult perspective within which this kind of criticism of our traditions of schooling may itself find context, and support. Hoping to incite support from the reflections of *Dædalus* readers, I draw it from classic texts. We are, after all, a bookish lot, suspect in principle of exaggerating the importance of text. So the texts I shall quote were addressed to others like ourselves, yet they manage to invert the metaphor I have been using, of text and context, and in so doing to help define just the style of early education our world needs.

The first of these writings is well known. It is from the pen of Galileo, a letter of reply to the criticisms of one Sarsi, criticisms directed at an account Galileo had published about the nature of comets. Galileo published this letter in his *Il Saggiatore* (The Assayer). Here is the text:

> In Sarsi I seem to discern the firm belief that in philosophizing one must support oneself upon the opinions of some celebrated author, as if our minds ought to remain completely sterile unless wedded to the reasoning of the other person. Possibly he thinks that philosophy is a book of fiction by some author, like *The Iliad* or *Orlando Furioso*, productions in which the least important thing is whether what is written there is true. Well, Sarsi, that is not how matters stand. *Philosophy is written in this grand book, the universe, which stands completely open to our gaze.*[3]

It was a dangerous act, that publication, since clearly it might lead to questions about the earlier astronomical texts which had been more or less incorporated into the received theology or, by some extension, to questions about the Scriptures themselves. Galileo is a hero for science, for the defense of those committed to the art of reading the book of nature. In the same spirit we can emphasize the need to support children's own attention and curiosity about that grand book, to the beginnings of their mastery of its grammar and syntax; so also we can emphasize the need to support their critical attention to the schoolbook. Among the authors of elementary school science texts, there are still Sarsis to be found.

What Galileo stands for is generally accepted, however imperfectly translated in early educational practice. Usually, however, it is linked only to the sciences. The concerns of early schooling in the humanities—history, literature, and the arts—are therefore still to be examined. This aspect of the curriculum, and the vitality of its introduction in the early years, has somehow been far less closely monitored than that of science and math. We have heard a great deal about the inadequacy of science education—if only for present and future research needs, job markets, citizen understanding of technological issues. It seems often to be taken for granted, however, that other educational deficiencies, if they exist, are less urgently in need of critical discussion. It is as though the growth of children's aesthetic capacities, their early cultivation of the historical, ethical, and political dimensions, their discovery and enjoyment of their own productive capacities were of secondary importance or else less in need of educational support. It may be that teachers do a better job here, less intimidated by science and math phobias implanted during their own earlier schooling. Yet classrooms which foster such engagements with the humanities at a high level are still rare—rare for the same reasons as those which foster good science are. Often it is the same classrooms which are able to do both.

I wish to make the same kind of argument for the humanities as for science, to find the same reversal of text and context—in which the book, however prized for itself, for its beauty or its depth, is still just context for some more alive and essential text—that of experience, which it can nourish and help extend, but not replace. To carry this emphasis further, then, I quote from the writing of John Donne. He was a contemporary of Galileo's, and what I shall quote was written, remarkably enough, in the same decade, possibly even during the same year as *Il Saggiatore*. It seizes upon the same metaphor, the same reversal. Perhaps it was a fresh fashion of the day among the literate. From one of Donne's sermons:

> The world is a great volume, and man the index of that Booke; even in the body of man, you may turn to the whole world.

Then again in his most famous devotion:

> All mankind is of one Author, and is one volume; when one man dies, one chapter is not torn out of the booke, but translated into a better language. . . . God's hand is in every translation; and his hand shall bind up all our scattered leaves again, for that Library where every booke shall lie open to one another . . . . [4]

The library, of course, is the Christian Kingdom of Heaven, which like the Happy Land of Shin Buddhism—all theology apart—is an image of a good society, one based on the mutual interchange of influence among its members, "open to one another." What I wish to make of it, however, is local and small-scale, nothing grandly conceived but only a description of that richly furnished classroom which I alluded to above, "charged with all the vehicles of communication." In such a world the diversity of children's strengths and needs can become manifest to a teacher for discerning and supporting their varied trajectories of learning. To each other, that same diversity brings recognition and enjoyment, sometimes a shrewd diagnosis of trouble or recognition of achievement which a busy teacher might miss. In their early readings of the book of nature, in their social play, their commitment to expression, one can see the point of those rather grand and lordly texts I have quoted, brought down to earth on a scale which permits analysis and understanding.

If the metaphor of the "booke" seems forced or strange at first, that is all the better for discussion. When one watches a young child's first efforts to pound a nail, or those of an older one committed to an accurate geometrical drawing, one doesn't describe the behavior— one *reads* it, rather, against a background observation, of familiarity with this particular child's ways of encounter and involvement. The posture, the motions of the hand and eye and facial muscles are of course observed; but they are observed in the way the words are in a text; they are transparent—or at least translucent—to a perception of the child's intent. What one observes is act or action, not merely "behavior." Of course the first intent is not to communicate, but only to seat the nail well or draw the parallels accurately; later it may become part of a request for help or even a display of competence. Only when the behavior becomes ambiguous to us do we give it attention in its own right. By the time we speak of "interpreting" it, it is in some degree opaque. So likewise, the words of a text get seen as opaque marks on paper only when the text's fluent control of our thought or imagination brings surprise or puzzlement. Teachers must be skilled in behavior reading, and children who work together must become acute at it. For the understanding of human affairs, and of themselves, this is their first language. Stories told, books read, all the expressive arts can be motivated, enjoyed, and translated from that understanding and can profoundly extend it; but they cannot of themselves create it.

Children first achieve competence. Next, they themselves recognize and enjoy its expression. Finally, they can achieve social recognition through sharing with others what they have achieved. This three-step process is just what is meant by *expression* in adult discussions of the arts. Expression among children may take the form of an art normally recognized by adults, but it is potentially present in all of their achievements. It has the quality of spontaneity, but spontaneity achieved through work and practice rather than thoughtless impulse.[5] This is why expression is a first language—often far subtler for children than anything they can say in words. Expression in this sense can convey a child's first readings of Donne's great "Booke."

When provided for in the good classrooms, children's science often has an appearance remote from the usual recitational stereotype. Taken seriously for children's learning, Galileo's injunction gives them the same privilege which he assigned to "philosophy." Man-made books may add, may indeed become indispensable, yet cannot replace the original. That this is as true for science education as for original scientific discovery may seem a dubious assertion. The knowledge of nature, once achieved, can surely be transmitted to others without repeating or paralleling the history, so often devious and slow. But this truism is beside the point. True, the classroom laboratory for elementary schools, like those for high school and college, is needed in some measure to certify that what is taught is so. The Sarsis should have no final say! That has always been the proud boast of science teachers, though the lab, with its cookbooks and exercises, does not always live up to it.

But there is a far more essential reason for students' involvement in the grand book of nature. Its language is that of the *phenomena* themselves, and it is those phenomena, closely observed, which give life and meaning to all scientific text and talk.[6] Without some deep engagement of observation and experiment, there is no growth of understanding, no enjoyment of the many novelties which lie just beyond the everyday world, no growth of the means of thought which shape choices, debate, and further learning.

From the earliest years children's innate curiosity can, at least for many, feed happily on a wide array of nature's phenomena. These involve light and color, motion and equilibrium, batteries and things they do, plants' growth and form, small animals' behavior, structures, siphons, bubbles, the sky . . . . The list of topics and classroom material which imaginative teachers can help evolve is practically endless—when they themselves are given adequate professional support. With some understanding that all those "elementary" phenomena lie close in one way or another to scientifically sacred ground, they can later become open doors to what is often, otherwise, seen only as a dark and forbidding pedagogical territory misnamed "science."[7] Understanding can also open doors to an ample and growing popular science literature which can give us all some entry to the walled cities of advanced and specialized research, so we can scale their walls and bridge their moats.

As I suggested at the outset, it is not just coincidence that the growth of public schooling has taken place over the same time period as the latter phase of the industrial revolution, the period marked by the growing impact of the sciences on technology. This period of the industrial revolution also saw a vast growth of population, and of energy consumption. A few wealthy countries gained and then lost control of the rest. Extremes of poverty in the poorest countries coincided with large pockets of economic despair even in the richest. The early educational reformers could not anticipate all this, of course. But they sensed that the older parochialisms were threatened, that the life-circuit of any citizen would traverse an ever widening territory of concern, and that this must be matched by the spread of education. What had been a culture of an elite minority must somehow evolve to become that of the majority. If they did not always understand the roots of literacy and the needed cultivation which their growth required, the ambition of the reformers was valid and their efforts have shaped us all.

Parochialisms are indeed threatened, beyond all early anticipations: those of locality and region, of social class and ethnic isolation, of national tradition. Even of "Western Civilization"? The preservation of tradition is still vital—long live the "Great Books"!—but so is the more ecumenical scrutiny of its failures and its resources for meeting world crises. These are crises which none of the great traditions of urban society ever anticipated—crises of industry, war, agriculture, massive human alienation, and the planetary ecosystem.

For any adequate comprehension of such matters within our culture—our popular culture or even much of that which considers itself high culture—there is as yet very little readiness. Since many of the human and terrestrial crises which face us develop gradually and are still ill defined and remote by the measures of inattention within daily life, there is time for an educational refocusing. The readiness to make any serious commitment to educational change must grow, however, far less slowly than ever before, and that puts greater demands on the media of literacy—the written word, first of all, and then on all the newer modes of communication, visual and digital, which have been more recently invented.

Given the premise that the educational quality of literacy is an expression, a continuation, of its experiential roots, then one must look at these newer media with that same premise in mind, now applied not just to the book, but also to the screen. Books are digital. We'd never mistake their illustrations for reality. But the screen can come alive, can impart to education much of the visual, of direct experience. That is an immense extension and potential boon—to capture the life in a drop of pond water, or the destruction of a rain forest, or to fly just above the nearby surface of the moon. But it can also blur the boundaries between reality and fiction, as some of our screens already too routinely do. There are Sarsis out there as well, in that camera-ready world. So it must be a figure of merit that in representing reality the screen should also lead us with fresh curiosity *back* to the concrete world of nature and of human affairs. Otherwise the screen confronts us with a danger far greater than any which confronted those of Galileo's time. In one classroom the teacher told me children were challenged to become serious "television critics." Along the way, as a result, they changed their viewing habits and inane recitations quite radically. In the same way, older children can be helped to cure themselves of addiction to adventure stories written by the plot machine, but the addiction to the screen comes earlier, is far stronger, and is far more effortlessly acquired.

So here again, for this extended meaning of *literacy*, one must ask for context, for the primacy, in the curriculum, of experience. Confronted with the pseudoreality of the screen, we run a greater risk than books ever presented—that the program and the script should lose the name of education, lose the deep commitment voiced in their different ways by Galileo and John Donne. To match their seventeenth-century commitment, then, here is another text, from E. B. White, one of the more lively and literate writers of our own recent past:

> Those last days! . . . Children early formed the habit of gaining all their images at second hand, by looking at a screen; they grew up believing that anything perceived directly was somehow fraudulent. . . . I think the decline in the importance of direct images dated from the year television managed to catch an eclipse of the moon. After that, nobody looked at the sky, and it was as though the moon had joined the shabby company of buskers. There was never a moment when a child, or even a man, felt free to look away from the television screen—for fear he might miss the one clue that would explain everything.[8]

14   David Hawkins

ENDNOTES

1Indeed, the essential content of the present essay can be found in a literature of reform, much of it buried, which goes back to the midnineteenth century. There is, to be sure, much chaff mixed with the wheat, but the good grain is there to be winnowed. The best reference is Lawrence A. Cremin, *The Transformation of the Schools: Progressivism in American Education, 1876–1957* (New York: Knopf, 1947).

2Do we forget the illiteracy of Homer? Storytelling is a medium and an art seemingly today outdistanced by all the others; yet it can flourish where print is absent or inconsequentially present. What Homer meant in his times is still a kind of wealth which prevails in many parts of the world. I owe to the late Sohl Thelejane of Lesotho the wry remark that the "European" schools would prosper, in tribal Africa, only when they learned to compete with tribal schools: children going, on moonlit nights, to hear stories told by grandmothers. From our own recent history one should read the transcription of Nate Shaw's autobiography, *All God's Dangers: The Life of Nate Shaw,* compiled by Theodore Rosengarten (New York: Knopf, 1974). This story was told by a man who, as one reviewer put it, was "illiterate—illiterate like Homer."

3The quotation is from *Discoveries and Opinions of Galileo,* trans. with introduction and notes by Stillman Drake (New York: Doubleday Anchor, 1957), (emphasis mine).

4The quotations are from Sermon LXXX and Devotion XVII. They are reproduced in *The Complete Poetry and Selected Prose of John Donne and the Complete Poetry of William Blake,* The Modern Library (New York: Random House, 1941).

5This formulation is that of John Dewey in his *Art as Experience* (New York: Minton, Balch and Co., 1934), chap. 2. I believe that Dewey's best writings relevant to education were often in his later works, but they are seldom, if ever, referred to in educational circles. The word *education* is not in the titles or even in any central way in his texts: *Logic, Art as Experience, Experience and Nature.* They express his maturest thought about human learning. He was a great pioneer of "cognitive psychology" still largely unrecognized in that trade.

6See my "Nature Closely Observed," *Dædalus* 112 (2) (Spring 1983): 65–89, where I have tried to spell out the meaning of the title phrase.

7There is much research, from recent years, which probes the troubled world of science teaching. Why do so many students fail to learn or soon forget? For a review see "Students' Untutored Beliefs about Natural Phenomena: Primitive Science or Common Sense?" by George L. C. Hills, *Science Education* 3 (2) (1989): 155–86. The paper contains a useful bibliography.

8E. B. White, *The Second Tree from the Corner* (New York: Harper and Brothers, 1954).

Historical Perspectives on Literacy and Schooling

Daniel P. Resnick

H ow can Americans begin to participate more *actively in the culture of language exchange and the printed word? Schooling can be a key. However, the author urges, a major change of historical course is required. School texts must shake free of the mold of catechism to encourage questioning and argument; language has to become an intellectual tool; and schooling for those age fourteen to eighteen needs to more effectively recognize the needs of both the adolescent and the workplace. Even though current practices developed for understandable historical reasons, we must acknowledge that in critical areas they reflect neither our most considered needs nor our boldest wants.*

Our current efforts to raise the standards of public literacy rest uncomfortably on a base of historically low expectations for school performance. These expectations, in turn, I shall argue, have their roots in archaic models for dealing with text, timid attitudes toward the pluralism of language, and unadaptive views of how to deal with older school-age children. Although some gains in school-based literacy can be made by incremental changes in current practice, reaching our most ambitious goals will require more dramatic challenges to the way things have been done in the past.

Daniel Resnick is Professor of History and Director of European Studies at Carnegie-Mellon University.

Current expectations for reading and writing in the school population build upon Reformation practices almost five centuries old. They were developed at a time when European populations were targets for religious conversion and political loyalties were closely tied to religious beliefs. The new technology of the printing press made text accessible to more people, but it did not remove old fears about the dangers of reading. Among established authorities, it raised those fears to higher levels. As a result, prescriptions by religious leaders for mass reading practice were fashioned to guard against subversion.

Reformation leaders of the first half of the sixteenth century wanted to educate believers, not thinkers. They did not have in mind literacy practice that would promote capacities for independent reasoning of the kind sought by Third World socially minded pedagogues like Paulo Freire or the leading edge of educational reformers, business leaders, and cognitive psychologists in our own society.[1]

If our mass readers seem passive, unadventurous, lacking in curiosity, unempowered by what and how they choose to read, and certainly unable to write, some measure of responsibility must be assigned to the early modern reading environment in which current expectations were shaped. Models for teaching and learning through texts passed from Church and home settings in the Reformation to primary schools of different kinds in the centuries that followed. Public primary school expectations for student performance have been exceedingly modest, whether in eighteenth-century Prussian and New England settings or in those of nineteenth-century France and England. Current levels of achievement for the bulk of our population meet those earlier standards.

One of the striking findings of the National Association of Educational Progress survey of the literacy of American eighteen- to twenty-four-year-olds is that virtually all (some 95 percent) command the basic skills of reading, writing, and calculating that are associated with the achievement of five to six years of primary school.[2] Our commentators have dwelled on the uncomfortable corollary—only a small portion is able to go beyond those norms. There is much to be gained, however, from exploring the primary finding—most of our adult population has the basic residues in skills and knowledge associated with completion of primary school. What does this mean?

The uncomfortable truth is that those skills are not enough to establish the foundations for reading and writing practice that meet current expectations about how adults should read, write, and reason. The focus of American mass literacy efforts, as in most developed nations over the past century and a half, has been on public schools for the young. We commonly express the focus of that experience in terms of basics—the mechanics of reading and attention to computation (addition, subtraction, multiplication, and division) in mathematics. Those basics are not rooted in the goals of higher-order thinking—conceptualizing, inferring, inventing, testing hypotheses, thinking critically—which are on the agenda of curricular reform. The model of basic learning for reading and writing has much in common instead with the Reformation pattern. Its limits are those we quite properly associate with catechism-dependent students, texts assumed to be authoritative, teachers who know all the answers, and repetition which passes as learning. Catechetical models that have come down to us from late Roman and medieval modes of oral instruction have been kept alive in many forms of Reformation and post-Reformation pedagogy.

AN ARCHAIC MODEL

Reformation catechism reflected an earlier set of misgivings about the spread of learning from texts. The Gospels and early patristic sources which, along with the Hebrew Bible, were the founding texts for the new religion, also had the power to subvert it. The authority of clerical bodies rested on an interpretation of the beliefs and practices of the early Christians. The disciples of Jesus had been missionaries who expected that the end of the world was imminent. Much of their argument, like that of Jesus, was oral, presented in terms of story and parable. The new religion was not founded on codified argument about the role of clergy, the nature of good works, and the number and efficacy of sacraments. As a result, positions on these issues— fundamental as they were—remained a matter of interpretation.

Medieval opposition to vernacular translations, lay movements, and lay preachers underlines the extent to which the texts of the Christian tradition, particularly the millenarianism of Revelation and the liberation theme of Exodus, challenged the distribution of power and the attitudes toward authority and justice in medieval societies.[3] In critical periods like the early thirteenth-century wars against the Cathars, the fears of vernacular translation were particularly strong in the clerical hierarchy. The fear within the clerical hierarchy of open access to text helps to explain the later focus on catechism as a way of controlling what was read and repeated to others.

Catechisms became the first mass primers, and a way of controlling literacy development in a period of increasingly abundant and relatively inexpensive text generated by the printing press. Luther's *Little Catechism* was translated into all the major European languages within a generation of its publication. The portion of the population introduced to reading via catechism was sizeable, particularly in areas where there were literacy campaigns. In the parishes of Lutheran Sweden in the seventeenth and eighteenth centuries, the literacy rates for men, women, and children in some parishes were as high as 80 percent. The standards for reading performance, however, were not high by contemporary standards. The text was familiar, read at home with the family, and reinforced in community settings by the liturgy of the Church. Interpretation was restricted by the constraints of a catechetical presentation of expected questions and desired and formulaic answers.[4]

The first school texts in the United States adopted, as in Europe, catechetical methods of presenting material and confirming student learning. *The New England Primer,* the most widely used early reader in American schools before the 1820s, with more than 2 million copies printed, appeared in many editions with a set of more than 100 questions and answers.[5] Elhanan Winchester's *A Political Catechism, Intended for Use of Schools in the United States of America* (1796) promised to explain the principles of liberty "by question and answer." Other texts followed suit and encouraged a pedagogy in which the reader was discouraged from behaving like an active learner who could frame questions, interpret materials, and reflect on the significance of what was presented.

Catechism, in this sense, has had a shaping influence on school traditions of both teaching and learning. Reading and writing demands both suffered, since no premium was placed on generating and inventing ideas or arguing about the truth or value of what others had written. The simple copying of portions of texts written by others—literally in copy books—took on value as writing practice. It did so because, among other reasons, the pedagogical tradition placed little value on developing the independent authority of a student's mind and placed a great deal of importance on confirming the authority of received texts. The ambivalence toward a critical and open examination of texts, so evident in the earlier Catholic tradition, was thus also expressed in Reformation and post-Reformation educational theories.

More ambitious programs for reading, writing, and using texts— both scientific-technical and humanistic—emerged only in European schools at an elite secondary level, shaping the curriculum of preparatory programs for younger children attached to academies and special schools. One French strand, for example, developed first in the seventeenth and eighteenth centuries in boarding institutions run by religious orders—Jesuit, Jansenist, and Oratorian—emphasized mathematics and science. Its curriculum and expectations remained important elements in the lycées created by Napoleon, and have become an enduring feature of French secondary education. A quite different strand, also elite but humanistic, can be traced in the Renaissance program of classical studies, which also became a major feature of lycée education. This strand, represented in England and America by the academic program of Scottish moral philosophy, is more easily recognized in our own colleges and universities as the traditional humanities program, rooted in classical languages and letters, history and philosophy.[6] It continues to shape the general education program in the liberal arts at the college level but has had little impact on what most American students actually study in high school. A large portion of American young people does not, in fact, encounter either of these historical strands of Western secondary education in their high school programs. Their preparation in an American comprehensive secondary school continues to be defined by the parameters of historically bounded primary education.

In the United States, a great variety of locally supported educational institutions flourished in the colonial and early federal period, from Sunday fee-paying and charity schools to classes in workhouses. The elementary common school that was ubiquitous by the 1850s grew out of a model of day-long weekday schooling, often fee-based, that developed in colonial times. By the 1850s, more than half of those seven to thirteen were enrolled for one or more years in some form of public schooling, although attendance was often irregular and seasonal. Best developed in New England, and less well rooted in the South, common schools offering primary education could be found by midcentury in every population center.

The growth of school enrollments between the Civil War and the turn of the century was rapid, yet largely limited to primary schools. Primary schooling became accessible throughout the society and more students attended for longer periods of time. By 1900, five years of attendance had become the modal pattern.

Years of attendance increased in the late nineteenth century, helped along by parental expectations that schooling would bring young people the opportunity to find and hold a better job, by child labor laws that raised the minimum age for holding certain kinds of employment, and by the increasing importance of white-collar skills in all sectors—transportation, industry, and agriculture, as well as the already paper-dominated fields of finance and government. By 1920, continuing through one year in a comprehensive high school had become common for most American young people and many stayed longer. The United States had moved ahead of all European countries, including Germany, the previous leader, in portion of the age group fourteen to eighteen enrolled in school.[7]

The rapidly expanding school programs, however, were driven from below by the pressure to integrate large numbers of students of different abilities and backgrounds in the same buildings. Teachers for the secondary school were often recruited from the same normal schools that prepared those heading for the primary school classes. To these new teachers, American universities did not pass on a core of humanistic and scientific learning. The university did not form them, and American secondary school teachers did not generally bond upward to the university culture. Secondary school teachers found their professional identity in associations with colleagues in primary schools.

The conditions that described American school expansion in the period 1890–1920 made it impossible to transfer the ambitions of earlier elite academic secondary programs to the new comprehensive high schools. The older academic high school had generally directed itself to the children of the more privileged classes, as the Committee of Ten of the National Education Association recognized in its description of school purposes in 1893. The function of the secondary school had been "to prepare for the duties of life that a small portion of all the children in the country . . . who show themselves able to profit by an education prolonged to the eighteenth year, and whose parents are able to support them while they remain so long at school."[8] The high school was not yet a mass institution. Of every hundred students in school at the turn of the century, only four were in a secondary school.

Students have suffered from the conditions under which the comprehensive high school emerged. Academic, general, and vocational programs were brought together in the same buildings and an unformed general program was allowed to take root and establish the school's tone and feel. A large sample of high school transcripts, as late as 1975–1981, indicated that less than half the general students who continued high school until graduation studied a foreign language, took any math beyond algebra, or studied any science beyond one year of biology. A year of American history, typing, physical education, algebra or general math, and biology, and two to three years of English made up the common elements. Students typically took no math or science in their last two years of high school.[9]

For most students, the classroom programs of secondary school maintained the limits of primary education, adding too little of the university's leaven to make it a qualitatively different experience. The textbook, *faute de mieux,* assumed an authority which the teacher often lacked. Reading and memorizing were never wholly separate. The purpose of reading was to answer the teacher's and the textbook's questions. In this sense catechetical primary school traditions entered the secondary school program. As Lauren Resnick argues in her contribution to this volume, this was not the relationship to text and author demanded by the most common forms of out-of-school literacy.

ONE LANGUAGE FOR NATION BUILDING

There were other flaws in the structural base of extended schooling, some of them tied to the cult of a single national school language. The American primary school had grown up in a society of relative cultural homogeneity. English was a native tongue, or close to it, for most of the American white population before the 1840s. At the same time, the ability of Americans to read and write was probably above that of England at the time, and, in 1840, on a level with that of Prussia.[10] It made sense to try to support the school culture with that of the home. It was relatively easy to do when the language of the home was English.

When the population began to change, some variations in this practice were introduced. From the 1840s to the 1880s, there was a great deal of dual-language public instruction in communities with active German communities (Cincinnati, Milwaukee, Indianapolis, and St. Louis were the most visible). This was, in part, an attempt to attract children of immigrants to public rather than Lutheran and Catholic German-language parochial schools, where there might be no English-language instruction at all.[11] A number of languages other than German—Norwegian, Polish, Italian, Spanish, and Czech among them—were also taught as language subjects in the elementary schools. Cincinnati, which had the largest German population outside New York, a higher ratio of German to other minorities than any other American city, and a pride in cultural innovation, took the lead. Germans, as the president of the Cincinnati school board reflected in 1853, "may well appeal to us to preserve between them that link without which all family and social ties are lost."[12]

Nonetheless, as the short life of these language experiments indicates, single-language instruction to foster a vernacular for the society, to knit its culture together, was always the first goal. Language, as Leon Botstein has argued in his contribution to this volume, has the potential to develop powerful currents of thought, to help individuals to reason about their world, but in order for it to play this role, it must be seen as an instrument for examining both private and public worlds. The English of the schools, however, was not perceived this way. It was first of all a lingua franca and a civic language that allowed children from different ethnic backgrounds to communicate about the public world in a minimal way. Second, it was the language of privileged native elites, its use reinforcing the deference to English institutions and culture. On the agenda of nation building, there was not a pedagogy of language designed to promote active and critical minds.

American schools were not alone in playing out their linguistic imperative, as examples from the history of France and Italy will illustrate. All three, and other examples can be cited, opened up fissures between school and home, imposing the language of an established elite on newer and poorer layers of society. The experience of school and language in French and Italian history illustrates this. The profusion of dialects was a strong obstacle to the creation of the modern nation-state. Everywhere in Europe, high on the agenda of schooling, one might say its "hidden curriculum" has been the creation of a common language in place of local dialects and foreign tongues. The creation of a shared mother tongue has been a major achievement of public schools. This resolution of the language question, however, alienated ethnic groups and created a gulf between the public language of the school and the language or dialect of the home. It also subordinated the linguistic task of sharpening minds to the goal of developing strong affective ties to the nation.

Formal opportunities for schooling at all levels in France were very limited under the Old Regime and remained so during the revolutionary era. On the eve of the Revolution, the clergy were the principal figures responsible for both primary and secondary schooling, and by New England or Prussian standards, they were not reaching out to a very large portion of the population. As Robert R. Palmer has indicated, primary schooling was a haphazard affair about whose conduct in the more than 30,000 communes we know very little.[13] It was regarded with great suspicion by religious and secular elites. With respect to secondary schooling, our best estimates are that no more than 2 percent of the age group twelve to twenty was enrolled. Despite the limits of these arrangements, there was not a popular demand for more access. No more than 1 percent of the rural parishes in the *cahiers de doléances,* the grievance registers submitted in 1789, voiced a demand for more schooling. Indeed, during the heated educational debates of the period 1793–1794, several speakers indicated that it would probably be necessary to force families to send their children to day or boarding schools. At that point, the state lacked the moral authority to impose such sacrifices.

To build legitimacy for the revolutionary state, however, France had to develop a language policy for the schools and invest in the creation of new institutions. One of the first actions of the revolutionary government was to examine the languages in which its citizens spoke. Under the Old Regime, the ability to sign could not guarantee what the spoken language of the signer would be like, and whether or not that spoken language existed in written form. Celtic in Brittany and Occitan or Provençal in the south were old linguistic streams. German in Alsace, Catalan in Roussillon, Italian along the Alps, and Flamand in the northeast were the result of seventeenth-century acquisitions. To these must be added countless dialects.

The Abbé Grégoire, then a priest and deputy to the National Assembly, made a survey in 1790 of what the French were reading, and in what language. He found it unacceptable that French was the language of the people in only one of every six departments. His reports directed attention to "the need and methods for extinguishing *patois* and universalizing the use of the French language."[14] The debates of this period point out the importance of the language issue in the making of national consciousness. Debate centered on whether or not the language of instruction should be French alone in primary schools that were to receive state support. A single national language carried the day in debate. Primary education, however, did not become universal, compulsory, and free until the 1880s. History textbooks in the French language became an important medium for building loyalty to the nation-state. Carlton Hayes, who reviewed more than a hundred of these books in the four decades before the First World War, found that their goal was to present the nation so that schoolchildren would "love it with emotional pride and religious zeal."[15] At the primary level, it was not a program to foster diversity or build independent minds.

Dialects in Italy were also targeted for extinction by nation builders. Estimates are that in the early 1860s, not more than 2 to 3 percent of the Italian population would have been able to understand Italian, which was still the language of the Tuscan region. The situation was perhaps less complex in France, but Eugen Weber estimates that, at about this time, with great internal variation, less than half the French population spoke French. What they spoke, in French and other language families, was a dialect.[16] Dialects encourage diversity and community, but they can undermine political unity. Dialects, as distinct from languages, the sociolinguist Gianrenzo Clivio argues, lack the authority of the nation-state: "from a strictly linguistic point of view . . . a language is a dialect that has an army and a navy and an air force; that is the only difference really from a linguistic point of view."[17] Public schooling in these nations lies on the ruins of buried dialects. Native language, which might have served as a bridge to home and community, was seen as a social and a national challenge to the state.

What distinguished American school-language development from that of France, Italy, and other European nations was the extent to which the school language became preoccupying, excluding attention to any foreign tongue. With rare exceptions, like the nineteenth-century German school programs discussed above, the opportunities for second-language learning have been limited to those in high school preparing to meet college entrance requirements. Since not all colleges and universities require study of a foreign language, only some in the precollege program will prepare in this way. Certainly most students in the general program have not studied a foreign language.

Attention to only a single language, which is spoken and read, more rarely written—all in the mold of school literacy—has deprived students of comfortable access to language as a way of reflecting on the culture of produced experience. It has cut students off from the pluralism of world culture and denied them a sense of powerfulness in approaching societies very different from their own. It is common for eleven- and twelve-year-olds in other nations to begin the study of second languages, even if they have no ambitions beyond a few more years of secondary school. The absence of second-language study in American schools contributes to the parochial nature of our schooling.

A WEAK DESIGN FOR ADOLESCENT SCHOOLING

A third weakness in the structure of extended public education was its poor mesh with the needs of a youth cohort fourteen to eighteen, halfway between the home and the workplace. Young people in this age group began to enter the schools in larger numbers at the end of the century. Work opportunities that had been available earlier for young people were disappearing; there were declining opportunities for apprenticeships. American adolescents were moving out of the work force and into the schools more rapidly than their European peers in the period 1870–1920.[18] Apprenticeship opportunities seem to have dried up more rapidly here as the scale of industry grew larger and more mechanized. The influx of immigrants, moreover, made stronger and older men more likely choices for positions in industry.

The schools responded to this change in the job market, welcoming the influx of new students. Professional educators and teachers thought they knew what the new entrants were capable of, and it was not sustained work of an intellectual character. On the basis of jobs held by parents and the language spoken in the home, young people were directed to school tracks where faculty had low expectations for their performance. Their primary school programs were extended, while more demanding courses in history, science, and foreign languages were reserved for college preparatory students.

Public school vocational education gained a foothold in 1917 with the passage of the Smith-Hughes Act.[19] Although the portion of those who took some or all of their courses in the vocational track grew in the next two decades, only a small minority of students were in full-time vocational programs and stayed on to graduate. Most remained in the general programs and were likely to drop out after a year or two. No more than 20 percent of those who entered high school were graduating in 1920, and only the Great Depression, which removed most of the opportunities for youth employment, was able to push the portion of graduates to 50 percent by 1940.

Could schools replace the workplace as a socializer and an educator of young people? Industrial workplaces had been sites where older workers could influence the behavior of young people. Schools were a problematic substitute for the social governance and apprenticed learning which those workshops and industries had provided. In place of more numerous older workers, there were vastly outnumbered teachers who had no pay envelope to offer and whose promise of skills and knowledge that would be useful in the workplace had little credibility.

Focus on social integration of the adolescent postponed questions about the school as a substitute for the workplace. The frenzy of school construction and expansion 1870–1930, the commitment to expansion of an emerging profession of school administrators, and the embrace by teacher-training programs of their expanded mission made enthusiasm a substitute for reflection. In any case, within our social system and market economy there was no other place than school for young people to go. Families, moreover, were for it. Family resistance to schooling had been conquered in the nineteenth century.

Family resistance emerges from historical research on school attendance as the single most important reason for early school leaving.[20] In the rural agricultural economy, as in the industrializing cities during the first half of the nineteenth century, extended obligatory primary schooling had met with strong resistance. By the end of the nineteenth century, however, that situation had changed. Even before the introduction of compulsory schooling laws in England and France, attendance rose rapidly. Thus, at least five years before the introduction of such legislation in France in the early 1880s, there was nearly universal attendance for some years by those in the age group six to thirteen. Although the reasons for this growth differ from region to region, almost everywhere there is evidence that the resistance of parents to public schooling had disappeared. A different kind of economy and different sorts of parental expectations had developed. A place had been made for public schooling in the moral economy of industrial societies.

Although formal family resistance had been overcome, the resistance of young people had not. The poor mesh of the academic side of school with the needs and expectations of adolescents expressed itself in many ways. The first casualty was the emotional response of students. A number of studies have noted the low mobilization of energy for high school courses, particularly evident in the general track. Boredom, tardiness, absence, and dropping out are part of a common pattern among those fifteen and older.[21] When Richard Marius reported in *Dædalus* less than a decade ago on the public schools he had visited, he commented on classrooms that teachers had turned into a "wasteland of tedium."[22] This indifference was not limited to those in the general program. A low level of directed emotional energy plays some role in the striking underachievement, by international standards, of American college-bound students.

The college bound also share in the youth culture, but they and their parents generally know why they are in school. They are there to meet the requirements for entry into college, and they spend more time on their studies. But they are not pushed to achieve. Entrance to good secondary schools is a function of where their parents can afford to live, not a record of earlier school achievement. The international comparisons of science and math indicate the collective deficit of the American college bound.[23] Only a small portion of the group preparing for college has been pushed to achieve the most of which they are capable.

The schooling arrangements we have for fourteen- to eighteen-year-olds have evolved without a clear sense of design. They took form in the social environment of the period 1870–1920 and have evolved very little since. Programs were created to socialize adolescents who could not enter the work force and to permit their delayed entry on favorable terms. Given the inability of the teacher to control the job market and the lack of a reward structure to encourage academic achievement, it is not surprising that the adolescent turned the tables and socialized the school.

The postwar baby boom, once it reached the high schools, created the foundation for a more powerful youth culture. The buying power of the young cohort made it the prey of cultural agents far removed from the precincts of the high school. Music, clothes, and cars—all possessed and paraded—were the cultural markers. At the same time, the moral authority of establishment institutions was degraded by violence at home and abroad. Teachers bought peace by tacit contracts.[24] If students respected the authority of the teacher to make assignments and keep order, teachers would not make too much fuss about the quality of what was produced. The contract is still in place.

High school has been the terminal educational experience for most of the American adult population. We have to worry about the way in which high school has shaped the taste for learning about the world and about the sense of self and language it has created. The reward structure of the high school does not lead young people to approach academic learning with the same intensity they direct to sports, other extracurricular activities, and out-of-school work. It does not develop a taste for independent study, for reading as a way to raise and answer questions about their world, much less for writing as a way of developing ideas and persuading others.

The forms of full-time schooling were not designed to appeal to the adolescent. They were developed for the mass of younger children and an elite among older youth. That does not mean that these forms cannot succeed with adolescents. Effective solutions, however, mean replacing the kinds of school experiences young people find boring with those that capture attention. It requires, as Mihaly Csikszentmihalyi has argued, "a seduction."[25] The features of that seduction are likely to require a closer relationship to the world of real work.

In a real work environment, as Lauren Resnick has argued, labor involves tools, cooperation, and tangible rewards. Of all the things students could be doing in school that would mirror the variety of performances demanded in the working world, they are doing little more than taking quizzes and tests. Rarely do they write papers or take on other projects, and even then they do so only for the teachers' eyes. Seldom is there an effort to encourage students to keep records of their work that can be shared with others. Employers of high school graduates and dropouts, moreover, have shown little interest in the achievement of general and vocational students. According to one survey, fewer than one in seven of those employers ask to look at transcripts of high school grades.[26] This disjuncture has had a very negative effect on motivation and achievement.

The adult literacy problem in a number of European nations has been traced to similar kinds of problems in the expansion of schooling for adolescents. When France made the decision in the late 1950s to raise the minimum school-leaving age to sixteen, young people who would have left school at fourteen or fifteen had to be absorbed into existing structures. Complaints were voiced, as they had not been before, about the widespread illiteracy of the school population.[27] This was true as well for English secondary school expansion in the same period, as the Black Papers protesting the lowering of standards indicate. These protests were loudest where there was a strong effort to create a comprehensive secondary school; there earlier elite standards were applied to more broadly representative student bodies. The protests were least audible in nations like West Germany, where early school leaving through apprenticeship programs was encouraged and where separate academic secondary schools were maintained.

IMPROVING ON THE PAST

America's response to the literacy-qua-schooling problem will require acknowledgment of the special conditions under which her school expansion proceeded. Catechism had an undeniable influence on American and European primary school programs. With respect to secondary schooling, the influence of catechetical models was far greater in America than in Europe. The catechetical mold of education, in which learning takes place on the basis of established questions and answers, was also reinforced in this country by the institutionalization in the 1920s of standardized testing. Examinations which required the elaboration of student-generated answers remained a more common element in European school assessment. To a large extent, steps taken to widen the ways in which school performance is evaluated hold the greatest promise of moving beyond the narrowness of current school practices. New forms of assessment can influence the content of textbooks and shape what is taught and learned in the classroom.

With respect to language policy, our nation may now be about to moderate somewhat its historic reliance on a single common school language. We are unlikely to see a return to the bilingual cultural programs that flourished in a few sites in the last two-thirds of the nineteenth century, but we can expect to see more focus on second-language learning throughout the school years. The impetus for this is external and economic, translated for the public through the initiatives of governors and other political leaders, and precisely because of this locus, may have the greatest potential for reaching out to the school programs of the nation's more than 15,000 school districts. Whether this will have the effect of promoting more reflection on language, it is difficult to say. Joined with the increasing emphasis on written English communication in the schools, however, this focus has some promise of developing a sense of language as a key to both thought and culture.

As we seek to move literacy expectations beyond a rudimentary ability to read, write, and calculate, the history of mass schooling indicates some of the obstacles in our path. Future attainments are constrained by the practice of earlier centuries: modest instructional goals, textbooks in the form of religious primers, language used primarily to create a civic culture, and mass schooling mainly for the primary years. The classroom practices and school structures of earlier generations are clearly unsuited to our ambitious goals. A study of the past can help us to appreciate the distance we need to place between our current way station and the peaks we seek to conquer.

ENDNOTES

[1]The current reform agenda with its cognitive underpinning is well described in Lauren B. Resnick, *Education and Learning to Think* (Washington, D.C.: National Academy Press, 1987).

[2]Irwin. S. Kirsch and Ann Jungeblut, *Literacy: Profiles of America's Young Adults,* National Assessment of Educational Progress, Report No. 16-PL-02 (Princeton, N.J.: Educational Testing Service, 1986).

[3]See Richard Landes, "Literacy and the Origins of Inquisitorial Christianity," in Andrew E. Barnes and Peter N. Stearns, eds., *Social History and Issues in Human Consciousness* (New York: New York University Press, 1989), 137–70.

[4]Daniel P. and Lauren B. Resnick, "The Nature of Literacy: An Historical Explanation," *Harvard Educational Review* 47 (3) (August 1977): 370–85; Egil Johansson, "Literacy Campaigns in Sweden," in Robert F. Arnove and Harvey J. Graff, eds., *National Literacy Campaigns: Historical and Comparative Perspectives* (New York: Plenum Press, 1987), 65–98.

[5]Charles Carpenter, *History of American Schoolbooks* (Philadelphia: University of Pennsylvania, 1963).

[6]Sheldon Rothblatt, in *Tradition and Change in English Liberal Education* (London: Faber & Faber, 1976), examines the migration of classical and liberal education.

[7]Arnold Heidenheimer, "The Politics of Public Education, Health and Welfare in the U.S. and Western Europe: How Growth and Reform Potentials Have Differed," *British Journal of Political Science* 3 (3) (July 1973): 319–22.

[8]Cited in David Tyack, *The One Best System: A History of American Urban Education* (Cambridge: Harvard University Press, 1978), 58.

[9]See Clifford Adelman, *Devaluation, Diffusion and the College Connection: A Study of High School Transcripts, 1964–1981* (Washington, D.C.: National Commission on Excellence in Education, 1982); Ian Westbury, "Who Can Be Taught What? General Education in the Secondary School," in *Cultural Literacy and the Idea of General Education,* Eighty-seventh Yearbook of the National Society for the Study of Education, Part II, Ian Westbury and Alan C. Purves, eds. (Chicago: University of Chicago Press, 1988), 171–97.

[10]Albert Fishlow, "Levels of Nineteenth Century Investment in Education," *Journal of Economic History* 26 (4) (December 1966): 418–36.

[11]Steven L. Schlossman, "Is There an American Tradition of Bilingual Education? German in the Public Elementary Schools, 1840–1919," *American Journal of Education* 91 (2) (February 1983): 140–86.

[12]Cited in Tyack, *One Best System,* 107. The decline in German immigration, nativist opposition, and later strong anti-German feelings during wartime brought this experiment to an end.

[13]Robert R. Palmer, *The Improvement of Humanity* (Princeton: Princeton University Press, 1985), esp. 8–12.

[14]See Palmer, *The Improvement of Humanity,* esp. 187–90. Michel de Certeau, Dominique Julia, and Jacques Revel, *Une politique de la langue: La Révolution française et les patois: L'Enquête de Grégoire* (Paris: Gallimard, 1975), 300–17, contains Grégoire's report. On Grégoire's survey of peasant reading tastes, see Roger Chartier, *Cultural History: Between Practices and Representations* (Ithaca: Cornell University Press, 1988), 151–71.

32   Daniel P. Resnick

[15]Carlton J. H. Hayes, *France: A Nation of Patriots* (New York: New York University Press, 1930), 52.

[16]Eugen Weber, *Peasants into Frenchmen: The Modernization of Rural France, 1870–1914* (Stanford: Stanford University Press, 1976), 67–94.

[17]Quoted in Jonathan Steinberg, "The Historian and the Questione Della Lingua," in Peter Burke and R. Porter, *The Social History of Language* (Cambridge: Cambridge University Press, 1987), 199.

[18]John Modell and Madeline Goodman, "The History of Adolescence and Adolescents," in Glen Elliot and Shirley Feldman, eds., *At the Threshold: The Developing Adolescent* (Cambridge: Harvard University Press, 1990).

[19]See the contributions by Larry Cuban, Joseph Kett et al., in Harvey Kantor and David B. Tyack, eds., *Work, Youth and Schooling: Historical Perspectives on Vocationalism in American Education* (Stanford: Stanford University Press, 1982).

[20]Mary Jo Maynes, *Schooling in Western Europe* (Albany: State University of New York Press, 1985), 83–102.

[21]John Bishop, "Why the Apathy in American High Schools?" in *Educational Researcher* 18 (1) (January–February 1989): 6–10, 42.

[22]Richard Marius, "Unscientific Ruminations," in *Dædalus* 112 (3) (Summer 1983): 162.

[23]International Association for the Evaluation of Educational Achievement, *Science Achievement in Seventeen Nations* (New York: Pergamon Press, 1988).

[24]Ernest L. Boyer, *High School: A Report on Secondary Education in America* (New York: Harper & Row, 1983).

[25]Mihaly Csikszentmihalyi and Reed Larson, *Being Adolescent* (New York: Basic Books, 1984), 205.

[26]Bishop, 8.

[27]See, for example, *La France illettrée* (Paris: Editions du Seuil, 1988). The school problem stands independently of the language problem introduced by immigrants and temporary workers.

Reconciling the Literacies of Generations
William Damon

Too *many students are turning away from the offerings of the American classroom. The disengaged youth are by no means functionally illiterate; rather, the literacies of the generations have become disconnected. The skills and knowledge that are valued by many of today's young bear little resemblance to the skills and knowledge that would serve them best. To restore the literacies link, our schools must acquire a surer feel for contemporary cultural conditions and craft academic programs that stimulate the intellectual and moral development of young people.*

It cannot be doubted that in the United States the instruction of the people powerfully contributes to the support of the democratic republic; and such must always be the case, I believe, where the instruction which enlightens the understanding is not separated from the moral education which amends the heart.
                                        —Alexis de Tocqueville
                                        Democracy in America

In the past decade, we Americans have experienced a crisis of confidence in our schools. Waves of critical reports have been followed by calls for radical reform and restructuring, each successive call seemingly more desperate than the last. The desperation goes to the heart of both our private and our public concerns. We naturally

William Damon is Professor of Education and Chair of the Department of Education at Brown University.

worry about students who never learn to write a coherent paragraph or to distinguish north from south on a simple map. But we also worry about the society that these students inevitably will inherit.

The quality of life within any society relies on the educational level of its members. But a republic is especially sensitive in this regard, because the very instruments of democratic governance derive directly from the citizenry's informed participation. A republic that loses large portions of its citizenry to civic ignorance and disinterest is as troubled as a school system that loses large portions of its students to illiteracy and early withdrawal. In contemporary America, we see warning signs of both. It is likely that the two problems are linked. It is certain that the two make an unholy combination in a democracy like ours, where full citizenship is universally granted and expected.

A poorly schooled, apathetic generation will not acquire the knowledge or values needed to make their democracy function as it should. As for the members of such a handicapped generation, how would they themselves get by? It is widely agreed that certain core literacy skills are necessary for optimal functioning in a civilized world: hence the common notion of "functional literacy." Are we right to fear the twin specters of civic and functional illiteracy in our coming generations? What, if anything, can we do about illiteracy?

I

In the days of tight-knit extended families, there was a piece of comforting advice that the elderly would pass along to nervous new parents: kids are resilient. For our current epoch, there are two things worth noting about this bit of traditional wisdom. First, children generally will find a way to adapt to their world. In fact, they often do so with astonishing skill and toughness. Second, in our habitual underestimation of our own offspring, we need to be reminded of this. It is an odd but true phenomenon that we do need to be so reminded, that we adults do not always take the adaptive intelligence of our own species' young as a matter of course.

If we can indeed keep ourselves reminded that children will adapt intelligently to their worlds, we shall see that our widespread concerns about the functional literacy of today's youth profitably may be refocused. For we shall start with the realization that children generally do acquire the functional skills that they perceive they need. The questions then become not whether children will become functionally literate; nor why they succeed or fail at becoming so; nor even how we can make them more so. Rather, the important questions become: What is the nature of the literacies that today's children are acquiring? What functions do the particular capabilities of today's children serve? Toward what goals, perceived or otherwise, are children's ineluctable adaptive skills now being directed?

Our real agenda in asking such questions, of course, must be that we ourselves are committed to certain types of literacy as well as to the personal and societal goals served by these types. Naturally, we wish to pass on these commitments to the next generation and wish to discourage other, conflicting commitments. Nor are our own commitments at all arbitrary. We can readily recognize, for example, the particular reading, writing, and arithmetic skills necessary for employability in our professional and corporate settings. So we define these as essential functional skills and expect our young to acquire them. As a socialization goal, this is both predictable and legitimate. But as an expectation, it is realistic only insofar as the young share our perceptions of what is functional in the world that they are growing into.

In Brazil, there are young children who spend most of their waking hours selling candy on the street.[1] Many of these children have little or no schooling and lack certain formal literacy and numeracy skills usually learned in school. For example, they are unable to decipher the standard orthography of the written culture. With respect to numeracy, this means that these children cannot read or represent large numeric values in the conventional multidigit manner of modern arithmetic. This would seem to put them at a grave disadvantage when it comes to making accurate calculations of any size.

In fact, however, unschooled Brazilian candy sellers as young as eight continually perform complex numeric calculations that might make our grown-up heads spin. Moreover, they do so with impressive speed and accuracy. Consider, first, the difficulty of the quantitative problems that these children routinely face in their daily work. To begin with, the candy sellers must buy large boxes of assorted candies at wholesale prices from outlet stores. Then the children must sort the candies into types, subdivide the amounts, and mark up the prices for their own retail street sales. This all requires a working understanding of ratios and fractions, a conceptual skill that elementary-age children often have great trouble mastering, even in the best educational circumstances.[2]

Yet in the candy sellers' daily jobs there is not only this substantial numeric demand but also a further quantitative perversity to be taken into account: Brazil's triple-digit inflation rate. Because some weeks pass between purchase and completed sales of the candy, the seller must factor the decline of the cruzeiro's purchasing power into the pricing decision. This requires a constant readjustment of the final price over the term of the deal. Of course each deal calls for a new calculation, since Brazil's rate of inflation fluctuates over time. When all this is figured in, the candy seller then must arrive at a pricing arrangement that is conveniently packaged in round numbers, such as two candy bars for Cr500 or five for Cr1,000. The cycle is completed when the candy is all sold and the seller shops for more supplies. Among other things, this final task requires the seller to keep track of the candy type in most demand, comparison shop among as many as thirty outlet store choices, and perhaps even haggle a bit to get the best wholesale price, again with the inflation rate constantly in mind.

Not only do the young candy sellers master their formidable mathematical tasks, but they do so without the aid of their culture's conventional symbol system. This precise type of orthographic ignorance, incidently, would place these children squarely in the category of the numerically "illiterate" by the standards of most official surveys.[3] How, we might ask, do these young children overcome this handicap?

The first thing to realize is that their "illiteracy" does not seem to be much of a handicap for the quite complex mathematics that these children need to perform. When compared with candy sellers who have some schooling, and thus who have a working acquaintance with the standard orthography, unschooled candy sellers are just as skilled at computing currency values, carrying out arithmetic operations, and manipulating ratios. What is more, the practice of selling candy in itself—without the aid of formal numeric reading and recording skills—enables children to acquire a working understanding of key mathematical concepts. When compared with both rural and urban nonsellers, the candy-selling children performed significantly better on a broad range of arithmetic tasks, and far better on some very challenging ratio comprehension tasks. This is a striking comparison, since the arithmetic and ratio problems are at the heart of mathematical logic, which in turn stands as a key contributor to critical thinking skills.

Since the young Brazilian candy sellers clearly are not incapacitated by their lack of a written numeric symbol system, what strategies do they use to solve their difficult daily mathematics tasks? Like many "primitive" groups studied by anthropologists, these children rely on concrete and figurative number-manipulation strategies for their calculations. They mentally group and regroup numeric terms according to the objects and spatial arrays associated with the terms and then perform systematic arithmetical operations on these terms.

For example, a child named Marcos with barely a first-grade education is able to determine a retail value for subdivided units of large boxes of wholesale candy by assigning sequenced numeric values to groups of candy located in different parts of the large box. Marcos begins by surmising that he will offer to sell three candy bars for Cr1,000. How will he check to see whether this price will make him a profit? If the large box contains ten groups of three candy bars each, Marcos gives the two groups on the leftmost section of the large box a value of Cr2,000, the next group a value of Cr4,000, and so on until he figures that the rightmost group has a value of Cr10,000. This he takes as the retail value of the whole large box. He knows that he paid Cr8,000 wholesale for the large box, or the value that he has assigned the next-to-last grouping. So his profit will be the price he receives for the last two groups of three he sells, or Cr2,000. He then must evaluate this final figure in light of the current inflation rate, a process that sets off another set of complex mental grouping and regrouping operations.[4]

Such strategies clearly are well adapted to the task at hand, as they are to any number of other essential computation functions found in nontechnological societies.[5] Brazilian candy sellers, therefore, acquire the numeracy skills that they need to adapt to their present world, despite a numeric illiteracy in the conventional sense of the term. Is it not reasonable to call what they have achieved a genuinely "functional" numeracy?

To place it in proper perspective, however, there are two further conclusions that must be stated about candy sellers' math. First, the skills that these children have acquired are well adapted not only to selling candy on the street but also to elementary school math in some of its most sophisticated reaches. As noted, manipulating ratios is among the most elusive of early math skills and a central indicator of sound conceptual understanding. So these young children have claims not just to a clever bag of streetwise tricks but to some facets of true mathematical intelligence. But we should not go too far in glorifying the quality of their knowledge. The second conclusion that must be stated is that these children's ignorance of the standard orthography is indeed a real handicap, even if it does not put them at a disadvantage in the worlds of street candy selling or related elementary school tasks. It is a handicap because facility with written symbol systems is essential for further progress into algebra, geometry, calculus, and all other forms of higher math.

As social scientists have uncovered this and other types of skillful functioning among "primitive" peoples (from children to native groups), there has been a tendency to romanticize the unschooled skill and to level the differences between it and the skills available through formal instruction. This understandable tendency comes as a reaction to an implicit devaluation of nontechnological modes of functioning in the works of many social scientists who have not carefully studied such modes. Still, it serves no useful purpose to imbue unschooled forms of knowledge with a sentimental gloss. Just as we should not lose sight of the remarkable adaptiveness of some unschooled abilities, we also must guard against expecting more from them than they can deliver.

All children acquire intellectual skills from their own experience outside school. These skills bring with them their own forms of literacy and numeracy, forms that inevitably will be adaptive to the child's own social situation—even where the situation requires some impressive facility with words or numbers, as in the case of the young Brazilian candy seller. But, although such directly acquired skills may overlap with some of those taught in school, they are not the same thing. In fact, the two types of knowledge can stand in a variety of distinct relations to one another, from mutual support to uneasy tension and conflict.

The distinction between unschooled and schooled knowledge has long been a familiar one to developmental psychologists. Vygotsky wrote of the gap between what he called "spontaneous" and "scientific" concepts.[6] Spontaneous ones arise directly from a child's own experience and are fully imbued with the vivid meaning and flavor of that experience. Scientific ones—among which Vygotsky included social scientific, literary, and historical ideas as well as concepts from the natural sciences—are learned as part of a systematic package of formal instruction. Whereas we might expect children to have more facility with spontaneous concepts, we cannot expect that the full range and complexity of higher-order thinking can be learned directly, in piecemeal fashion, from one's own experience. The advantage of schooling is that it gives a culture the opportunity to impart "scientific" ideas (in the broad Vygotskian sense of the term) coherently and systematically to its young.

There is no question that the ideal learning environment combines the immediacy and excitement of the child's spontaneous concepts with all the rigorous standards and complexity of the culture's more formal ones. Creating such environments has been the goal of educational innovation all through the modern era.[7] But we probably are no closer to such an ideal in our schools now than we have ever been. So we cannot simply stop at the easy old conclusion that schooled learning needs to be more tightly integrated with unschooled skills and interests. We must ask why this goal eludes us, perennially but especially today.

This requires us to examine our standards for the legacy of skills and ideas that we wish to impart to our children. Moreover, we must examine these standards in relation to the skills and ideas that children themselves are generating as they adapt to the world as they find it. Finally, we must examine our standards as objectively as possible, without being unduly influenced by the idiosyncrasies of our own experience. In other words, we must determine, apart from any accidental inclinations that history has bestowed on us or them, the extent to which the standards that we hold for our children's learning establish a rational program for their intellectual futures.

Examining our standards in this manner will make us quickly aware that most serious educational issues go beyond the matter of intellectual skills into the realm of moral and cultural values. Our gravest misgivings will always focus on values rather than competence. It is one thing to wonder whether children's spending time selling candy on the street will put them at a math advantage or disadvantage to their more schooled peers. It is quite another thing when the street substance that is bought, sold, and exquisitely quantified is crack instead of candy. At such points our values must come into play. In contemporary America, unfortunately, children selling crack on the streets is no idle academic example. The intensity of our concern in such cases is magnified far beyond any worries about these children's intellectual skills.

Crack dealing is a clear enough case. The destructiveness and criminality of the activity itself poses no real moral question for us as responsible adults. Even if studies were to show that this was the world's best forum for children to learn and practice math in, we must still unequivocally oppose it. But our values also become engaged in a host of less straightforward choices for our children's schooling. The heated debates that constantly swirl around these choices leave no doubt that our expectations for cultural transmission via school learning include more than the fostering of the three Rs.

Many urban communities throughout the United States teach math to beginning Hispanic students in their native language. Studies have shown that children exposed to such programs perform better on math achievement tests both before and after their conversion to English than children who have had to struggle through early math instruction in a language that is barely comprehensible to them.[8] Yet in many of our communities, teaching math in Spanish to Hispanic children remains fiercely controversial. Objections persist apart from all evidence concerning the academic merits of the programs. These objections are directed more to the cultural than to the intellectual effects of bilingualism. They have far more to do with nationalistic values than with competency instruction. As an aside, it is noteworthy that, in the objectors' view, the nation's future is seen as more imperiled by an imagined loss of its cultural identity than by the real and present danger of a mathematically illiterate populace.

Consider too the case of slang, alternative dialects, and other forms of nonstandard English. Practically every English teacher will correct children when "street talk" intrudes into the classroom. This sets up an implicit standard for linguistic competence, a standard that is used to evaluate children and assess their educational potential. We might well defend this standard on the ground that it reflects the kind of speech needed for the children's future employability and general adaptation to our society. The children, of course, may not see it this way. They may be more interested in picking up the skills that they need to function in their own social worlds. A gap then can be created between a child's present literacy skills and our beliefs about what constitutes a literacy that will serve that child well in the future. We may try to close this gap through persuasion, instruction, or coercion, but we may not often be very successful. The continued gap cries out for an interpretation.

Among professional educators, there has been a tendency to interpret any such gap as an indicator of the child's competence rather than as an indication that the child does not share our values concerning linguistic adaptation. Not surprisingly, this interpretation frequently has been used to denigrate the communicative competence of underclass or minority children and their families.[9] A linguist's defense of children who primarily speak a slang that he calls "Black English" is instructive:

> Unfortunately, these [detracting] notions are based on the work of educational psychologists who know very little about language and even less about Negro children . . . . in fact, Negro children in the urban ghettos receive a great deal of verbal stimulation, hear more well-formed sentences than middle-class children, and participate fully in a highly verbal culture; they have the same basic vocabulary, possess the same capacity for conceptual learning, and use the same logic as anyone else who learns to speak and understand English."[10]

It is not always easy for us to sort out the nature of our objections to behavior that is jarringly different from our own. But when the behavior is typical of younger generations whom we are trying to influence and educate, it is critical that we do so with some precision. We might object to children's nonstandard language use on several distinct grounds: we might consider it vulgar, illogical, vague, clumsy, misleading, and so on. Each of these objections has its own significance and says something particular about the speaker and the speaker's relation to the conversational context. When we fail to keep these distinct, and instead express a global dissatisfaction with the child's poor literacy, we make the kinds of mistakes that the linguist Labov complains about in the passage above.

The point here, as earlier, is that there are many ways to gauge the functionality of literacy and numeracy skills. By some standards, the literacies that children acquire through their own experience will inevitably be functional: otherwise they would not have acquired them. Of course this does not mean that these spontaneous literacies will retain their functionality as children enter new spheres of social commerce. It is our anticipation of this situation that fuels our sense of responsibility as educators and transmitters of the culture. But we often fail because we are not careful to identify either what is right or what is wrong about the skills that children themselves have cultivated. Our imprecision on this score broadens the gap between the skills that children assume work well in their lives and the skills that we assume we have needed in ours. It is not easy to communicate across such gaps, and it is not possible to educate without communication.

II

In the first part of this essay, I have drawn a contrast between, on the one hand, some of the literacies that children have found functional and, on the other hand, our adult values with respect to functional literacy. My purpose was to point out that we stand on one side of a gap that must be bridged if we are to teach children to function according to our own mature values. The first step toward accomplishing this is recognizing that there is already something of substance on the other side of the gap. An awareness of, and a respect for, the functionality of children's own spontaneous achievements is necessary if we are to communicate our values, knowledge, and skills effectively to them. Such an awareness also enables us to harness for learning purposes the abundant natural energies flowing from children's spontaneous activities. In this era of apathetic and alienated students, so likely a source of educational motivation is no small matter.

In order to make this point, I have referred to the adult side as a unitary "we." But among ourselves we adults have multiple agendas for educating the young, reflecting multiple views of what constitutes true literacy and numeracy. Not all of these views are compatible with each other. Nor are they all equally in tune with the present and future needs of the young.

E. D. Hirsch has given us the notion of "cultural literacy," which he defines as "the basic information needed to thrive in the modern world."[11] Hirsch's notion has struck a responsive chord in the American public, perhaps because other influential educators and political figures have been saying similar things.[12] The energy behind the notion is fueled by the appalling worldly ignorance often demonstrated by today's young. My own favorite Hirsch example is the schoolgirl who assumed that Latin cannot be a dead language because it is spoken in Latin America. ("At least she had heard of Latin America," Hirsch notes with some relief.) Hirsch's comment explicitly frames his position as a reaction against the "contentless" forms of instruction that he believes have swept modern pedagogy. "Contentless" instruction, a Deweyesque creature, supposedly focuses on pure thinking skills at the expense of specific facts and knowledge.

If there are indeed educational programs in place that try to instill abstract thinking apart from knowledge, Hirsch may have a point. I personally have never encountered any of these and doubt that they are as common as Hirsch supposes. My guess is that the shocking ignorance that so many observers have reported in today's children derives more from the failure of traditional school settings to engage their interest than from Deweyesque pedagogy, which is really the exception rather than the rule in American schools. But I readily grant the validity of Hirsch's main concern. The culture is indeed in trouble when there is as great a loss of shared knowledge between generations as we see in America today.

Is Hirsch's cultural literacy the answer to this concern? Is it important, to use one of his examples, that businesspeople know English literature well enough to produce and appreciate Shakespearian allusions during commercial transactions? Would our essential communication needs be less well served if the shared referent instead were drawn from last week's newspaper? And what about children's developmental needs—are these better served by Shakespeare than by Bloom County Comics (no pun on Allan intended)? Hirsch's belief is that, yes, there is a specific set of facts that must retain a privileged position in our culture for both communicational and educational purposes.

There is no question that Hirsch's point becomes more compelling each time we hear a young person say that Toronto must be somewhere in Italy. But as a program for education (and Hirsch's book does claim to be the "hidden key to effective education in America"), what does the notion of cultural literacy have to offer us? It is, at its core, no more than a program for "accumulating" (Hirsch's own word) a broad array of "background information" disembodied from any procedures, theory, or context that could establish the usefulness of this information. As such, it offers the student familiarity without insight. It is a program for fostering the knack of dilettantism.

Hirsch himself, at least, is true to his own principles. In his book he cites a number of psychological sources. Most of these are either obsolete or tangential to the problems in human learning and development that he addresses, but some are not. Several college courses could be taught on the distortions that may be found in Hirsch's use of these psychological sources. For my present purposes I shall note only one of these, an error that is both common among laypersons and yet central to the problem of cultural transmission between generations.

Hirsch sets up a predictable but empty opposition between Rousseauian nativism on the one hand and Platonic environmentalism on the other. He deplores the "natural development" theories that liken the child to an "acorn" growing into a "tree"—theories which he claims have spawned the "new kind of teaching"—and sets himself on the environmental-acculturation side. Whatever rhetorical fruits there are to be gathered from such an opposition, it certainly does not represent the current state of thinking in developmental psychology.

Virtually all contemporary developmental theorists are interactionists. No serious scholar in child development today could disavow the dynamic interplay between culture and individual growth. No scientific position holds that children develop like acorns. The controversies in the field revolve not around the question of whether interaction occurs, nor even on whether it is critical to development, but rather on the form and direction of the interaction. Here we do find differences among those who would emphasize biological processes, those who would emphasize social processes, those who would emphasize linguistic processes, and so on. One would think that a scholar who presumes to set an agenda for educational reform—and particularly a scholar who claims to be committed to the accumulated knowledge of cultures—would attempt to understand and use the best knowledge available about such matters. But the intricacies of human development elude Mr. Hirsch, just as I am sure the intricacies of history or geography would elude any student whose education consisted of learning Mr. Hirsch's lists. A passing acquaintance with facts does not define the depths of functional literacy, "cultural" or otherwise.

I note the importance of interaction in development not simply to goad Mr. Hirsch—whose treatise, I suspect, will itself have only a passing and shallow effect on schooling—but to frame some fundamental assertions concerning the literacy and numeracy of our children. The general problem, now as ever, is the intergenerational transfer of skills and knowledge. But the special problem for now, as I have posed it earlier in this paper, is the disjointed perceptions of functionality between young and old in our society. The symptoms of this are everywhere, including in the reports that E. D. Hirsch, Bloom, and others have entertained and disturbed us with. And it is correct that school is the institution in society that must address this problem. Yet it does not help to delude ourselves about the nature of schooling or its relation to the developing child.

Schooling is nothing more nor less than a set of engagements between the child and a formal program of instruction. The quality of these engagements is all-important in determining what the child learns from them. Some school engagements generate learning and others do not. We know that children can and do emerge from years of schooling knowing very little. All the subjects of the recent disturbing reports, after all, have spent most of their young lives in our society's compulsory educational system. On the other hand, many (if not most) children come out of school with a reasonable assortment of advanced skills and knowledge. It would be a mistake to condemn the entire system on the basis of a limited set of documented failures. The fact is that schooling is only as good as the engagements that it fosters but that, however imperfect these engagements may be, they still offer children an irreplaceable opportunity for developing their intellectual powers.

Among the Vai peoples of Liberia, some children receive formal schooling and others do not. The children who attend formal schools learn literacy in English. Many of the children who do not attend such schools, however, still acquire alternate forms of literacy. There are two main alternative forms: an Arabic literacy that is tightly linked to reading and memorizing the Koran and the Vai written language, used mostly for local commercial transactions and personal correspondence. Because some Vai become literate in only one and not others of these three ways, social scientists were able to examine the distinct learning effects of the schooled versus the unschooled literacies.

The investigators found that the Vai who acquired literacy in the formal school setting were better able to provide extensive verbal descriptions and explanations of their own cognitive performances. They expressed well-articulated insights about the principles they used to carry out the logical and syllogistic tasks given to them in the study. This could be a sign of self-reflection, critical thinking, or simply a greater linguistic adeptness. The Vai, on the other hand, who had confined their literacy learning to the local language or to the Arabic Koran showed little facility with explanations or reasoning on the logical tasks:

> Under conditions obtaining in Vai society, neither syllabic Vai script nor Arabic alphabetic literacy was associated with what we considered the use of taxonomic skills on any task designed to test categorization. Nor did either contribute to a shift toward syllogistic reasoning . . . .[13]

Schooling is the primary context in which children learn the most advanced forms of thinking available in a culture. This does not mean that schooling is always strictly necessary for the attainment of useful thinking skills. Young Brazilian candy sellers perform effective mathematics in their daily lives without relying on schooling. Still, even these precocious candy sellers will find their further mathematical progress hampered without the formal symbolic tools best learned in school. In the long run, a lack of schooling will place these budding mathematicians at a serious societal disadvantage.

If schooling, therefore, is not strictly necessary for the development of advanced thinking, it certainly is close to necessary. But by no means is it sufficient. We have heard enough stories about the less-than-educated children who populate our school systems to assure ourselves on this point. What is the missing link between the potentials and the realities of schooling in late-twentieth-century America?

The missing link, I believe, is the connection between the literacies of generations. The current connection is not as strong or as apparent as it needs to be for the purpose of inducting our young into the worlds of skills and knowledge to which we have committed ourselves. We have been unable to convince large numbers of contemporary youth that they should spend their time mastering the literacies and numeracies that we consider even minimally functional for modern living. This is not because today's youth are afunctional. Close examination of any youth group will reveal a literacy and a numeracy that is closely matched to the adaptive needs perceived by the group (though not many will match the dramatic capabilities of the Brazilian children who need to sell candy for a living). Our educational problem is one of mismatch rather than afunctionality, and to cope with it we need to recognize it as such.

We will not solve this problem by resorting to nostalgia. The burgeoning, multicultural populations of children residing in our cities will not be convinced to read Shakespeare because we express a fondness for how Shakespearian verse shaped our own intellects. Nor will exhortations or threats do the job. We simply do not have the requisite control over these children's lives to implement instructional agendas through coercion. And stonewalling, always a tempting recourse, is self-defeating at best. Maintaining that "we have our standards and the young can take them or leave them at their peril" does little more than run away from the problem. In order to educate children to function in the world of their own futures, we need to communicate culture to them rather than guard it from them. In the end, there is no substitute for helping children find a use in their own lives for the skills and knowledge that we want to teach them.

III

The quotation that I began this article with was only part of de Tocqueville's passage. Here is the rest:

> But I would not exaggerate this [educational] advantage, and I am still further from thinking, as so many people do think in Europe, that men can be instantaneously made citizens by teaching them to read and write. True information is mainly derived from experience; and if the Americans had not been gradually accustomed to govern themselves, their book-learning would not help them much at the present day.[14]

Whether applied to civic virtue or cultural knowledge, de Tocqueville's statement makes sound pedagogy. Ideas and values finally are mastered only through direct experience. In the American schooling tradition, this principle is most closely associated with Dewey. But strains of it run through virtually every systematic approach to human learning, from Hull and Piaget to the "situated thinking" thrust of cognitive science today.

The skills and values that we cherish can be imparted to younger generations only through action-based experiences that open for them new worlds of knowledge. Direct participation is the road not only to democratic values (à la de Tocqueville) but also to literacy in its many senses.

But this does not mean direct participation in lieu of schooling, but rather as a part of it. Ideally, schools create the main links between a society's cultural heritage and its students' personal experience. But in order to do so, the schools must bridge the gaps between the goals, skills, and values of generations. As I have maintained throughout, too few of our schools in recent years have been able to do so.

We have some principles that could lead us to a better way. The first principle is that there is not one literacy but many literacies, each acquired as a functional adaptation to a particular social need. It is clear that the type of literacy required for reciting the Koran by rote will not necessarily bear the same criteria as the literacy required to compose Broadway musical comedies. Nor is the distinction limited to "background information." Each literacy brings with it its own logical flavor and creates its own characteristic discourse opportunities.

This leads into the second principle. Although *literacy* in a generic sense implies nothing about advanced thinking (how could it when it has so many variants?), some forms of literacy are indeed implicated in creative and critical thinking of the best sort. These, and not the intellectually empty lists of our contemporary phrase makers, are the truly privileged forms of literacy. They are privileged in a developmental sense, because they enable persons to maximize their cognitive and moral potentials. Often these are the literacies that accompany formal instruction in systematic bodies of knowledge: "book-learning," as de Tocqueville called it. Schooling for all practical purposes is necessary for sustained progress along these lines. Unfortunately, as de Tocqueville rightly surmised, it is not sufficient. This brings us to the third principle.

If we wish schooling to impart the kinds of literacies that engender creative and critical thinking, we must be sure that schooling engages children in activities that require these skills. This principle is a simple reflection of the direct participation point that opened this section. To anyone acquainted with educational theory and research, the point may seem so obvious that it is almost tautological; but it still needs to be stated in these days of cultural literacy lists.

It also needs to be stated in light of what most schools actually do with students. Few schools provide children with the kinds of experiences that fully exploit the learning potentials of the formal literacies.[15] For example, elementary school reading exercises often focus on decoding letters and words rather than on comprehending texts.[16] During reading instruction, teachers spend far more time talking about assignments and procedures than exploring core concepts in what the students have read.[17] As a result, findings issued by the National Assessment of Educational Progress suggest that "while students seem to be acquiring the necessary basic skills associated with literacy, there is little emphasis being placed on the instruction of higher-level, critical thinking skills."[18]

With regard to this and a host of other missed pedagogical opportunities, we know more than we are currently putting into practice. The reading shortfall readily could be rectified by a "reading for meaning" strategy of the type advocated by many contemporary educational researchers.[19] One such approach, called "reciprocal teaching," builds upon the dialogical and communicational functions inherent in all reading activities.[20] Writing that "dialogue does not appear prominently in our system of formal education," the researchers orient their own approach toward creating productive dialogue between teacher and student.[21] The focus of the dialogue is a narrative text, and the student is encouraged to engage in a number of comprehension-fostering activities through participatory exchanges with the teacher and the other students. These activities include making predictions concerning forthcoming passages, generating questions, summarizing what one has read, clarifying the explicit and implicit purposes of the text, monitoring one's progress, drawing inferences concerning unstated textual implications, and testing such inferences.

Reciprocal teaching represents one formal instructional mechanism for setting reading in a context of classroom communication. As a general principle beyond this one approach and this one skill, communication is the strategic key to our current educational problems. It is also the "missing link" that I have mentioned above. It is missing from the many school literacy programs that fail to emphasize the communicational function at the heart of reading and writing. More disturbingly, it is missing in the cultural stances of today's generations. If we have been unable to convince many of the young to study our literacies and numeracies, it is because we have not adequately communicated to our young their present and future need for these.

Socialization means communicating goals as well as skills and information to the younger generation. Developmental theory tells us something about how this is accomplished. It is not done as easily or as directly as some impatient public figures have assumed. For example, lecturing is useless; and of course you cannot simply send a letter to your children outlining what you expect of them. Rather, the process entails an intricate process of support, collaboration, and negotiation that has been called, alternatively, "scaffolding," "guided participation," and "respectful engagement."[22] Through recognizing the child's agenda while never losing sight of one's own, the adult over an extended period of time works toward transmitting an entire perspective on the world to the child. Such a perspective brings with it a set of motivating goals and the intellectual tools to carry them out.

Transformation of the child's goals takes place only gradually and in a context of mutual engagement. To achieve this engagement, an initial match of goals is necessary. This requires some accommodation on the part of the adult. For example, a mother wants her two-year-old son to learn table manners. She starts by getting him to use his fork and spoon, and he joins in eagerly in a spirit of play. In its initial phases, the child's use of silverware bears little resemblance to table manners: it is erratic, rambunctious, and incompetent, and it ends up making more of a mess than if the boy used his fingers. The mother bears with him. Eventually, through assistance, demonstration, admonishment, and constant cajoling, the mother guides her son's playful behavior into an organized system of tidy eating. This system is accompanied by a whole perspective on table manners and their societal implications. The boy, for example, may devalue the offensive behavior of those who eat sloppily and may even come to disrespect the persons themselves. Once the boy assumes this perspective on his own, it requires less and less reinforcement from the mother (except perhaps during some hair-raising teenage interludes, but that is another story entirely). The scaffolding metaphor has been used to denote the gradually reduced need for adult support during this transformative process.

Though illustrative of socialization principles, table manners are not, of course, socialization's most critical product. Elsewhere I have described how adults may nurture in the young the more essential values of charity and fairness.[23]

The principles are much the same: we must engage the younger generation's own goals while at the same time we maintain a commitment to our own moral beliefs. I have called this the principle of "respectful engagement." The desired outcome is a kind of "moral literacy" that enables the child to make autonomous judgments while mindful of the values we all cherish. I also have made the case that it is precisely this kind of moral literacy that is required for mature functioning in a democratic society. And de Tocqueville has made the case for the republic's need for just this kind of functioning on the part of its citizenry. With de Tocqueville, I believe that democratic values are most firmly established when "the instruction which enlightens the understanding is not separated from the moral education which amends the heart." Moreover, I believe that this is the best route to, and the finest social purpose for, the higher forms of literacy.

When passed to a new generation, the higher forms of literacy serve both as maintainers of our culture and as enablers of the child's intellectual and moral potential. This process of generational transmission relies on the same principles of communication as any socialization achievement. There must be an initial match of interests. This does not mean capitulation to the child's agenda but rather commitment to an agenda that is mutually negotiated and temporarily shared. With persistent guidance, the agenda eventually will develop in the direction of cultural wisdom. In many ways, but not all, it will emulate the elder's perspective. Not all, because new generations do find ways to progress beyond the old ones.

ENDNOTES

[1]Geoffrey B. Saxe, "The Mathematics of Child Street Vendors," *Child Development* 59 (1988): 1415–25, and "Candy Selling and Math Learning," *Educational Researcher* 17 (4) (1989): 14–21.

[2]Herbert P. Ginsburg, *Children's Arithmetic: The Learning Process* (New York: Van Nostrand, 1977); Jean Piaget and Barbel Inhelder, *The Growth of Logical Thinking from Childhood to Adolescence* (New York: Basic Books, 1957); and Lauren B. Resnick, "The Development of Mathematic Intuition," in M. Perlmutter, ed., *Perspectives on Intellectual Development*, vol. 19 (Hillsdale, N.J.: Erlbaum, 1986).

[3]C. C. McKnight, F. J. Crosswhite, J. A. Dossey et al., *The Underachieving Curriculum: Assessing U.S. School Mathematics from an International Perspective* (Champaign, Ill.: Stripes, 1987); Harold W. Stevenson, S. Y. Lee, and James W. Stigler, "Mathematics Achievement of Chinese, American, and Japanese Children," *Science* 231 (4739) (1986): 693–99.

[4]Saxe, "The Mathematics of Child Street Vendors," and "Candy Selling and Math Learning."

[5]Michael Cole, John Gay, Joseph Glick, and David Sharp, *The Cultural Context of Learning and Thinking* (New York: Basic Books, 1971); J. Lave, M. Murtaugh, and O. de la Rocha, "The Dialectic of Arithmetic in Grocery Shopping," in Barbara Rogoff and Jean Lave, eds., *Everyday Cognition: Its Development in Social Context* (Cambridge: Harvard University Press, 1984); Geoffrey B. Saxe, and Maryl Gearhart, eds., *Children's Mathematics* (San Francisco: Jossey-Bass, 1988).

[6]L. S. Vygotsky, *Thought and Language* (Cambridge: M.I.T. Press, 1962).

[7]Lawrence A. Cremin, *The Transformation of the School: Progressivism in American Education* (New York: Knopf, 1964).

[8]Patricia G. Ramsey, *Teaching and Learning in a Diverse World; Multicultural Education for Young Children* (New York: Teachers College Press, 1987).

[9]Basil Bernstein, "A Sociolinguistic Approach to Socialization: With Some Reference to Educability," in F. Williams, ed., *Language and Poverty: Perspectives on a Theme* (Chicago: Markham, 1970); R. Hess and V. C. Shipman, "Early Experience and the Socialization of Cognitive Modes in Children," *Child Development* 36 (3) (1965): 869–86.

[10]William Labov, "The Logic of Nonstandard English," in V. Lee, ed., *Language Development* (New York: Wiley, 1979).

[11]E. D. Hirsch, Jr., *Cultural Literacy: What Every American Needs to Know* (New York: Vintage, 1987).

[12]Allan Bloom, *The Closing of the American Mind* (New York: Simon & Schuster, 1987).

[13]Sylvia Scribner and Michael Cole, *The Psychology of Literacy* (Cambridge: Harvard University Press, 1981).

[14]Alexis de Tocqueville, *Democracy in America,* vol. 1, the Henry Reeve text (New York: Knopf, 1945), 317.

[15]T. E. Raphael, ed., *The Contexts of School-Based Literacy* (New York: Random House, 1986).

16R. P. Parker, "Schooling and the Growth of Mind," in R. P. Parker and F. A. Davis, eds., *Developing Literacy: Young Children's Use of Language* (Newark, Del.: International Reading Association, 1984).

17Ibid.

18As summarized by Raphael, 19.

19David N. Perkins, *Knowledge as Design* (Hillsdale, N.J.: Erlbaum, 1986); A. L. Brown, A. S. Palincsar, and B. B. Armbruster, "Instructing Comprehension-Fostering Activities in Interactive Learning Situations," in H. Mandl, N. Stein, and T. Trabasso, eds., *Learning and Comprehension of Text* (Hillsdale, N.J.: Erlbaum, 1984); and Anne-Marie Palincsar and Ann Brown, "Reciprocal Teaching of Comprehension-Fostering and Comprehension-Monitoring Activities," *Cognition and Instruction* 1 (1) (1984): 117–75.

20Palincsar and Brown.

21Anne-Marie Palincsar, "The Role of Dialogue in Providing Scaffolded Instruction," *Educational Psychologist* 21 (2) (1986): 73–98.

22Barbara Rogoff, "Adult Assistance of Children's Learning," in T. E. Raphael, ed., *The Contexts of School-Based Literacy* (New York: Random House, 1986); William Damon and Anne Colby, "Social Influence and Moral Change," in W. Kurtines and J. Gewirtz, eds., *Moral Development through Social Interaction* (New York: Wiley, 1987).

23William Damon, *The Moral Child* (New York: The Free Press, 1988).

"What's the difference between the United States and Hungary, Bulgaria, and Romania?" A Romanian friend asked me this the other day, and when I said I didn't know, he told me, "The United States still has a Communist party."

We also have a school system that operates like the command economies these countries are busy getting rid of. It's top-heavy, rule-bound, and inefficient, and when the bureaucrats in Budapest and Bucharest go out of business, it probably will be the worst-managed system in the universe.

We felt superior to these Communist regimes, but we were terrified by them too, so we spent more money than anyone can count to be sure they wouldn't bury us. Why aren't we terrified about what this generation of poorly educated students will do to our society? Why won't we commit a fraction of the resources to education that we once committed to preparing for a possible war? Why do we find it easier to bury ourselves than to admit that our schools don't work and set about rethinking them? Damned if I know.

Albert Shanker
President
American Federation of Teachers

There are as many as 60 million illiterate and semiliterate adults in America today. Because poverty and illiteracy go hand in hand, the poor are disenfranchised, cut off from the democratic process. Any account that does not discuss the political interests served by allowing a large proportion of the American people to remain disenfranchised does not touch the heart of the matter. Before the Civil War in the United States, it was illegal to teach slaves to read, for reading was acknowledged as the tool needed to understand the social, historical, behavioral, and physical laws that control the human condition. An apprehension of those forces invests human beings with the capacity to alter the conditions of their lives. It is not too farfetched to draw an analogy between slaves in the nineteenth century and illiterate Americans today.

Joseph Murphy
Chancellor
City University of New York

Damaged Literacy: Illiteracies and American Democracy

Leon Botstein

T*he historical role of literacy has framed our current assumptions, institutional arrangements, and expectations. We often think of illiteracy in terms of the poor and the disadvantaged. But the state of literacy among the presumed models of society—the affluent and the privileged—is also of concern. I offer not a nostalgic critique but a candid analysis of illiteracy's political and cultural consequences throughout the population.*

In philosophy it's always a matter of the application of a series of utterly simple basic principles that any child knows, and the—enormous—difficulty is only one of applying these in the confusion our language creates. It's never a question of the latest results of experiments with exotic fish or the most recent developments in mathematics. But the difficulty in applying the simple basic principles shakes our confidence in the principles themselves.
—Ludwig Wittgenstein
Philosophical Remarks (1930)[1]

The poignant paradox in the crisis of literacy in the United States is that, on the one hand, the basic principles of language use—as Wittgenstein would have it for philosophy—are simple enough to be grasped by children. Fancy inventions, complex circumstances, and novel pedagogical strategies that pretend to account for the special conditions of modern life cannot hide the fact that, at an early age,

---

Leon Botstein is President and Professor of Music and Music History at Bard College.

reasonably complex verbal and linguistic operations are mastered by most people. On the other hand, that very ease of learning fails to prevent the abuse of language. In the encounter with formal schooling, it may even work against attaining a literacy sufficient to clarify and communicate within contemporary life.

Developing the childhood experience of language acquisition and use into serious widespread adult literacy of a high order has proven truly difficult. The challenge of achieving mass literacy with quality becomes even more difficult when the habits and rules of language that need to be taught and employed are defined by the demanding context of writing. Writing—the documentation, distribution, and preservation of all that language makes possible—exponentially augments the complexity of extending to the skills required by adult life what the child learns to do by listening and speaking. The task of teaching individuals to follow actively in adulthood (even when speaking) the most crucial basic principles of language use in writing has met with little success.

The problem is exacerbated by the fact that we live with a false sense of sufficient literacy. Pseudoliteracies have flourished. Despite schooling on a broad scale, the tolerance in society for crippled and limited literacy has only grown. That tolerance results in passivity. Most high school graduates and therefore most Americans believe they can read and write well enough, and so they are resistant to corrective intervention.

Before the age of mass literacy in the nineteenth century, illiteracy meant simply the almost total inability to read and write.[2] Today, illiteracy has become a species of the ability to read and write, a severely crippled and limited form of literacy. Redressing this state of affairs is more difficult than alleviating gross illiteracy. It is as if a game or a set of procedures (such as learning to play a sport or musical instrument) were being learned on a broad scale but passed on wrongly, so that in order to progress beyond an embarrassingly primitive level, one had first to break habits, because the existing habits themselves were barriers to improvement and to a serious command of the necessary skills.

Literacy—and therefore language—in the form in which it is taught and learned fails adults when they encounter the intricate and sophisticated issues of public and private life. There are two reasons for calling the current results a failure:

1.   The actual command of the spoken and written word, on the basis of widespread empirical observation, is insufficient to grasp, much less command, the realities in which we live. What passes for basic literacy is, objectively, too limited when compared with the content and logic of the political, ethical, and social issues of our time. Even the literacy that permits the privileged in our society to graduate from high school and college is too compromised in these terms to be called a high order of literacy. Behind this empirically grounded conclusion is an underlying conception of the ideal requirements for literacy given (a) the contemporary political imperatives of democracy and freedom and (b) the commercial imperatives of a global and technologically based economy in which the United States no longer dominates.

2.   There is no convincing argument or objective evidence that schooling, now that it is nearly universal, cannot, in principle, bring about adequate literacy. Conversely, there is no scientific basis for invalidating the political hypothesis behind universal education, that all segments of the population can, in theory, command language at a much higher level than they do now, and at levels which could effectively approximate an ideal of literacy.

The conclusion derived from contemporary criticism of the actual levels of literacy normally now attained by the school-going population need not be to condemn as utopian the project of universal education with high standards on a mass scale. Therefore, the source of the failure to achieve literacy through schooling ought not to be defined as the fragmentary, complex, and subtle character of reality itself. The modern form of illiteracy—inadequate literacies—is perhaps most devastating and widespread among those who otherwise would qualify, demographically, as part of a social and economic elite capable of serious literacy.

The simple, single principle of truly adequate literacy that has failed to be transmitted through the modern project of universal literacy is that the way we use language constitutes what and how we think.[3] At stake in the debate about literacy are, ultimately, not issues of style, civility, ornament, or decoration. Language is not the arbitrary external form of thinking. It is not the clothing of ideas but rather their substance. The failure to communicate that central principle constitutes the crux of the contemporary problem of illiteracy. Owing to damaged literacy, written language in our culture therefore functions more as a barrier, a limiting instrument—as a source of confusion and not enlightenment. Illiteracy in its many forms in the late twentieth century—from the straightforward inability to read and write to the incapacity to use language meaningfully without confusion and nonsense—is therefore a complex set of social forms that condemns individuals to thoughtlessness. That thoughtlessness is evident in the wholesale confusion and conflict created through language by people who have been through formal schooling. It is perceptible also in silence—not of the profound mystic but of the many individuals who have chosen (or been relegated to) a detached passivity and for whom thinking and writing seem to be impossible or to hold little or no allure.

The failure to combine language and thought is evident in the student with high SAT verbal scores who writes papers free of errors of usage but without a considered argument. Writing is accepted as a school-based ritual and not the medium for sustained thought. There is little sense that literacy is needed for the formulation, expression, and defense of ideas useful or desirable outside school. The failure to grasp the link between language, thinking, and life is equally responsible for the eighteen-year-old who cannot learn how to construct a coherent paragraph or sentence and for whom the rules of grammar in written work are, often despite reasonably correct usage in speech, seemingly a mystery.

In the United States, formal schooling teaches grammar and usage with regularity but without the proper context for their use.[4] It is as if young children were first taught the official written rules of baseball before playing, or ever trying to throw or hit a ball. In terms of written literacy, they are taught merely to observe rules and not to play, perhaps to read or decode but not to write. This pattern persists well into high school. Yet it is only after there is a genuine attachment to, or premium placed on, playing and winning that children quickly learn the complex rules of any game. They realize that without the rules, there can be no hits, no runs, no errors, no score, and no winners. So it is with grammar and usage. If we do not reveal what playing by the rules can achieve in the use of written forms of literacy for both private and public life, the teaching of rules alone will remain in vain for the privileged as well as the disadvantaged·child and young adult. What modern illiteracy in the United States demonstrates is that there is pitifully little realization in society that written literacy, independent of oral usage, permits the creation and extension of ideas—the generation of what in the best sense might be regarded as one's intimate self.

I

In the analysis of the origins of today's crisis of literacy, little attention has been paid to the special historical context language acquisition possessed in America in the late nineteenth and early twentieth centuries. An analogy can be made between the history of ordinary language literacy and the history of literacy in music. The development of active skills, memory, and the use of technology in musical literacy since the mideighteenth century provides illuminating insights for the understanding of the evolution of today's conceptions of literacy. Music education underwent a fundamental change in the late nineteenth century. This change was later accelerated by other more modern technologies of musical reproduction, including the player piano, radio, and phonograph. Skills of pitch reproduction and the active manipulation of musical elements (including improvisation) were replaced by the habits of employing gadgets designed for easy sound reproduction (beginning with the modern piano) whose use was not dependent on musical literacy. Today the listener who regards himself or herself "literate" in music and able to recognize a work of Beethoven and follow it can do so because of repeated hearings through recording, without any reference to a printed text. At best, a very few laypersons can still follow a score (usually single lines), retrospectively, while hearing music but without being able to anticipate sound or meaning as a result of reading notation alone. Reading music in this sense is reactive and passive. The analogous circumstance in language would be individuals who believed they knew Shakespeare by hearing and watching his plays but who could not read the texts or jot down in writing what they heard so as to form an attitude towards interpretation divorced from specific renditions.

It is an analogous transformation of the conception of ordinary literacy since the early nineteenth century that justifies the claim that we live, to some extent, not only with a problem of illiteracy in the traditional sense but in a "Potemkin Village" of literacy. A substantial percentage of our citizens possess fragments of skills of literacy that seem sufficient for them to survive painlessly. This constitutes the most difficult barrier to reform, since this condition of self-satisfaction mirrors the idea that to be literate is, in some sense, now merely a matter of passive recognitions. A new definition of reading has become dominant, one divorced from writing. It is as if decoding were an autonomous, simple skill, detached from an individual's capacity to create written language. The definition of reading as encoding has become circumscribed and deracinated.

Owing to the stress on reading skills in their contemporary definitions, literacy has become an act of passive response, a skill of reaction, documentation, and adjustment, all on a very rudimentary level. From the start of schooling, reading is taught without a parallel emphasis on teaching writing. The child, then, never reads as a writer or a potential writer. Therefore, the capacity to ask questions about what is written, to frame a critical perspective on the use of language of others, is severely limited.

The individual who does not employ writing (or has no memory of doing so) as an active dimension of self-discovery, rumination, description, and observation as well as argument cannot bridge the gap between the spoken and the written word, an essential skill in a political culture based on law and the elevation of written documentation as evidence of action, thought, and truth. The linguistic construct of reality, transmitted through journalism, in print and on television, becomes much harder to appropriate, challenge, and resist.[5]

The unique historical link between literacy and political life in America has bequeathed significant residues and a revealing legacy that may be useful in the task of formulating strategies to elevate, for future generations, the national level of literacy attained through schooling. We have drifted, not in recent history but as early as the late eighteenth century, from the presumption evident in *The Federalist* that reading and reflecting on that strikingly high level of written argument constituted the proper standard of literacy for democratic participation. The ratification of changes to the Constitution would hardly take such a form today—a fact that is true not only for the present but for the far distant past. The issue is not the debasement of an aristocratic model of literacy in the historical or empirical sense.

Rather, the egalitarian extension of democratic power and the institution of universal schooling for children and adolescents in the two centuries since 1787 have not been accompanied by an achievement of literacy among the population adequate to the ideal political premises of democracy—the exercise of government by free people through the use of reason and communication and not through the use of violence.[6]

Unlike most European nations, America, from the late eighteenth century onwards, suffered from linguistic insecurity in the sense that it did not possess its own national language. Political independence was obtained without cultural autonomy in linguistic terms or an emphasis on language as a mark of national identity.[7] After the Civil War, as a nation increasingly of immigrants, the learning of the national language was often the learning of a second language, albeit often the first to be learned in written form. In the cases where English was the first language learned in writing, the oral tradition in a familiar native language became contrasted with a limited expressive capacity in writing the new language. While English became an essential element in the formation of new citizens, the links among personal survival, national identity, and language in America worked against placing a high premium on a high standard for written literacy among the populace.

Despite the ideology of Horace Mann and the common school, American public schools, unlike those of other Western nations, have remained highly decentralized. The patchwork quilt of local and state control has worked against the development of a national standard of literacy. National identity in America, which began with a derivative linguistic national character, underwent, in terms of language, a differentiated evolution with the experience of immigration. For example, during the last century America did not develop a normative accent or model national language style comparable to Parisian French, Weimar German, or Muscovite Russian.[8] The survival of the links among status, class, and region that sustain an ideal of "the King's English" barely exist. Not with universal schooling but with the advent of radio did a normative style of American speech evolve, one that was not traceable to region or class. The internal social premium on developing a highly valued standard American English, particularly in written form, however, has remained relatively weak. Insofar as it did exist for the upper classes in the late nineteenth century—the era of Henry James—it was still tied to English standards and therefore was ambiguous in terms of how language functioned as part of national politics.

The tolerance of local diversity in education helped establish a more minimal standard of literacy, particularly as it related to political life. The survival of pluralism, the relatively open access to citizenship to non-English-speaking groups and the historical pressure toward egalitarianism conspired against the establishment, through schooling, of a high standard of common written English for public life.[9] Already in antebellum political campaigns, a trend toward slogans and packaged language occurred. These familiar dimensions of modern American politics, which assist in both framing and limiting debate and discourse, reflect the weak reliance on literacy in the American political tradition. Finally, the American tradition of literacy stressed a minimalist definition sufficient for work in the industrial workplace, a standard arguably inadequate for full political participation.[10]

The use of language in the formation of national consciousness was nevertheless still crucial. But citizenship and language in America never became as closely allied as in Europe. By the late nineteenth century, there had been a special emphasis placed on the public school as a critical instrument in the fashioning of Americans out of immigrant populations. In this sense the role of language instruction was to provide the central instrument of assimilation. Since the teaching of English was often as a second language, for many families English was an official state language. Native languages persisted at home and on neighborhood streets. Intimate conversation and close communication within family circles and close-knit groups were not necessarily associated with English. Hence, an uncomfortable tension persisted among Old World languages, hybrid forms of slang, regional and ghetto speech, and the pressure to cultivate a utilitarian (but rudimentary) American English mode of expression, particularly in writing.

Belonging in the New World occurred on two linguistic levels, with different languages attaching to the private and to the public arena. The memory of this duality has persisted in social attitudes toward language even when the original language and its residues have vanished from the scene. On the one hand, American English has been enriched by the integration of foreign linguistic patterns. On the other hand, the context of immigration cast English, and thereby its acquisition and teaching, into the role of a translating language. English was the documenting language, the formidable public language. The new language was positioned against the old. The former was personal, local, and informal, useful for the expression of sentiment and private thoughts. The latter was a necessary instrument with a national reach whose rudimentary command was crucial to elementary survival as a citizen. In late-nineteenth-century America, English gained the mark of a language of assimilation, officialdom, and economic and social advantage and opportunity. In that process, English obtained the aspect not of a language of thinking, but of a language one uses to interact with "others"; the language one needs to communicate, minimally, often with strangers.

Therefore, the desired literacy facing the immigrant population was peculiarly imitative—the copying of some perceived accepted local regional style of speaking and writing. English took on qualities of strangeness and artificiality (in the sense of being not tied to cross-generational domestic and family patterns of speech) which were hard to shake. It was frequently not associated with the ability or desire to express one's deepest sentiments and reactions. In the first generation, English was not the exclusive language, or even the favored language, of private thinking.[11] Rather, it was English through which one's ethnic self was converted into one's acquired American personality. Language, in American English, became the cautious mode of expression, the form in which one said what one might have thought in another language, one's "mother tongue." The national memory of the immigrant absorption of English and the premium on the language as an instrument through which one could hide and mask ethnic (and regional) origins and symbolize a break with the past remain with us in the circumscribed and cautious contemporary attitudes of subsequent generations in the twentieth century toward language acquisition and the meaning of literacy.[12]

In political terms, the practical emphasis on English as a common means of communication across ethnic and regional lines and the divorce from private thinking rendered language, as public instrument, theatrical. It was an instrument of imitative formulaic simplicity. The emphasis was on rhetoric, not argument, debate, and dialogue. Eloquence became a limited and anachronistic virtue by the midtwentieth century.

The paradox that language in American democratic politics and citizenship was tied to historical patterns of use divorced from intimate expression (as a language whose political uses were detached from private uses of language, argument, and the process of the original formulation of ideas in close circles of friends and family) became most pronounced in the twentieth century. The legacy in terms of late-twentieth-century politics is clear, as the primitive limited national use of written language in entertainment, commerce, and the political process of presidential campaigns reveals. The decentralized school system continues to perpetuate a context in which citizens believe that only a minimal and ritualized use of language is required for common economic and public life.

Furthermore, the historical process by which written literacy in English became linked, during the age of immigration and the early twentieth century, with the effort to achieve social mobility and acculturation led to an undue stress, in schooling, on language as stylistic; as an imitative surface skill sufficient to camouflage origins and establish a new identity. This legacy only bolstered the remnants, particularly in colleges and universities (particularly in New England), of an Anglophilic obsession dating from the revolutionary era. The combination of the immigrant absorption of English and a marked insecurity within the dominant host culture regarding the social and cultural status of American English has resulted in the still strong tendency among Americans and their schoolteachers and college professors to construct literacy in its highest senses too much as a matter of style, as an emblem of civility and not as the indispensable instrument of argument, ideas, and imagination.[13] The elevated model of language use is rhetorical in the pejorative sense, aesthetic, and derived, ironically, from the Old World—England. In contrast, diversity (only strengthened by immigration) has led, on the rudimentary level, to the acceptance of too minimum a standard of literacy despite the lingering upper-class allegiance to an English model.[14]

To be literate, then, is at once to achieve merely basic marks of Americanism, and at the same time to recognize a yet higher realm of literacy, associated by Americans with England. This puts the weight in the matter of language on adaptation to particular surroundings and styles in accent and usage. The powerful American ideology of individualism—the premium on personal style—in its social, collective sense, becomes reinforced by the notion that one's language may be used, much like matters of fashion and personal taste, as an external mark of one's individual identity. The notion of written language as a central national instrument of communication across social boundaries becomes diminished and secondary.

Therefore, from a historical vantage point, civilization and culture may not be the crucial concerns in the contemporary analysis of problems of literacy and the development of strategies for reform. Rather, the credibility of our primary political concepts is at issue. In the face of a proper respect for heterogeneity and social pluralism, can we teach and encourage literacy at a level commensurate with the exercise of democratic rights and processes?

During the first decades of the twentieth century, the critique of language became a central activity of English and Continental philosophy. In the era of Wittgenstein's *Tractatus,* that critique extended beyond professional philosophical discourse. Wittgenstein's observation that "the tacit conventions on which the understanding of everyday language depends are enormously complicated" was coupled with an intense identification of ethics with standards of language use. Authenticity in thought was linked to "the striving after clarity and perspicacity" and the expression of purity and "goodwill" through language.[15]

The villains in the abuse of language in the first historical era of mass literacy (the late nineteenth and early twentieth centuries), according to critics such as Fritz Mauthner, Karl Kraus,[16] and Wittgenstein, were nonsensical philosophical talk and all forms of journalism, particularly of the sophisticated cosmopolitan sort. By the end of World War II, two additional terrifying political betrayals through language had become evident: the camouflage, obfuscation, and justification of evil through linguistic manipulation and bureaucratic jargon and the misappropriation of the appearance of truthfulness characteristic of the language of science by the instruments of modern mass politics. These realities were in part the negative consequence of the success of the spread of literacy in the West.

A shift occurred from a generalized view that literacy, particularly on a large scale, was, if not a positive good, at least benign. A culture of doubt took its place, based on the recognition of the evils committed by literate societies using language. The disastrous perversion of mass literacy in this century must frame any late-twentieth-century discussion of what and how literacy should be achieved in society.

The admonition in Wittgenstein's early work that perhaps the most serious issues of life cannot be spoken about and must be "consigned" to silence was in part a political claim. If truth value can be assigned only to a quite limited set of propositions, then matters that, for example, in World War I led to death and destruction and that seemed to be unconditional truths—complex claims on the issues of ideology, religion, patriotism, and ideas of justice and nobility— might have been not only nonsensical but better left unsaid and unwritten. If even the linguistic act of naming the other as foreigner and enemy is, although commonsensical, arbitrary nonsense, particularly as a justification of killing, then silence might be a political virtue. The eighteenth-century notion that freedom and reason are tied to language and therefore to literacy within the body politic becomes thereby suspect. The notion that literacy enables discourse and debate and enhances the pursuit of justice and equity is challenged. Is, then, the social project to achieve in parallel fashion the extension of rights and the attainment of mass literacy justified?[17]

The United States in the late twentieth century must now confront, in its pedagogical strategies, the challenges of the critique of language that emerged a century ago. The contemporary debate regarding the need to improve the state of literacy among Americans must confront the heritage of a heightened sensitivity regarding the complexity of ways in which language can both camouflage and clarify. What do we mean when we argue for greater literacy? We must become clear with respect to what the definition and level of literacy should be. The quite sophisticated assumptions regarding the connection between literacy and liberty inherent in democratic theory must then be reconciled with how we teach language. How can justice and freedom in the ever larger and more complicated world of the Americas in the late twentieth century actually be sustained through literacy?

II

What follows is an interpretation of the state of literacy in contemporary America in light of its underlying social and cultural causes and conditions. The views are polemical, but not entirely divorced from verifiable observation, particularly of high school and college students. The central thesis here is that the nature and function of language use in contemporary life reveal profound discontinuities with past expectations and assumptions. Therefore, insofar as schooling can and must work to achieve widespread literacy among citizens adequate to the demands of contemporary America, pedagogical strategies must take actual current realities into account without uncritical optimism or nostalgia. Past conditions were never so wonderful as to condemn the future from the outset by facile comparisons.

Six boundaries of our current condition demand consideration. First, illiteracy in its modern form (particularly when it masquerades as literacy) cuts across social and economic divisions in society. Illiteracy is not exclusively visible among the poor and minorities. Symptoms of inadequate command of language appear throughout the normal distribution of the population, however the population is measured. The actual inability to read and write among the poor is as much the result of the absence of opportunities as it is the consequence of a failure to develop sources of motivation to learn. That motivational collapse is revealed as well in the thoughtless use of language and the limited skills of literacy characteristic of the middle class.

Therefore, it can be said that the problems of literacy are distributed in quite comparable ways throughout the population. Therefore, a reform strategy (e.g., changing the way reading is taught in relation to writing) which can raise the minimum standard, owing to the wide distribution of the problem, may be able to improve the quality of skills over the entire distribution of the school population. Consequently, the very highest level of attainment can be raised by uniform approaches, since the root of the problems of literacy (e.g., the relation of language to thought) is common to pupils from all sectors of society.

In order for this to be accomplished, however, the matter of motivation must be addressed. Jeremiads about Japanese competition and the decline of America will not suffice among schoolchildren. Writing and reading have to become useful and important to pupils and not remain merely school-based activities whose only evident importance is as school-imposed skills with school-based rewards.

The need to strengthen the motivations for literacy extrinsic to school is tied to the second boundary. The traditional symbiosis between literacy (and education in general) and democracy, through the alteration of the processes of contemporary politics, has disfigured the child's perception of what defines adequate literacy and what literacy can achieve. Children have little idea why high-order literacy is necessary. According to the traditional nineteenth-century view, literacy was necessary for the effective extension of democratic political rights. Access to power within a democracy was contingent upon the ability to read and write sufficiently to defend rights and translate dimensions of the rule of law affecting personal and communal life into common ordinary language. The capacity to evaluate arguments, for example, delivered by elected leaders in a democracy seemed to require the corollary skill, the asking of commonsense questions of experts and those with privileged knowledge. In this sense, adequacy, in terms of written literacy, partly became cast, by the late nineteenth century, in relation to conceptions of the issues and procedural requirements of democratic government, both the formal legal processes and the informal instruments of a democracy—caucuses, meetings, debates, elections, due process, the transfer of information, the issuing of broadsides, and a free press, for example.

What has occurred is that the external apparatus of democracy continues to function—although not entirely to the satisfaction of all concerned—despite levels of literacy in the nation which in fact cripple the potential of these routes to effective participation in democracy. A circular dynamic has taken place in which the governed and those who govern have become accustomed to the persistence of democratic forms theoretically dependent on written literacy but actually supported by a highly limited exchange of language and new means of communication. What the schoolchild sees is the appearance of the transference and exchange of, in linguistic terms, limited information. Sustained and effective critical response to processes and issues among adults using written language is hard for them to find.

There is little observable capacity among the citizenry to limit, using literacy, the extent to which technical expertise conceals political value judgments. Although the lay citizen is insufficiently literate to question, criticize, and respond (except with visceral mistrust derived often from religious frameworks) or to challenge the barrage of claims coming from professional politicians, civil servants, scientists, and technical experts, that fact remains hidden.[18] Given a weak and perhaps invisible link between literacy and democracy outside school, why become literate in more than a rudimentary sense?

Third, although a level of functional literacy is deemed essential for employment and leisure, the overwhelming impression gained from the culture is that a decent standard of living, if not fame and wealth, including the pleasures of recreation and the satisfactions of intimacy, is accessible without a high degree of literacy. The premium on freedom in the society has shifted from an eighteenth-century balance between freedom of movement and freedom of thought to an overwhelming twentieth-century emphasis on freedom of movement, insofar as that category includes the exercise of the freedom to shop and consume goods.

The voluntary restriction of political discourse that stems from the de-emphasis in modern culture on the exercise of the freedom of thought as an active, daily part of life has reduced the tolerance for dissent expressed not through life-style, but sustained argument. The consequence is that while the First Amendment remains in force, however interpreted, dissent itself becomes rare. When it occurs, it is frequently imitative, managed, centered on groups, and routinized into slogans. Dissent becomes a mirror image of the vague, passive, and detached consensus of conventional wisdom which defines the majority view on most issues. The reduced will among individuals to dissent (and tolerance for it) reflects a limited literacy which in and of itself further renders less probable the desire to think new thoughts and gain the skills to differ. From the point of view of generating motivation, schooling is quite helpless in working against this boundary characteristic of adult life.

Fourth, although much has been made of the role played by television in the lives of adults and children, the ease of travel, its declining per-mile cost in this century, and the relatively cheap access to telephone communication have all been more crucial to the displacement of writing by oral conversation in the transaction of both economic and private activities. The intimate sphere of life and the workplace have, in turn, a decisive influence on the character of public life. The telephone has helped shape the way we use language.

The initial premium on brevity, owing to cost, has vanished. Despite remnants of a telegraphic verbal style, the habit of direct informal verbal communication has replaced much of writing in the conduct of daily private life. Love letters with content beyond the declaration are a rarity, as is any extended regular personal correspondence. Within families, the relative one writes is often the relative one least wishes to see. Writing as the medium of self-expression, from the child's viewpoint, is hardly imaginable.

Negotiation between groups and in the workplace is carried on verbally without use of writing. When writing is required, often a technical expert is used to document and summarize. Written documents either represent the end of negotiation or argument, or formal strategic or legal maneuvers. Furthermore, writing in the workplace is often used to induce fear and hierarchical distance. It is frequently bereft of candor and designed intentionally to misinform. In this context, writing takes on the qualities of insincerity, indirection, caution, reserve, circumspection, economy, and formality. One writes often in anticipation of possible judicial conflict. One writes to justify, to document, to allude indirectly, or to deflect attention from other issues at hand. Consider, for example, the language of recommendations for college attendance, employment, and evaluation of work done.

In bureaucratic behavior, writing can become the surrogate for action, a delaying tactic or a defensive procedure against charges of incompetence or irresponsibility. Last, but not least, conflict resolution is not conducted by individuals in common language but given over increasingly to a specialized cadre, lawyers, who command a self-referential sublanguage specific to modern conflict resolution. In sum, writing in the contemporary environment assumes an aspect in contradiction to ideas or activities associated with truth, candor, spontaneity, intimacy, ambiguity, speculation, or authentic sentiment. The child is aware of the marginal social role assumed by written documentation. Warnings and bad news come in written form. Good news comes in person or on the phone.

The fifth cultural boundary which any reform strategy must confront is the fact that the language we encounter has become, by and large, streamlined in periodicity and phraseology. The great success of advertising language and slogans, cast within the context of television time units, has had the effect of demanding, on the surface, maximum efficiency within the shortest period. This has permitted the development of specialized vocabulary and jargon which effectively refer to or denote notions or events and at the same time standardize references. Sentences are constructed by clichés, densely packed single words and phrases, and not by a flexible range in the combination of common-language words.

The child receives little reinforcement for the notion that language can be appropriated as a personal tool of expression. When one speaks of distinct subjects, one imitates a particular phraseology. This imitation now extends to increasingly uniform sublanguages and vocabularies of professions which signify conventional rituals and concepts. The most egregious example is the wholesale appropriation of pseudotechnical terms derived from psychology in the way we talk about ourselves and our relations with others. This appropriation is not informed by theory and is therefore not based on particular knowledge essential for clarity. Rather, the vocabulary is a surrogate for thought and obviates the need to think anew in comprehensible ways about personal issues.

On the informal level, in ordinary speech, expressive language has become emancipated from its possible written image. Speech has become an accompaniment to facial gesture and vocal, tonal emphasis—a result of the greater ease of physical and aural contact. The oral tradition has triumphed over the written. This is most evident in popular music, where the language serves, in a subservient role, the music and not the reverse.[19] The simplification and standardization of language, one might argue, restrict the range of expression and thought, even silent internal rumination. In this sense, eloquence and even originality, from the perspective of the classroom, have become superfluous. The use of the standard words and phrases of common language as indirect allusive referents and not instruments of individual argument or thought complicates any effort to teach individuals to command language apart from the accepted clichés to enhance communication within a highly differentiated community.[20]

Sixth, among the most highly trained class of citizens—traditional professionals such as physicians, scientists, engineers, and practitioners of service vocations, including education—the literacy achieved, at often high levels, is restricted, untranslatable into common language, and imitative of itself. Jargon is learned in professional training and is replicated through the institutionalization of training. Technical sublanguages are utilized within defined rules and circumstances. Sublanguage use is repeated and adapted but rarely subjected to scrutiny by ordinary writing and speech. The society has witnessed an explosion of technical languages with specific vocabularies behind which professionals and practitioners, aided by the generous use of technical terms in print and television journalism, hide from critical scrutiny and the general public.

From the perspective of children and adolescents, these boundaries in the use and function of language and literacy in society result in a reduced motivation to learn, concentrate on, and remember how to use language in the sense of learning how to think and write with language in any complex or extended fashion. The command of formal rules of grammar and syntax, the riches of vocabulary, or the capacity to adapt and modify language and its rules as vehicles of individual expression are not encouraged by the culture external to the school. The premium on thinking, inquiring, and remembering is low. Even though the teaching of language in the schools fails to stress active literacy on a high level, the problem may be not so much that the link between language and thought (or between reading and writing) is not being taught. Rather, the problem may be that there is insufficient motivation for anything to be remembered and used.

The causes of poor performance by American students across the board, measured by either ideal expectations or reasonable standards applied as a result of past patterns, may have less to do with input than the context in which teaching takes place. Learning language seems divorced from reality. It is so disconnected as to inhibit concentration and memory, much less curiosity. This condition exists throughout all social and economic distinctions. Reform in teaching language use must directly attack the boundaries of contemporary language use.

III

The collapse of a motivational structure and environment for schooling has several additional causes apart from the uses of literacy in the culture.

A Sense of Powerlessness

Despite the overt claims of democracy, a sense of individual powerlessness reduces the force of the argument that serious literacy is necessary to assume one's proper role as a citizen. The child lives in a world in which there is little observation that individuals use language and knowledge to influence government. There are few town meetings left. Fighting city hall is difficult at best. Perhaps local school boards are one remaining venue of democratic participation. Voting, signing petitions, and answering opinion surveys are insufficient environmental factors outside the school for inspiring the achievement of serious literacy. They are, like modern literacy, rudimentary and passive. The sense of powerlessness is most striking in the much-discussed issue of war and peace in the nuclear age. Popular knowledge is sufficient for most citizens to realize that nuclear combat demands surprise and speed. This makes the traditional constitutional protection of a joint session of the House and Senate to debate and then declare war meaningless. The process of representation and considered delegation of power seems therefore useless in controlling the fundamental matters of life and death. Why, then, must one be literate and informed?

The Dominant Cultural Conception and Social Use of Time

On the matter of time, education is a social process which places a premium on delayed benefits for one's life. The child senses (or is told) that he or she is embarked on a twelve-to-sixteen-year journey whose results will be evident five or ten years after the journey's completion. The time frame for sustained effort and concentration toward a realized gain is therefore about twenty-five years. In the context of a culture that frames life in terms of generational time, the ratio between adult expectations and behavior and the demands placed on the child through schooling might be reasonable. Within a nineteenth-century framework of the perception and use of time the expectations of the child might have been convincing.

Consider, however, the conception of time in contemporary life. Rewards in business are measured in months, if not days, and at best in single years. Five years on a job is considered long. Living in a single community for between ten and twenty years is considered long. Few families possess vocational consistency over more than one generation. Relationships are measured in short time periods. Fashion and style are products of seasonal changes. The entire conception of time and its crucial units works against the demands placed on the child. If no adults have the patience for or habit of waiting for desired results for more than months or a few years, how can one expect sustained concentration by children on a process which lasts decades? Who, from politicians to industrialists, thinks in generational terms? Fame, fortune, and careers are quickly achieved and rapidly forgotten. If one adds to this dynamic any lingering suspicion that the future is itself not assured, why is one then surprised that little is learned and less remembered by children? Long-term memory, historical awareness, patience, and sustained expectation are consistently undermined by adult culture. Training the memory in teaching language using written fragments of a cultural past can encourage the sensitivity to the historical and the reflective. But in the present condition literacy, the essential instrument of cultural continuity and memory, appears as an anachronistic value, entirely out of step with the temporal framework of modern life and culture.[21]

The Absorption of a Pessimistic Historical Teleology into the Culture

Schoolchildren in the late twentieth century in America are the heirs of nearly a century of historical pessimism. This pessimism has been reinforced by the past decade of debate about the deterioration of values, culture, and civility in America. It has been underscored by the wide discussion since the presidency of Jimmy Carter of the economic and political decline of America. How can schoolchildren be expected to be enthusiastic about the benefits of education in this context?

This particular American incarnation of historical pessimism is part of a larger twentieth-century dilemma. Language and learning were, from the eighteenth-century perspective, tools of progress. This progress was to be historical and therefore to be reflected in the future moral, material, and political betterment of mankind. The conceit of men such as Hume, Jefferson, and Condorcet (not, however, Rousseau)—even Marx—was not borne out by nineteenth-century history.

It is not, however, the doubts of Dickens, Nietzsche, or Burckhardt that weigh (albeit indirectly) on the problem of schooling for the 1990s and after. Rather, the wide awareness that mass literacy and the spread of literate culture and knowledge failed to prevent barbarism in the twentieth century cuts most deeply against the project of mass literacy and learning. The nuclear arms race, the persistence of violence and poverty in our world, and the legacy of

Nazism, Stalinism, and the Vietnam War severely compromise facile claims about learning and the capacity to better the world and the way people normally behave. The illiterate and ignorant have not been the worst perpetrators of evil in the twentieth century. A Kantian faith in enlightenment is hard to sustain in the light of modern history. The link between ethical progress and the extent of culture and learning—the so-called liberal arts—has, at best, become suspect.

No earlier generation of schoolchildren—not the children of the 1930s, 1950s, or 1960s—possessed so severe and stark an obstacle to the incentive to perform in school, exercise curiosity, and cultivate a sense of hope and ideals tied to the acquisition of written language and knowledge. The good, the beautiful, and the just are not associated with the attributes and rewards of literacy. A sense of decline, deterioration, and futility hangs over the American classroom. In its trivial form it is expressed in the myth that pupils and schools have been better in the past. That commonly held notion, however, is merely a sign of a larger societal paradox which demands an answer within the process of education if progress is to be made in motivating children to learn to be literate. At best, the child and adolescent cling to the notion that the successful completion of school and its attendant certification are necessary for short-term personal survival and comfort. However, purely private and personal incentives may be too weak for serious literacy to be achieved on a wide scale.

The Disappearance of an Amateur Class of Highly Literate Citizens

As has been suggested by the discussion of language use in adult culture, the child, by and large, does not observe serious literacy being used voluntarily outside a school context or by individuals who are not paid to be highly literate. The corollary of this fact is the condition that most activities within the culture that demand high degrees of literacy have been professionalized and often institutionalized in school and university structures. In other words, there is no amateur or lay audience of any size that writes, philosophizes, or actively engages in politics, culture, and the arts that does not do so for a living. It is therefore no surprise that high-quality magazines of general opinion and subject matter have been on the decline, as has been the percentage of readers (not absolute numbers) for serious nonfiction (and fiction) from among the total of potential readers (those with the presumably sufficient formal schooling).

The common standard of literacy remains low, and the higher reaches are reserved for those who intend to use such literacy for utilitarian ends, as a profession. The absence of a large nonprofessional literate class that engages in serious discourse dampens the likelihood that schoolchildren can be motivated by a desire to imitate grown-ups. Even schoolteachers give little evidence of using their skills of knowledge and literacy except as part of their stated professional tasks.

Peer Interaction in Adolescence

Finally, while peer culture, particularly in the crucial ages of puberty and adolescence, has never been prized for its noble content or judicious values, the ability of school to compete for the attention of young adults during the crucial years from twelve to twenty has probably never been weaker. This is in part fueled by the severe age segmentation in our culture. The psychological emphasis on group membership and approval according to particular ages has become an increasingly dominant aspect of adolescence.

Given the earlier onset of maturation, relaxed standards of conduct, increased freedom for adolescents, and the lure of values spread by a pervasive commercial culture, the school fights, often in vain, against the anti-intellectual passions and patterns of American adolescent culture. In turn, adolescent culture is at the center of the movie industry, the music business, television, and the fashion industry. These enterprises know that habits are formed in these years. Despite the enormous energy put in by young people in home-grown rock groups, for example, the internal structure and exterior significance of rock-improvisation performance and listening militate against the sustained use of language as a vehicle of expression. In terms of language acquisition and science and mathematics education, the adolescent years are critical. Any school reform strategy must confront the contemporary challenge of adolescent culture, which may be, in turn, just a symptom of the other cultural and social forces working against the motivation to acquire serious literacy.

IV

Given these cultural conditions, formal schooling must now try to become more effective and decisive in creating motivation and literacy than it has been in the past. It can be argued, however, that the project to attain universal literacy at higher levels than now apparent—even if possible—is romantic and quixotic. Would an improvement of the bottom level and the elevation of elite standards in a common language actually increase the probabilities that justice, equity, and freedom will flourish? Since what is needed is not the imposition of a pseudohistorical model of aristocratic usage, but the development of thought through language throughout the population, this doubt can only be answered with a counterfactual answer. Are we better off not trying? Is there a modern or a futuristic surrogate for literacy and its potential to enhance private and public life? At a minimum, it is reasonably certain that democratic theory depends, for the moment, on the possibility of communication through written as well as spoken literacy.

Considering the restraints external to schooling, the effective spread of literacy will be dependent more than ever on schools and institutionalized educational strategies. Trying harder to achieve higher standards without challenging the real conditions in which learning takes place is futile. Links must be forged with other mediating institutions, including the workplace, civic organizations, public libraries, and the like. The strategies needed to achieve genuine literacy on a large scale, in school and outside, are general in character and adaptable so that near universal applicability is plausible.

Language must be taught, from the start, as an active instrument of speculation, creation, and personal expression—of thinking—which can be possessed by every individual. It must be seen as an evolving instrument appropriated by the individual but effective in communicating with strangers. The teaching and use of writing must exist throughout the curriculum and be emancipated from the exclusive focus on finished examples of expository prose. The keeping of notebooks, the use of free writing, despite the limitations of class size, must be used from the start. Collaboration among pupils in editing, responding, and rewriting must be encouraged. Pupils must see their teachers use writing to express themselves and must learn to enjoy writing. The teaching of reading, therefore, must run parallel to and be integrated with a stress on the active use of written notation. Grammar and usage then can be taught and remembered as the indispensable tools of realizing the potential of language to communicate in writing beyond speech.[22] At the same time, the cultivation of the skills of oratory and speech must parallel the development of the skills of writing.

Philosophical and reflective considerations and materials must be introduced into the teaching of language beginning with the elementary grades. The child must see that language is the instrument of argument and logic; of description and discovery; of the asking of fundamental questions in epistemology and ethics. The source can be the tradition of ordinary-language philosophy, the philosophy of language, the history of philosophy, and the exploration of the structure of language.[23]

Ordinary language must be used in the teaching not only of social science subjects such as history, but also of mathematics and experimental science. Only if common language is used to translate and explicate symbolic languages will the motivation and comprehension for both literacy and numeracy increase.[24]

Make writing public. It could even be part of the sports life in the school, from the huddle after the game to the planning of a strategy. Writing should be part of other public activities in the school building. Pupils rarely see that writing and its distribution has impact and meaning, and results in action and enjoyment. Modern desktop publishing apparatus makes it possible for a school building to have its own publication and distribution network, for all ages, including teachers. Make writing consequential. Give it a social function and communal meaning within the school, as communication and part of governance. Teach the fact that written argument, and its merits, can convince and change ideas and opinions.

Reading aloud, public speaking, and memorization of texts and materials are too neglected. The memorization of model uses of language (from various cultural and historical traditions) creates a fund of differentiated and retained language and an appreciation for the beauty and variety of language. The testimony of twentieth-century political prisoners and concentration camp inmates vindicates the link between memory and spiritual survival. Although there is a long-standing prejudice in America against rote learning, the retention of texts creates the opportunity for variation, invention, and contrast in the use of words and the formulation of thoughts. Memory is an ally—not an enemy—of originality in the sense that it frames the source of the new.

The etymological and historical character of words should be part of the development of an understanding of culture and history from the elementary grades on. This can be done in a playful way by using the notion of family resemblances in language uses and the variability of meaning in terms of the context of language use. The notion of language as a living and developing instrument, not as a fixed, scholastic, and abstract quantity, must be transmitted.[25] In the teaching of foreign language, stress the teaching of translation skills in writing from the start, reciprocally, from both languages.

The texts used in school should be ones which eschew jargon and bureaucratic prose. In their variety, they should reflect an abiding care for language and be worth reading. They should be compelling, important, and occasionally humorous.[26]

Language should be taught in conjunction with the pictorial and the musical, so that the interplay and contrast between these various forms of expression is understood.

Apart from teaching strategies, the techniques and instruments of testing should never be multiple-choice, identification, or "choose from column A" tests. Pupils and students should always be called on to express themselves by creating their own sentences. This standardization in writing of how knowledge is transmitted not only conforms to the experience of life, but demands that the attributes of memory and concentration be strengthened.[27]

In order to attack illiteracy among young adults and adolescents, the approach must find a way to reach adults such as parents in tandem with the school pupils. Only if the school building is seen by the out-of-school adult as the source of learning the critical skill of writing can the motivation be increased among high school and junior high school students. Literacy training, especially remedial forms, at all levels, should be intergenerational. All public agencies, from social welfare agencies to law enforcement and judicial agencies (and even the Internal Revenue Service), should collaborate in appropriate ways with school systems in a national effort to stimulate and improve literacy among adults and children.

V

This paper began with an excerpt from one of the texts Ludwig Wittgenstein wrote as he formulated a philosophical position different from the 1918 *Tractatus*. It is appropriate to close with a fragment from Wittgenstein's later position. It expresses the fact that, despite the limiting conditions facing teaching literacy in the late twentieth century, there is no alternative to embracing written language and its effective teaching as the crucial strategy for the future of humanity. In 1949, Wittgenstein wrote:

> One can imagine an animal angry, frightened, unhappy, happy, star-tled. But hopeful? And why not? . . . Can only those hope who can talk? Only those who have mastered the use of a language. That is to say, the phenomena of hope are modes of this complicated form of life. (If a concept refers to a character of human handwriting, it has no application to beings that do not write.)[28]

The point is clear. If indeed the categories of freedom, justice, truth, and humanity are to flourish, a language must be mastered. That language, in the American context, must be mastered at a level in speech and writing well beyond current achievements for most, if not all, our citizens. It must be done in a fashion which connects language and thought.

We need to retard the evolution of thoughtless language use exemplified, ironically, by the way we use the word *hope*. It is now accepted (and has been since the 1950s) to use the adverb *hopefully* as a replacement for the phrase *I hope*.

Consider these uses: "Hopefully, inflation won't be too severe"; or "Hopefully, I will get a raise"; or "Hopefully, we will have better leaders"; or "Hopefully, these guests will leave soon." All these formulations, once considered incorrect, now are accepted.

This extension of grammatical tolerance, however, is more than an example of the evolution of style. A shift in thinking is perceptible in the linguistic change. In the shift one can perceive a distancing from the idea of personal responsibility and a weakening of faith in personal efficacy. "I hope," the older formulation, makes clear the presence of the speaker as actor. Indirectly, one knows that the speaker not only holds the view but is in a position to say the next logical point. "I hope," if used, can and ought to be followed by "since I hope, I will . . . ," or "I think . . . ," or "I urge . . . ," and so forth. The older formulation carries with it the assumption of personal responsibility to act on hope and expresses the potential of utility in hoping, speaking, and acting.

The abuse of *hopefully,* in contrast, signals the idea that what happens is the result of neither one's beliefs nor one's actions, that one is powerless and subject to amorphous circumstances and impersonal forces apart from one's existence. The current use of *hopefully* reduces hope to a mere feeling, an emotion, a sentiment which is at once vague and inarticulate. Therefore one is impotent to realize in the present and future any aspiration implied by hope. As the correct usage suggests, the speaker is, in fact, the only one who can hope. Through the command of a language which functions, the only possible actor in a position to realize hope and render it meaningful as an idea and factual is the speaker, the possessor of a language.

In the shift in our usage there is camouflaged a pessimism and an exhaustion—a sense of the superfluity of individual belief and influence. This cuts against Wittgenstein's suggestion and (perhaps) admonition that we command a language sufficient for authentic hope. Since hope is contingent on language, real hope derives from a confidence in human knowledge and action. In this sense, it is the dissemination of language and its consequent capacity to spread hope—the essential meaning of literacy—on which the future depends.

ENDNOTES

[1] Ludwig Wittgenstein, *Philosophical Remarks* (Chicago: University of Chicago Press, 1975), 153–54.

[2] See, for example, the poster issued right after the Russian Revolution which illustrated the phrase "To be illiterate is to be blind—on all sides lurk failure and unhappiness," no. 4 in A. Radakov, ed., *Russian Revolutionary Posters 1917–1924* (Leningrad).

[3] While the argument that follows links literacy and Anglo-American democratic theory, one should not forget that the link between language, canons of truth, and human experience has been elaborated in an influential manner through a different philosophical tradition, that of Martin Heidegger. Ironically, the Heideggerian logic supports the claims made in the argument that follows. See "Poetically Man Dwells . . . " in *Poetry, Language, Thought,* trans. Albert Hofstadter (New York: Harper & Row, 1971), 215–16.

[4] See John I. Goodlad, *A Place Called School* (New York: McGraw-Hill, 1984); George Hillocks, Jr., *Research on Written Composition, New Directions for Teaching* (Urbana, Ill.: National Council of Teachers of English, 1986); and Arthur N. Applebee, with Anne Auten and Fran Lehr, *Writing in the Secondary*

School: English and the Content Areas (Urbana, Ill.: National Council of Teachers of English, 1981). I am indebted to Professor Paul Connolly, the director of the Institute for Writing and Thinking, Bard College, for his invaluable comments and suggestions.

5See Craig H. Roell, *The Piano in America 1890–1940* (Chapel Hill: University of North Carolina Press, 1989); and Leon Botstein, *Music and Its Public: Habits of Listening and the Crisis of Modernism* (Chicago: University of Chicago Press, forthcoming), and "Patrons and Publics of the Quartets: Music, Culture and Society in Beethoven's Vienna," in Robert S. Winter and David Martin, eds., *The Beethoven Quartets: A Listener's Guide* (Berkeley: University of California Press, forthcoming). The analogy is particularly instructive for our understanding of the concept of reading. Wittgenstein's discussion is relevant. See his *Philosophical Investigations*, 2d edition (New York: Macmillan, 1958), 61e–70e.

6See Juergen Habermas's work, *The Theory of Communicative Action*, particularly vol. 2, *Lifeworld and System: A Critique of Functionalist Reason*, trans. Thomas McCarthy (Boston: Beacon Press, 1987).

7This discussion differs from the well-known argument in de Tocqueville. I would, however, contend that insofar as de Tocqueville saw language in America as strengthening egalitarian democracy and patriotism, it was with the concession (appropriate to a pessimistic but liberal aristocrat) that language would become inevitably leveled, and with it culture and genius. See Alexis de Tocqueville, *Democracy in America*, vol. 1, chap. 2 and vol. 2, chap. 16.

8See Theodore Zeldin, *Intellect, Taste and Anxiety*, vol. 2, *France 1848–1945* (Oxford: Oxford University Press, 1977), especially chap. 4. The effort by Noah Webster to create a specifically American language in the beginning of the nineteenth century (the blue-black spelling book and the dictionary) and the almost artificial lengths to which he went to achieve his goal are historical instances supportive of this analysis regarding the absence of a specifically American language. See Joseph J. Ellis, *After the Revolution: Profiles of Early American Cultures* (New York: Norton, 1979).

9These trends are not, obviously, in and of themselves negative. Cultural uniformity and political solidarity need not be mutually necessary or desirable, particularly for contemporary America. However, these social virtues and the survival of spoken dialects and foreign languages only underscore the need, at the same time, for a common English language, particularly in written form, for political life. The responsibility for achieving this rests with universal schooling.

10See Harvey J. Graff, *The Literacy Myth, Literacy and Social Structure in the Nineteenth Century City* (New York: Academic Press, Harcourt Brace Jovanovich, 1979).

11This discussion applies to Italian, Greek, Armenian, Slavic, and German immigrants. Consider, for example, the remarkable tradition of personal letter writing in the Yiddish daily papers in New York. See Isaac Metzker, ed., *A Bintel Brief: Sixty Years of Letters from the Lower East Side to the Jewish Daily Forward* (New York: Ballantine Books, 1972).

12A good contrast to this condition can be found in those circumstances—different from the American immigrant experience—in which multiple written languages existed in homes and in public. In the Habsburg Empire before 1914, particularly for Jews, multiple languages heightened the critical sense of language and its connection to thought. See Fritz Mauthner's recollection of his childhood in his 1918 *Prager Jugendjahre* (Frankfurt: Fischer Verlag, 1969).

13The tendency to depoliticize language by failing to underscore the relation of language to nature and language to thought in the teaching of language through an excessive literary bias and domination has taken a nasty turn with the advent of deconstruction. New literary theory places severe doubt on language as instrument of truth or reality, as instrument of potentially shared communication. One need not adopt either a primitive epistemology or a conception of language to sustain a subtle analytic defense of the categories of reason, truth, and communication. An extreme but now popular and widespread sophisticated subjectivism derived from a literary, aesthetic construct of language and texts can be rejected reasonably. See, for example, Juergen Habermas, *Reason and the Rationalization of Society*, vol. 1, *The Theory of Communicative Action*, trans. Thomas McCarthy (Boston: Beacon Press, 1984), 94–101.

14Consider, for example, the premium still placed on classic works such as Strunk and White's *The Elements of Style* and the pedagogical emphasis that remains in school texts on a simple, journalistic, and "clean" objective style, irrespective of the philosophical or substantive requirements possible among language users potentially at odds with such normative literary standards urged on students seeking a higher degree of literacy.

15Ludwig Wittgenstein, *Tractatus Logico-Philosophicus* (London: Routledge & Kegan Paul, 1961), 37, and "Foreword" in *Philosophical Remarks*.

16Readers who do not read German should consult the essay on Kraus by Erich Heller in *The Disinherited Mind* (Cleveland: Meridian Books, 1959); Elias Canetti's essay, "Karl Kraus: The School of Resistance," in *The Conscience of Words* (New York: Farrar, Straus & Giroux, 1979); the fine biography by Edward Timms, *Karl Kraus: Apocalyptic Satirist* (New Haven: Yale University Press, 1986); and Harry Zohn, ed., *In These Great Times: A Karl Kraus Reader* (Manchester, U.K.: Carcanet, 1984).

17See in this regard the analysis of speech and language in the work of Hannah Arendt: *Eichmann in Jerusalem* (New York: Viking, 1963), *The Human Condition* (Chicago: Chicago University Press, 1958), and *On Revolution* (New York: Viking, 1963).

18See George Steiner, "The Retreat from the Word," in *Language and Silence* (Harmondsworth: Penguin Books, 1969), 31–56; and Leon Botstein, "Imitative Literacy," *Partisan Review* 48 (3) (1981): 399–408.

19See Leon Botstein, "Politics, Language and Music," in Leonard Michaels and Christopher Ricks, eds., *The State of the Language*, vol. 2 (Berkeley: University of California Press, 1989).

20See Richard Hoggart's *The Uses of Literacy* (New York: Oxford University Press, 1970).

21See Norbert Elias, *Ueber die Zeit* (Frankfurt: Suhrkamp, 1988). As Wittgenstein remarked in the preface to his dictionary for schoolchildren, "oral information leaves a much weaker impression in one's memory than words one has seen," in

Ludwig Wittgenstein, *Woerterbuch fuer Volksschulen* (Vienna: Hoelder Pichler Temsky, 1926, 1977), xxv. See also Ludwig Wittgenstein, *Zettel* (Berkeley: University of California Press, 1970), 114e.

[22]See Lev Vygotsky, *Thought and Language* (Cambridge: M.I.T. Press, 1962); Nancie Atwell, *In the Middle: Writing, Reading, and Learning with Adolescents* (Portsmouth, N.H.: Heinnemann, 1988); and Donald Graves, *Writing: Teachers and Children at Work* (Portsmouth, N.H.: Heinnemann, 1982).

[23]See Wittgenstein's *Zettel*, note 22, 73e–76e; see also the provocative paper (unpublished) by Ranjit Chatterjee, "The Battle for Intelligence: Wittgenstein as Educator" (1989), and Leon Botstein, "Language, Reasoning and the Humanities," in Diane Ravitch, Chester Finn, and Robert Fancher, eds., *Against Mediocrity* (New York: Holmes and Meier, 1984).

[24]Paul Connolly and T. Vilardi, eds., *Writing to Learn Mathematics and Science* (New York: Teachers College Press, 1989).

[25]See Ludwig Wittgenstein, *Philosophical Investigations*, 2d edition (New York: Macmillan, 1958), 31e–42e. The dictionary cited in endnote 22 was organized in part to enable this sort of approach. As Heidegger put it, "But that is not to say, ever, that in any word-meaning picked up at will language supplies us, straight away and definitively, with the transparent nature of the matter as if it were an object ready for use," in Heidegger's *Poetry, Language, Thought*. George Steiner has remarked, "Language is in perpetual change," a point which needs to be stressed so that new generations seize literacy as a means for their own thoughts, not as a rigid inheritance. See George Steiner, "Understanding as Translation," *After Babel: Aspects of Language and Translation* (Oxford: Oxford University Press, 1975).

[26]This simple and commonsense objective is more difficult to achieve than it appears. The reading material in schools is heavily censored by regulating public authorities, from local school boards to the states, in often seemingly trivial ways. The source of the regulation and—to put it more bluntly—censorship is presumably the exercise of democratic rights by factions seeking to protect children in schools from so-called offensive religious views and secular values (e.g., eating junk food). However, all this does is to help rob reading of its desirability. If there is no critical conflict, no mystery, and nothing remotely taboo associated with reading—which is important and can be debated and discussed in group settings (and not in secret or in private)—then why read? The excessive regulation shuts off much of the great writing and literature and limits subject matter. Ironically, the passion expressed over what public school libraries collect and what is assigned reflects a nonliterate or a semiliterate ignorance and an exaggerated fear of the influence of reading. If it were only so powerful!

[27]See S. Witte and Lester Faigley, *Evaluating College Writing Programs* (Carbondale, Ill.: Southern Illinois University Press, 1983).

[28]Wittgenstein, *Philosophical Investigations*, 174e.

The Difficulties of School: Probable Causes, Possible Cures

Howard Gardner

School *may never have been easy for most students, but evidence accrues that it poses enormous problems for large segments of the American population today. Some of the contributing factors have long been present but have only begun to be understood in recent years: for example, the surprising disjunction between the intuitive knowledge which individuals have about the physical world and the kinds of understandings which are captured in formal codes and notational systems. But other factors of more recent vintage—chiefly those having to do with the deteriorating social supports and the anti-educational biases in the American value system—impose virtually insuperable obstacles on many American public schools.*

I. INTRODUCTION: THE PROBLEM

Those of us who routinely read scholarly articles may balk at the claim that literacy, numeracy, and critical thinking are often difficult to acquire. After all, whatever our family background or early schooling, most of us learned to read, write, and compute without undue problems. Moreover, it is likely that our children also accomplished these academic milestones with relative ease. Many of us (and our children) have selected those professions that presuppose literacy,

Howard Gardner is Professor of Education and Codirector of Project Zero at Harvard Graduate School of Education.

numeracy, and critical thinking (hereafter LNC); and we expect that those with whom we are in contact will also exhibit these skills.

To be sure, once we assume a different perspective, we recognize that a significant proportion of our population lacks these skills. As documented throughout this volume, many youngsters from impoverished backgrounds, and not a few of those from more privileged classes, have difficulties in mastering both "basic skills" and "higher-order thinking skills." On nearly every scholastic measure, the average performance of American students compares unfavorably with that of their counterparts in most industrialized countries. A growing number of our youngsters are being labeled as learning impaired.[1] Thus, we have become aware that LNC can no longer be taken for granted; and indeed we may be confronting a major educational crisis.[2]

Faced with the uncomfortable disjunction between our own experience and the current educational malaise, there is an understandable temptation to "blame the victim." If everyone were to put his nose to the grindstone, we could achieve much higher levels of LNC. The faults lie in our inadequate teachers, undemanding parents, and/or our lazy students. A dosage of Japanese (or Singaporean or Hungarian) medicine should cure America's learning maladies.

This prescription has its merits. If all those with responsibility for the schools made greater demands on others *and on themselves,* we could significantly raise test scores—and perhaps even the skills and knowledge that they are supposed to signal. Yet I believe that current reform efforts in this vein are likely to fail, because they are based upon an inadequate analysis of the learning process and on an anachronistic view of American society.

A better strategy calls upon us to rethink both our educational goals and our means for realizing them. Such rethinking must take into account three sets of factors which underlie the difficulties of school in America today. From a *psychological* perspective, specific developmental, cognitive, motivational, and/or neurological conditions may interfere with the acquisition of the school literacies. In terms of *secular* trends, numerous aspects of contemporary American society combine to make school an increasingly inhospitable environment for many children. Finally, a major contributing factor is the dominant *value system* of our society. The tension that exists between "traditional" and "progressive" values, as well as the particular historical and contemporary circumstances affecting American education, merit special scrutiny.

Hence, in what follows, I first review some historical aspects of education and schooling. I then consider the trio of factors that seem most important in accounting for our current situation. Only if we understand these conditions, and attempt to deal directly with them, can we come up with a prescription which will enhance the scholastic performance of significant numbers of children. In conclusion, I sketch out the principal features of "individually configured excellence," the approach most appropriate for American education in our time.

II. VARIETIES OF EDUCATIONAL INSTITUTIONS

Education has a much longer history than schooling. Throughout human existence, youngsters have learned from their parents (and from other elders) simply by observing them in their daily activities and by following their simple instructions or adages. Such learning begins shortly after birth and continues until the basic competences of the culture have been mastered, presumably somewhere between the ages of seven and adolescence. In cultures where specific crafts need to be mastered, apprenticeship systems have gradually evolved. Youngsters are explicitly assigned to masters and undergo a (usually lengthy and often arduous) educational process, frequently marked by a specified sequence of ranks. In this instance as well, learning takes place chiefly by observation and informal coaching, though the procedures for posing problems and evaluating performance are likely to be more formal than those adopted in the home. While apprenticeships are often narrowly conceived and harshly administered, they nevertheless embody important insights about the ways in which human beings come to achieve excellence in a domain.

Until acquisition of the basic literacies became an important societal goal, there was little reason to invent "schools." These institutions were designed in the first instance to teach the reading of text (often in a language other than the vernacular). Over time, they gradually increased in curricular scope, so that they encompassed a variety of literacies, reasoning skills, and scholarly disciplines. And, instead of having an exclusively religious or moral orientation, they came to serve a diversity of cognitive, social, economic, political, and civic purposes.

It would be a mistake to romanticize these early schools, with their harsh procedures and elitist clientele. But whatever their limitations, their scholastic activities were highly prized within the wider community. Parents placed a great value on the acquired literacies; teachers were considered the trustees of a sacred charge; the first day of school was marked as an important community event; and the "good" student (however defined) was held up as an ideal.[3]

For the most part the tracks of school and of apprenticeships have proceeded largely in parallel rather than in convergent ways. Youngsters enrolled in school or in apprenticeships; apprenticeships emphasized learning in context, while schools highlighted learning in a relatively antiseptic and remote setting. Only occasionally—as in progressive schools in the United States, or postgraduate training around the world—have attempts been made to integrate apprentice and scholastic models.

Nonetheless, aspects of the tension between apprenticeships and scholastic approaches have sometimes been echoed in the schools themselves. One can distinguish between two primary approaches to the acquisition of knowledge.[4] The traditional or "mimetic" approach emphasizes the mastery in a relatively rote manner of what has been thought, spoken, and written by earlier generations. The result of such a regimen is that nearly every student achieves a reasonably high level of competence, because redundancy in content and manner of presentation is so great. On the other hand, signs of innovation or originality are rare, and many students become ultimately estranged from schools in the wake of this essentially passive approach to learning.[5]

Contrasted to this traditional approach is a more "progressive" orientation toward education. In this vein, associated with the writings of Rousseau, Froebel, and (especially) John Dewey, it is assumed that individuals learn best when placed in a stimulating and meaning-rich environment. In such a highly contextualized setting (more reminiscent of the atelier than the traditional classroom), students have the opportunity to explore materials, pose and solve provocative problems on their own (or with their peers), or carry out their own projects. When well realized, such an education produces students who have initiative, imagination, and a lifelong commitment to learning.[6] Less well executed, however, progressive education can become a license for "anything goes" or "nothing happens." The *variability* of performance is likely to be much greater in a progressive school: some students attain outstanding performance, while others achieve far less than those shaped in a traditional setting.

While the tension between traditional and progressive approaches can be found throughout the world,[7] it has permeated American society in general, and American education in particular.[8] While Americans hold education in high regard, they have been less inclined to restrict it to the classroom, more inclined to recognize the educational importance of the home, the church, the workplace, and the media; and on occasion they have looked to the schools to counter the unwarranted influence of these other educational forces.[9] By the same token, Americans have been relatively open to the progressive philosophy, according to which school should extend well beyond—and perhaps give less weight to—the academic subject matters taught in a didactic manner. One must note as well a recurring ambivalence about "progressive experiments": there are periodic hankerings for a more traditional approach.[10] But an enduring accent on progressive themes is a vital part of the American heritage (while it is absent or a distinct novelty in most other societies): this element must be taken into account in any analysis of the current difficulties of school and in any prescription for American education.

III. PSYCHOLOGICAL FACTORS

While historical and social factors are often discussed in isolation from psychological factors, any consideration of the educational landscape ought to treat them in as integrated a way as possible. In recent years, much fresh evidence has been gathered about factors involved in teaching, learning, and human development. Interestingly, this research pulls in two directions: on the one hand, it underscores the tremendous receptivity of the young child to a wide variety of domains; on the other hand, it throws into sharp relief the formidable challenges involved in genuine mastery of scholastic materials.

The milestones of learning emerge with dramatic swiftness and potency in the opening years of life. Given environments that are not grossly impoverished, all children will learn how to speak and understand their native languages (and other languages in their surround) with ease and facility; acquire basic understandings of the operation of the physical world (the constancy of matter, the principles of cause and effect); understand key aspects of the social world (the way to convince another individual, the detection of benevolent or malevolent motivation); and use a range of symbolic codes, such as those involved in picturing, gesturing, and making music, in order to express and derive meanings. These and related capacities are daunting and yet seem to require relatively little direct tutelage. Indeed, as has been often noted, adults do not know *how to teach* many of the most important forms of knowledge which every normal child acquires as part of her birthright during the first years of life.[11]

We can describe a set of general principles that governs such early learning. During infancy, children's knowledge grows directly out of their *sensory* and *motor* interactions with the world of objects and with the circle of other persons. Many of these sensorimotor skills ultimately attain a high level of sophistication, as displayed for instance in riding a bicycle or throwing a ball. During the years of early childhood, children become facile at using the *symbols* valued in their culture—words, pictures, gestures, numbers. Then, at least for those youngsters who live in a literate culture, their task upon entering school is to master a more abstract form of symbolization—various cultural *notations*—such as those needed for reading, writing, performing arithmetical operations, and learning history, geography, and "general science." Once in school students also must learn *formal concepts and principles,* which have been discovered by scholars over the centuries, including those that may directly conflict with the *intuitive* knowledge that they built up during early childhood.

Until recently, due to the enormous (and largely beneficent) influence of Piaget,[12] it was thought that these principles—and this developmental sequence—operated quite generally across all areas of knowledge. However, it is now widely acknowledged that Piaget's scheme was too neat, and it has not been borne out in the wake of more careful examination of developmental trajectories in individual "domains of knowledge."[13] Piaget focused almost exclusively on "universal" domains of knowledge—those forms of learning which can be assumed across all cultures. But of increasing importance in our world are forms of learning which may be specific to certain cultures, such as the literacies and disciplines required in school.[14] While such areas as reading, or studying history, or composing music may well be characterized by stages of competence, the stages found in one domain may have little resemblance to, or correlation with, those regnant in other domains.

By the same token, even in those areas of learning which appear to be universal, all forms of learning do not develop in synchrony. Rather, human beings differ in the manner in which, and the speed with which, they express various mental capacities or "intelligences."[15] Thus, an individual may be quite advanced with her musical capacities, or her spatial reasoning, without any implication that she will be equally advanced with logical capacities or the understanding of other persons. The reasons for these relative proficiencies or deficiencies are not well understood but, at least in some cases, neurological deficiencies may be implicated,[16] making students more "at risk" in some intelligences than in others. More generally, it is quite clear that individual students have very different kinds of minds: the notion that they can all be taught in the same way, and that they will all learn or represent or recall knowledge in the same way, has lost plausibility.

The breakdown of the "Piagetian synthesis," which asserted that the same cognitive stages and structures of development obtained across all domains, has profound implications for our understanding of the learning processes. While "universal" capacities can perhaps be counted on to develop naturally, it is simply a mistake to expect that more culturally specific competences—such as the understanding of discipline-based concepts—can unfold without explicit tutelage. Generous endowment in one or two intellectual spheres may make certain aspects of school easy for the student; for example, students talented in language and logic may do well on standardized tests and in large segments of the standard curriculum. But the vast majority of students must somehow improvise effective approaches to various concepts and disciplines based on their own configuration of intellectual proclivities and deficits.

Enhanced appreciation of the complexity of learning has revealed a fascinating disjunction in many students' understanding of specific disciplines and domains. Relatively early in life, students develop an intuitive or "common sense" understanding of basic physical and social concepts. They also learn to parse the perceptual and symbolic world in certain ways—for example, grouping together members of the same species or segregating picture books from "pure" texts.

Once they have entered school, they encounter a different order of knowledge: one expressed in abstract symbolic codes (like written language, arithmetical symbols, maps, graphs, and the like). With greater or lesser difficulty, they begin to master these "notational" forms of knowledge. Researchers have compellingly documented how frequently these orders of understanding exist in splendid isolation from one another, with students failing to appreciate the relation between their long-lived intuitive knowledge and the way in which related concepts are customarily expressed in school.[17]

Let me mention instances of this disjunction drawn from three different domains. In the case of the understanding of physical properties, children just entering school appreciate that when water of ten degrees is mixed with water of ten degrees, the resulting mixture is also ten degrees. Somewhat older children, however, argue that the resulting mixture is twenty degrees, for one must always add such numbers together. "Common sense" has been overwhelmed by an algorithm which stipulates what to do with numbers.[18]

In the apprehension of a musical pattern, students without training in formal notation will display a "figurative" understanding. That is, they will appreciate which tones belong to the same phrases (even when they happen to occur in different measures) and where an accent should fall (even if it occurs in the middle of a measure); but they will fail to appreciate the exact temporal relations which obtain among individual attacks, because they lack the concept of meter. Students who have learned "formal" notation can accurately transcribe a pattern (they know just how much time elapses between attacks, and they will put the proper number of beats in a measure); but they will often appear insensitive to broader expressive aspects which elude standard notation. The task for the skilled musician is to reintegrate her formal knowledge of musical representation with the intuitive or figural sense of expression.[19]

Finally, in the realm of elementary physics, university students who have taken a course in Newtonian physics are able to answer challenging problems on a final examination. Yet, shortly after completion of the course, they fail to solve problems which exemplify the very principles that they had supposedly mastered; the students' answers reflect the same "naive" (Aristotelian) physics concepts that individuals untutored in physics exhibit.[20] Because they did not fully understand how the formalisms actually relate to intuitions, but had only memorized the contexts in which they appear in class, they cannot reconcile intuitions and formalisms when they are encountered in other settings.

In such diverse instances, a common pattern emerges. Students dutifully learn the symbolic, notational, and formal/conceptual accounts that are presented in a scholastic setting; when the identical eliciting circumstances appear, they can spew back the correct answers. Yet, there has not been a successful rapprochement between these new forms of representation and the more elementary sensori-motor and intuitive forms of knowledge which students acquire by virtue of their own long-term interactions in the practical world. In the absence of such connecting tissue, these forms of knowledge continue to exist independently from one another, so isolated that a contradiction may escape the learners entirely.

Here, then, we confront directly a major, though hitherto ignored, difficulty of school. "School knowledge" is typically presented and apprehended in a way remote from the manner in which that knowledge is customarily mobilized to solve problems and fashion products outside of a scholastic context. So long as testing is geared exclusively to "school knowledge," this disjunction can be ignored; but once we researchers begin to probe the flexibility and depth with which such knowledge has been acquired, we encounter a most unsettling conclusion. By and large, knowledge acquired in school helps one to progress in school, but its relation to life outside school is not well understood by the student, and perhaps not even by the teacher. The credentials provided by school may bear little relevance to the demands made by the outside community.

In sum, then, recent psychological investigations document the facility of child learning in many areas, even as they underscore the complexity of the task faced by the child who would master the curricula of school and then draw upon this knowledge to tackle issues in the larger society. Further, the evidence suggests that, in any culture, certain students will be at risk for failure in one or more school subjects and will not have an easy time in acquiring the basic and higher literacies. The relation between school achievement and success in the wider community remains vexed,[21] especially in a pluralistic society like America.

In addition to considering cognitive factors, it is necessary as well to take into account psychological factors of a motivational and affective sort. Students' learning potential reflects not only their "actual" capacities—however these might be defined or measured—but also their evaluation of their own capacities and the potential of those capacities to change as a result of effort or instruction.[22] Students who believe that they are competent, have reasonable self-esteem, gain pleasure from engagement, and feel that they can improve through application are in a much more favorable position than students who feel incompetent and lack the motive to better themselves through effort. Of course these ascriptions do not arise in a vacuum and may sometimes reflect genuine differences in capacity or energy. Yet, there is evidence that parents and teachers can influence these ascriptions and that a change in attitude may effect significant changes in performance.[23]

IV. SECULAR TRENDS IN CONTEMPORARY AMERICAN SOCIETY

While psychological factors can be considered without respect to a particular geographical setting, secular trends must necessarily be viewed with respect to a specific cultural context. In considering American society today, one risks being overwhelmed by the numerous factors at work in the culture, many of them seemingly at odds with the traditional (and even the progressive) model of school.[24]

In this essay I can do little more than list the "usual litany" of factors. There is, to begin with, the tremendous and growing heterogeneity in the population,[25] including very large proportions coming from disadvantaged backgrounds and, in contrast with most earlier waves, having little educational tradition in the family. There are the growing pressures on the family structure and much strain on local support networks.[26] There is the rapid pace of the society—epitomized by television, videogames, and interactive technologies;[27] and there is as well the sense of instant access to the many life-styles, fashions, practices, and options available around the world, some of them being potentially very destructive to the individual.[28] Probably none of these factors was completely absent in earlier eras; and it may be futile to attempt to demonstrate that the pace at which society alters is *more* rapid, or the disintegration of family life *more* pathological, today than it was a century ago. (It is less controversial to assert that these trends are heightened in the United States as compared with other cultures.) In any event their accumulated impact at the present time is enormous and difficult to contemplate in tranquility with reference to any of our institutions, least of all the schools.

Even more crucial than these trends, however, are the pressures to which the schools themselves are being subjected. On the one hand, the expectations surrounding schools are enormous. In generations past, high schools served only a small minority of our population and "dropping out" was common; nowadays, we like to see all of our students graduate from high school and a majority go on through college. At the same time, the expectations of primary and secondary education have increased. Whereas in an earlier time, the basic literacies were the *raison d'être* of school, it is now expected that students will master concepts in several increasingly complex disciplines (ranging from social studies to physics), exhibit higher-order thinking skills, learn to use computers, and distinguish themselves in extracurricular activities as well.

Yet at the very time when the schools are expected to educate everyone to a high level, the support surrounding the school system has weakened, where it has not completely collapsed. Teachers are drawn from the least well-prepared and least able segment of the college population;[29] taxpayer revolts have lessened the financial basis on which most schools must draw; bitter struggles among parents, school administrators, unions, court officials, and other interest groups make the classroom seem the pawn of educational conflict, rather than the primary locus of educational progress.[30]

Most strikingly, the high regard in which the schools were held until fairly recently has almost completely disappeared. In decades past, even those segments of the population with little educational experience looked to the schools as a primary avenue for improvement of one's life chances. The meritocratic potential of schools was widely appreciated. Nowadays, however, with the notable exception of the Asian-American populations, there is far less conviction that the schools can provide the means for personal self-improvement or for greater success in American society. Indeed, to some individuals, the schools appear increasingly anachronistic—a design or set of practices that may have made sense in an earlier era no longer seems appropriate.[31] To others, however, it is the schools that have changed in unpalatable ways: were they to revert to their earlier form, American education would be better off than it is today.

V. THE VALUE COMPONENT: PROGRESSIVE AND TRADITIONAL THEMES IN AMERICA TODAY

In discussing the recipes favored by different educational commentators, we touch directly the third of our factors: the values held in American society today. There may be agreement that our schools are inadequate; there may be consensus that all schools need effective instructional leaders or motivated students; but there remain disagreements over what our schools ought to be teaching; by what methods they ought to be teaching; how knowledge and skills should be assessed; and how schools should relate to the broader community. These discussions in turn reflect fundamentally competing value systems embraced in our country today. I will touch here on the competition between progressive and traditional values; the general value placed upon education in contemporary America; and the particular set of values that underlie my own program of improving education in our country today.

In the complex matrix of competing values, almost any generalization is at risk. Still, it seems reasonable to suggest that in American society, over the past century or more, there has been a relatively steady trend in the direction of progressive values.[32] Especially "in the streets" our culture honors values of choice, flexibility, individuality, self-motivation, and the pursuit of "fun" and "relevance" to a greater degree than does any other contemporary society. Within schools, the progressive element is perhaps less pervasive, at least in part because schools have been locales that honor a contrasting set of values— structure, regimen, externally imposed motivation.[33] Yet in many corners of our society, such as preschools, children's museums, and certain independent schools and liberal arts colleges, progressive values are alive and well.

Any claim with respect to the progressive nature of our society must take into account certain pulls in the alternative direction. First of all, there has always been in our culture a strong traditionalist— indeed, fundamentalist—strain, which is profoundly uncomfortable with the progressive values, particularly as they are embodied in a school.[34] (At least some fundamentalists are quite eager to see laissez-faire principles at work in the marketplace or on the streets.) Second, the ethnic groups which, over the decades, have relied on the schools as a route to success have embraced a regimen of hard work on hard subjects and have had little use for "experimental" approaches. Third, following an accent on progressive values during the 1920s and 1930s, and once again in the 1960s, there has been a quite pronounced swing away from progressive education as an avowed value—so much so that, in certain circles, one can elicit guffaws simply by explicit references to Dewey or to his ideas.

There may be genuine reasons for a disaffection with progressive practices, at least as they were implemented in their most recent or most radical guises.[35] Perhaps because of the permissive values in the society at large, and the breakdown of controls in many homes, an additional pull by the schools in the same direction proved destructive. And there is certainly reason for the complementary neoconservative desire for a return in the schools to "basic skills," "core values," and even "literacy, numeracy, and critical thinking."

Yet, in my view, current efforts to restore order and discipline and to promote greater learning in the primary and secondary schools of America have taken inappropriate forms and are unlikely to work. In its most prevalent guise—which I have termed the "uniform school"—the emphasis falls on a regimen in which teachers offer a highly restricted curriculum.[36] Students receive daily "basic skill" training through ubiquitous workbooks. Standardized tests are administered regularly, test results are promulgated widely, and students, teachers, principals, school districts, and entire states are evaluated on the basis of the average performance on these instruments. As the number of testing requirements increases, the degree of freedom allowed the teacher has steadily decreased, so that a great many teachers have little time to deal with anything except the prescribed curriculum. In the current argot, the students are workers, expected to "punch the clock" each day as they pass through the many hurdles supposedly en route to higher levels of literacy and more critical forms of thinking.

This portrait may have a caricatured flavor to it, but it probably describes with accuracy the pressures being felt by the vast majority of classrooms in America today.[37] Where the late 1960s featured an excess of choice and flexibility, the late 1980s feature uniform curriculum, uniform test scores, uniform performance standards—

and sometimes even uniforms! The evidence so far is that test scores have improved marginally, but even this result has been called into question because of the so-called Lake Wobegon effect—the ability of overly eager educational statisticians to make each student look as if she or he is "above average."[38]

Reactions to this re-Taylorization of American education have been twofold.[39] Those committed to a traditional approach say that the only solution is to impose even more severe and more specific requirements. Those committed to a progressive approach call instead for a loosening of requirements, fewer standardized measures, and greater professionalization of teachers.[40] The "new progressivism" is being attempted in several pockets of America: the various "restructuring experiments" have yet to exert a significant impact on the 15,000-odd school districts in the country.

While personally more sympathetic to the progressive approach, I am not sanguine that either the traditional or the progressive path will prove equal to the challenge of improving American education significantly. Neither has considered deeply enough the need for a solution that is built on and effectively integrates our three central factors: the psychological dimensions of learning, the secular trends at work in the society, and the dominant value systems in America today.

In considering educational values it is necessary to revisit and delineate more carefully a paradox which has pervaded America through most of its history and which increases the burden faced by the schools today. Few societies have paid as much lip service to the importance of education, which has sometimes played the role of a "secular religion" in our country; and no society has held universal education as a goal with the tenacity of the United States. And yet it seems necessary to say as well that education—and particularly the schools—have often held a dubious position in the value scheme of the larger society.

Why so? First of all, as noted above, knowledge rooted in the past has inevitably held an ambiguous place in a society founded upon the rejection of one's own heritage. America has always been hospitable to the notion of "second chances" or "alternative paths" and the lack of an education (or pedigree) has never been fatal. Our leaders have rarely been scholars or intellectuals; most have taken pride in identifying with the "common man"; and many of our celebrities (including our leaders) openly embrace an anti-intellectual stance. Teachers—and especially those of young children—receive meager compensation and occupy low niches on most measures of community status.

While many of us who are involved in intellectual or scholarly activities are understandably embarrassed or angered by this state of affairs, it would be disastrous to ignore it in any consideration of the ills of contemporary American education. American students assimilate these anti-intellectual attitudes, even as they absorb the attractive way in which the media portray "street smarts" and the sadistic manner in which "eggheads" get their comeuppance.

Any program for American education must be charted under the harsh light of these value factors: the struggle between progressive and traditional forces, and the widespread (if sometimes veiled) disdain that many Americans have for education and for educators. Further, any effort to prescribe an educational regime must perforce reflect its own scheme of values. In this spirit, I put forth my own framework for a more effective education in America.

VI. THE EDUCATIONAL TRIAD

While mastery of specific facts, or acquisition of the basic tools of literacy, might once have sufficed, such accomplishments are clearly inadequate today. Students must not only possess the skills of reading or of arithmetic; they must know how to use these tools, understand where they are relevant in and out of school, and acquire the capacity to continue learning once formal schooling is at an end.[41] Furthermore, they must attain sufficient depth so as to be able to integrate formal notations and concepts with intuitions and practical knowledge. To my mind, these represent a complex of "targets" which we must today embrace if our youngsters are to have a reasonable opportunity to fulfill their own intellectual potentials and to compete fairly in the future.

In speaking of intellectual potentials I make explicit a value central to my own educational philosophy. The primary task of educational institutions is to provide individuals maximum opportunities to develop their own potentials to the fullest possible extent, so long as they do not thereby prevent other individuals from developing their own potentials.[42] Stated so baldly, this educational goal seems utilitarian and egocentric, if not narcissistic. (One might quip that it is American in the worst connotation of the word!) At least on the surface such a vision contrasts sharply with an educational ideal that underscores the importance of knowledge accumulated in the past or a regime that focuses on the development of citizenship, cooperativeness, morality, or a religious strain.

Accordingly, I need to provide context for this value. First of all, I am in no way belittling the importance of knowledge or skills accumulated in the past. To realize one's potential, one must "work through" what has been known and thought in the past—else one will at best simply reinvent the knowledge accumulated in earlier eras. Second, I am not promoting a selfish or a self-centered regime. Indeed, I believe that individuals are most able to work cooperatively and to want to join forces for the wider good if, on the one hand, they have had the opportunity to develop their potentials, and if, on the other hand, they are able to make contributions that draw on their particular strengths and styles. Finally, I am in no way endorsing unbridled individualism. It is part of the community's role, and eventually, the individual's own obligation, to make sure that the development of his own potential does not collide with the development of other individuals or with the "common weal" of his society.

Having laid out in brief compass an educational value scheme, I turn to the issue of how best to achieve it. Here we must return to a consideration of the aforementioned trio of factors. In light of the many documented differences among youngsters, it no longer makes sense to administer to all children the same educational regimen. To be sure, it is appropriate—and perhaps even necessary—for all children to acquire the basic literacies and to study more "advanced" subjects like history or geometry. But *there is no reason why children should all have to study the same subjects at exactly the same time and in precisely the same way*. Rather, education can become far more individualized, with students encountering materials when they are deemed ready to master them, learning about these materials in ways that are congenial with their own learning styles and their profile of "intelligences," and being assessed in ways that are appropriate to the materials and that adequately capture the conceptions being taught in the student's class.

Effective education needs to take into account as well the secular trends and the overall value system of the society. In the America of the late 1980s, parents implore their children to read, write, and study; but they do remarkably little reading themselves (while watching many hours of television each day). Teachers' reading habits are not much better than "the general public's,"[43] and they rarely document for students the utilities of literacies in their own lives. Societal leaders call for critical thinking but tolerate in public debate a level of analysis which can be kindly characterized as sophomoric. A demand for discipline and decorum in the classroom is often put forth by the very individuals who countenance disorder, if not bedlam, in the marketplace. The messages—and the values—in the wider society are disconsonant with almost all of the educational practices being invoked by hand-wringing spokesmen.

Struck by this blatant disjunction between life in school and life in the society, students fail to appreciate the reasons for formal education. When they watch television or employ interactive technology, they have at their fingertips exciting phenomena from the entire world and can move among them with great facility. When they attend a children's museum, a science museum, or a discovery museum, they have an opportunity to learn about materials firsthand and to deploy intellectual capacities that are highly useful in the wider society but are often ignored—or even discouraged—in school. When they see the individuals who are most feted by the society—athletes, entertainment figures, politicians, and celebrities (those famous for being famous)—they behold a population that definitely exhibits skills but scarcely those valued within the walls of school. No wonder that so many children—whether privileged, ordinary, or at risk—find schools to be a boring, if not a downright alienating, experience.

Anyone sensate in American society today must also be struck by the incredible diversity of the society. Our society is as pluralistic and "nonuniform" as at any time in our history.[44] Members of diverse groups embrace different values and exhibit different styles of interaction and learning.[45] While certain aspects of uniform schooling might perhaps make sense in a relatively homogeneous society like Japan or Sweden, they are manifestly inappropriate—and probably unworkable—here.[46]

Sometimes, in a laudable effort to reconcile these different pulls, educators attempt to create an amalgam.[47] They offer some classes which emphasize traditional education, while others are more progressive; they reach out sporadically into the community or occasionally bring the community into the classroom; they conduct in-services on learning styles or developmental levels and attempt to inform their classes by these concepts. To be sure, such efforts do no harm, but these interventions are usually modest, or insufficiently thought through, and so they have relatively little lasting impact on their intended audience. What is needed is an integration on a far broader scale, one deeply rooted in the most enduring American values, our knowledge of individual development, and our understanding of the congeries of circumstances that constitute American society today.

VII. INDIVIDUALLY CONFIGURED EXCELLENCE: AN APPROACH TO SCHOOLS

Given vast differences among individuals and the brevity of human existence, it is patent that individuals cannot learn everything. Nor is there any reason to try to teach all individuals the same body of knowledge, let alone to teach common bodies of knowledge in the same way to all individuals.

Such considerations have led me to call for a form of schooling that is centered on the particular needs and potentials of each individual and that seeks to develop these to the highest possible extent. In such schooling, individuals have considerable choice in the kinds of materials with which they work and the ways in which they work with them; they begin from an early age to master certain skills which may be helpful to them in future vocational and avocational pursuits; their learning is regularly monitored in an informal and context-sensitive manner by others, even as the students themselves assume self-monitoring over the course of time. In such schools, all students participate in apprenticeships as well as traditional classes; indeed, each student becomes an apprentice from an early age in one art form, one bodily activity, and one academic area. Much time is spent working on long-term meaningful projects, reflecting on the course of those projects, presenting them to others, and preserving them for subsequent examination. Because I have written quite extensively about such schools elsewhere, I can make a virtue of necessity and be brief here.[48]

It is crucial to counter possible misconceptions about individually configured excellence. First of all, such schooling definitely involves certain obligatory skills and areas of content. Everyone masters the basic literacies and everyone studies something about the history and literature of his country and other countries; basic competencies in the arts and sciences are also acquired. But there is considerable flexibility on how and when these skills are acquired, even as there is choice of which arts and sciences are singled out for the careful study. Most important, even when there is obligatory content, there is flexibility concerning the manner in which this material is acquired and the means by which its mastery is assessed.

Individually configured excellence is by no means devoid of rigor. Indeed, in consultation with knowledgeable elders, students select areas for concentration and are then expected to undertake an apprenticeship of several years in those areas. As part of those apprenticeships students must carry out specific projects and acquire skills characteristic of ever higher levels of expertise. A student advances to a new level not when she has spent a certain number of hours in class but when she has demonstrated significantly enhanced competencies. Students work directly with individuals of unquestioned competence in the domain; accordingly, the need for rigor and the attainment of quality emerge as matters of common sense and not as seemingly arbitrary requirements. Students are encouraged to develop their knowledge and competence to the highest possible degree—hence my use of the term *excellence*.

Finally, as noted above, individually configured excellence should not be confused with self-centered education. Cooperative learning, peer learning, and group learning are entirely appropriate, as students master skills of consequence in their society. Indeed, if anything, it is the decontextualized "standardized test regimen" which seems to put a premium on individualism, isolation, and competitiveness. It is my hope that students involved in individually configured excellence will emerge as adults who are competent in several areas and who feel good about themselves; such self-confidence and self-esteem *ought* to result in more of a communal and selfless spirit.

I am opposed to efforts to mandate just how such individually configured excellence ought to be achieved. Especially in our country, "top-down" mandated educational reform does not work;[49] it is essential to adapt any approach to the particular circumstances of an individual region and school.[50] In lieu of a blueprint or receipt, I would simply offer a few guidelines.

First of all, some assessment of learning must occur in any school; it is unrealistic to expect citizens to invest in an educational experiment without some assurance that the experiment is working and some plans for adjustment if it is not. But it can be fatal to use inappropriate means for assessment; and so I have been devoting nearly all of my own research efforts to the development of new forms of assessment which are sensitive to particular intelligences and which can document the kinds of learning that take place "in context" when students are carrying out projects of some scope.[51]

A second consideration has to do with the matching of students with appropriate curricula and technologies of learning. It is fine to pay lip service to individual learning styles; but in fact the appropriate linking of students with materials, particularly when classes have thirty or more students, is no easy matter. Such "happy marriages" are most likely to work if systematic evidence has been accumulated about each student's learning profile and made available to future teachers and to the students themselves.[52] The use of teacher aides and older students who embody different teaching approaches can offer students a range of learning options within their own classrooms. Technologies also harbor the potential of delivering subject matter in ways that complement particular students' profiles of intelligences.

A final point has to do with the arbitrary limitations imposed when education is restricted to the schoolhouse. Typically, a myriad of educational opportunities exists in the wider community, including apprenticeships, mentorships, and other relations with competent professionals. These opportunities are particularly important for those students who have intellectual potentials that are not well served by the present formal school system. In my view, finding some topic or skill with which one feels "connected" is the single most important educational event in a student's life.[53] It is unreasonable to expect schools as currently constituted to cater to all intelligences and styles; however, it is reasonable for the school to help students connect with individuals and institutions that are relevant to their strengths, styles, and interests.

In this context, it is worth singling out the institution of the children's museums. While children's museums (and their close relations, science and discovery museums) are relatively new phenomena, their educational power is being convincingly demonstrated. For example, children's museums have a particular genius at drawing together the different forms of knowing—intuitive, skilled, symbolic, notational—which are either treated separately or ignored in the schools but which must be fused if an individual is to attain deep knowledge of a subject area.[54] In my view the interactive technologies currently being developed by museums and computer companies offer exciting possibilities for education which bridges different forms of knowing while linking scholastic with broader communal concerns.

Enhanced school-community links are of great importance for this endeavor. As noted above, so much of the community is seen (often appropriately) by children as being irrelevant (or even inimical) to the activities of school. It is crucial to identify those individuals and institutions in a community that do harbor the potential to make educational contributions, and to bring children into firsthand contact with educationally viable role models. A strong relationship with a caring adult or mentor is the single most potent predictor of success in an at-risk population;[55] in the many instances where such a relationship does not arise spontaneously, the schools can help to bring it about via productive networking with relevant community leaders and institutions. Where educators do not take the initiative, community leaders should.

I have left until last—though I hardly need say it is not least—a consideration of the role of parents and teachers in individually configured education. The best curricular materials are destined to fail unless there is, at the very least, support of educational goals and objectives on the part of those most significant in the life of the child. Correlatively, such support can make a big difference for students, whose security and efficacy can be significantly affected when they feel that "important others" are "in their corner."

Still, as our discussion of psychological factors has indicated, good intentions and active support systems are not enough. Much of what has to be learned in school is difficult; and at least some children are not well equipped to master the materials of school, which range from complex notational systems to bodies of technical knowledge. Even flexibility, sensitivity to individual differences and developmental differences, elaborate guidance, and technological prosthetics cannot substitute for the hundreds of hours of hard work, drill on materials that can only be learned in that way, and occasional frustration that accompany any serious intellectual endeavor. Excellence continues to correlate highly with perspiration.

Of the various impediments to productive learning, none is more entrenched than the disjunction among the various forms of knowledge which a youngster encounters as he grows up in a complex technological society. Here, I think, my own discipline of developmental psychology can teach us something vital. In any reasonably rich environment, young children show a strong desire to explore, to capture their knowledge in some kind of symbolic form, and to communicate their knowledge to other persons. Thus six- and seven-year-olds in our culture want to master notations and to comprehend principles of the world (though they may not be able to articulate either of these goals). We should help them to go as far as they can on the basis of these strivings and encourage them to develop their own notational systems, to articulate their own principles, and to attempt to communicate them to others.[56] As their own understandings become deeper, they are then in a much better position to relate these explicitly to those notational and explanatory forms that have developed over a much longer period of time in the wider culture.

In this process there will inevitably be disjunctions and confusions; indeed, these make learning initially frustrating, and ultimately enjoyable, as one learns one's way around the frustrations.[57] But so long as students perceive that they are engaged in a cooperative effort to figure out these systems, they are likely to persevere and ultimately to unravel the relations among these different forms of understanding. Moreover, it is on those occasions and in those skill areas where students have worked out for themselves the connections among the various forms of knowledge that they will be most likely to achieve true mastery and to be able to put that knowledge to appropriate—and even original—uses in the future.[58]

It is too much to expect that we will be able to undermine the competing and often mindless messages which pervade the wider society. But perhaps it is not essential that we do so. So long as individuals can locate a model of serious study, reflection, and application in the world that is meaningful to them, that model may be enough to sustain them. Indeed, nearly all adults have at least some preserve in which they feel committed and engaged. If we can so arrange "the contingencies" that all students have at least some exposure to adults engaged in such activities—and apprenticeships should ensure that—we may be able to mitigate the often destructive "countereducational" messages of the culture.

When I have described my vision to audiences of educators, I have often been greeted with the following response: "I am entirely in sympathy with what you would like to do. But it is simply not practical. However much we might like an education founded on individually configured excellence, we are compelled by economic considerations to impose a more uniform-style school and to police it with standardized tests."

While I recognize the rhetoric of the speaker, I find myself in fundamental disagreement with his premises. In my view, the model of individualized schooling is entirely possible to achieve. It makes sense in terms of what we know about human cognitive and motivational diversity; it makes sense from the perspective of secular trends in American society; and, if I may be personal, it makes sense in terms of a value system of individual growth, excellence, and cooperation, which many Americans embrace.

Our reluctance to pursue individually configured excellence reflects not so much a paucity of resources as a failure of will. Should our society decide to commit itself to such an educational course (with the same dedication which it has exhibited with regard to militaristic missions), I have no doubt that we could move speedily and effectively in that direction. Indeed, some efforts in which I am myself involved have already shown that features of individually configured excellence are within our grasp today.[59] It is possible to offer students far more meaningful scholastic choices; to assess their skills and capacities with measures that avoid the limitation of standardized tests; and to integrate their studies with opportunities for growth and stimulation in the wider community.

Admittedly, it takes effort to institute such changes. In the past they have been most likely to come about in those communities and institutions "on the margin," where experimentation is easier to carry out. Today, they are most likely to occur in those metropolitan areas where partnerships have been formed among scholastic, corporate, and philanthropic entities and where school administrations and unions have forged flexible contractual arrangements.[60] Pittsburgh is one operating example; Rochester promises to be another. Not every experiment works; and individually configured excellence may not be the optimal "choice" for every municipality and social group. But that most communities could offer an education that allows more individually configured excellence seems clear.

In this essay I have argued that current knowledge about human development and cognition should allow us to develop educational regimens that achieve a reasonable level of literacy, numeracy, and critical thinking for nearly all students, and a high level of competence for many of them. If we are to achieve these goals, however, we must attend carefully to the educational values that we are embracing and to the cultural ambience in which we are working. These goals are best achieved by embracing an individualized form of education, which takes seriously differences among students in abilities and proclivities, and which seeks to fuse aspects of traditional education, progressive education, and apprenticeships. Such an educational regimen should yield students who are more competent, who feel better about themselves, and who are more likely to become productive and cooperative members of the community. Achieving such an educated society may not be easy, but it is far more a matter of committed will and of values than it is a matter of additional resources. Whether or not this approach would have been optimal at other times or in more remote places, it is clearly the best approach for American society today.

ACKNOWLEDGMENTS

In addition to my fellow contributors, I would like to thank Jeanne Chall, Patricia Graham, Stephen Graubard, Jonathan Levy, David Perkins, and Edward Yeomans. I owe a special debt of gratitude to Mindy Kornhaber, who was a real partner in the preparation of this essay. The work described in this essay was supported in part by the Spencer Foundation, the Rockefeller Foundation, and the Lilly Endowment.

ENDNOTES

[1]Thomas Armstrong, *In Their Own Way* (Los Angeles: Tarcher, 1987); Gerald Coles, *The Learning Mystique: A Critical Look at "Learning Disabilities"* (New York: Pantheon Press, 1987); Arthur Jensen, "How Much Can We Boost IQ and Scholastic Achievement?" *Harvard Education Review* 39 (1) (1969): 1–123; and D. Lipsky and A. Gartner, *Beyond Separate Education* (Baltimore: Paul Brookes, 1989).

2A. Applebee, J. A. Langer, and I. V. S. Mullis, *Learning to be Literate in America: Reading, Writing and Reasoning* (Princeton, N.J.: National Association of Educational Progress, Educational Testing Service, 1987); Susan Berryman, "Education and the Economy: What Should We Teach? When? To Whom?" Occasional Paper No. 4, a lecture presented at the Graduate School of the City University of New York's Distinguished Speaker Series in Adult Learning, March 30, 1988; Allan Bloom, *The Closing of the American Mind* (New York: Simon & Schuster, 1987); E. D. Hirsch, *Cultural Literacy* (Boston: Houghton Mifflin, 1987); Diane Ravitch and Chester Finn, *What Do Our Seventeen-Year-Olds Know?* (New York: Harper & Row, 1987); and National Commission on Excellence in Education, *A Nation at Risk: The Imperative for Educational Reform* (Washington, D.C.: U. S. Department of Education, 1983).

3Bruno Bettelheim and K. Zelan, *On Learning to Read: The Child's Fascination with Meaning* (New York: Knopf, 1982).

4Howard Gardner, *To Open Minds: Chinese Clues to the Dilemmas of Contemporary Education* (New York: Basic Books, 1989); Philip Jackson, *The Practice of Teaching* (New York: Teachers College Press, 1986); and Seymour Sarason, *Schooling in America: Scapegoat and Salvation* (New York: Free Press, 1983).

5Gardner, *To Open Minds*.

6W. Aiken, *The Story of the Eight-Year Study* (New York: Harper and Brothers, 1942); Lawrence Cremin, *The Transformation of the School* (New York: Vintage, 1961); Patricia A. Graham, *Progressive Education from Arcady to Academe* (New York: Teachers College Press, 1967); and Patricia Minuchin, *The Psychological Impact of School Experience: A Comparative Study of Nine-Year-Old Children in Contrasting Schools* (New York: Basic Books, 1969).

7Gardner, *To Open Minds*.

8Bernard Bailyn, *Education in the Forming of American Society* (Chapel Hill, N.C.: Publication for the Institute of Early American History and Culture at Williamsburg, Virginia, University of North Carolina Press, 1960); Oscar Handlin, *The Uprooted* (Boston: Little Brown, 1951); Richard Hofstadter, *Anti-intellectualism in American Life* (New York: Knopf, 1963); George Spindler, *Education and Culture: Anthropological Approaches* (New York: Holt, Rinehart & Winston, 1963), chap. 7 and 8.

9Bailyn; Lawrence Cremin, *American Education: The Metropolitan Experience 1876–1980* (New York: Harper & Row, 1988).

10Robert N. Bellah, *Habits of the Heart: Individualism and Commitment in American Life* (New York: Harper & Row Perennial Library, 1986); Hofstadter; and David Riesman, Nathan Glazer, and R. Denney, *The Lonely Crowd* (Garden City, N.Y.: Doubleday, 1953).

11Noam Chomsky, *Reflections on Language* (New York: Pantheon, 1975).

12Jean Piaget, "Piaget's Theory," in P. Mussen, ed., *Handbook of Child Psychology*, vol. 1 (New York: Wiley, 1983).

13Peter Bryant, *Perception and Understanding in Young Children* (New York: Basic Books, 1974); Margaret Donaldson, *Children's Minds* (Glasgow: Collins/Fontana, 1978); Kurt Fischer, "A Theory of Cognitive Development: The Control of

Hierarchies of Skill," *Psychological Review* 87 (6) (November 1980): 477–531; Howard Gardner, *Frames of Mind: The Theory of Multiple Intelligences* (New York: Basic Books, 1983); and Rochel Gelman, "Cognitive Development," *Annual Review of Psychology* 29 (1978): 297–332.

[14]David Feldman, *Beyond Universals in Cognitive Development* (Norwood, N.J.: Ablex, 1980).

[15]Gardner, *Frames of Mind*.

[16]Norman Geschwind and A. Galaburda, *Cerebral Lateralization* (Cambridge: M.I.T. Press, Bradford Books, 1986).

[17]Sylvia Scribner and Michael Cole, "Cognitive Consequences of Formal and Informal Schooling," *Science* 182 (4112) (1973): 553–59; Rochel Gelman, Melissa Cohen, and Patrice Hartnett, "To Know Mathematics Is to Go beyond Thinking that 'Fractions Aren't Numbers,' " *Proceedings of the Eleventh Annual Meeting of the North American Chapter, International Group for Psychology of Mathematical Education*, September 1989, Rutgers, N.J.; and Lauren Resnick, "Learning In School and Out," *Educational Researcher* 16 (9) (December 1987): 13–20.

[18]Sidney Strauss, ed., *U-Shaped Behavioral Growth* (New York: Academic Press, 1982).

[19]Jeanne Bamberger, "Intuitive and Formal Musical Knowledge," in S. Madeja, ed., *The Arts, Cognition, and Basic Skills* (St. Louis: CEMREL, 1982); and Jeanne Bamberger, "Revisiting Children's Descriptions of Simple Rhythms," in *U-Shaped Behavioral Growth*, ed. Sidney Strauss (New York: Academic Press, 1982).

[20]Andrea A. DiSessa, "Unlearning Aristotelian Physics: A Study of Knowledge-Based Learning," *Cognitive Science* 6 (1) (January–March, 1982): 37–75; Michael McCloskey and R. Kargon, "The Meaning and Use of Historical Models in the Study of Intuitive Physics," in S. Strauss, ed., *Ontogeny, Phylogeny, and Historical Development* (Norwood, N.J.: Ablex, 1988); and Alfonso Caramazza, Michael McCloskey, and Bert Green, "Naive Beliefs in 'Sophisticated' Subjects: Misconceptions about Trajectories of Objects," *Cognition* 9 (2) (April 1981): 117–23.

[21]Christopher Jencks, *Inequality: A Reassessment of the Effect of Family and Schooling in America* (New York: Basic Books, 1972).

[22]Ann Brown, John D. Bransford, R. A. Ferrera, and Joseph C. Campione, "Learning, Remembering, and Understanding," in P. Mussen, ed., *Handbook of Child Psychology*, vol. 3 (New York: Wiley, 1983); Mihaly Csikszentmihalyi and Isabella Csikszentmihalyi, eds., *Optimal Experience: Psychological Studies* (New York: Cambridge University Press, 1988); Carol Dweck and E. Elliot, "Achievement Motivation," in P. Mussen, ed., *Handbook of Child Psychology*, vol. 4 (New York: Wiley, 1983); and John Ogbu, *Minority Education and Caste: The American System in Cross-Cultural Perspective* (New York: Academic Press, 1978). See also John Ogbu's article in this issue.

[23]James Comer, "Educating Poor Minority Children," *Scientific American* 259 (5) (November 1988): 42–48; Dweck and Elliot; and Harold Stevenson, *Child Development and Education in Japan* (New York: W. H. Freeman, 1986).

24Sarason.

25Harold Hodgkinson, "The Right Schools for the Right Kids," *Educational Leadership* 45 (3) (February 1988): 10–14.

26Nathan Glazer, *The Limits of Social Policy* (Cambridge: Harvard University Press, 1988).

27John Naisbitt, *Megatrends: Ten New Directions Transforming Our Lives* (New York: Warner, 1982); and Neil Postman, *The Disappearance of Children* (New York: Delacorte Press, 1982).

28Christopher Lasch, *The Culture of Narcissism* (New York: Norton, 1978); and Marshall McLuhan, *Understanding Media* (New York: McGraw-Hill, 1964).

29Carnegie Forum on Education and the Economy, *A Nation Prepared: Teachers for the 21st Century: The Report on the Task Force on Teaching as a Profession* (Washington, D.C.: The Forum, 1986), 32; and Gary Sykes, "Contradictions, Ironies and Promises Unfulfilled: A Contemporary Account of the Status of Teaching," *Phi Delta Kappan* 65 (2) (October 1983): 87–93.

30For an account that exemplifies the struggles among these various parties, see J. Anthony Lukas, *Common Ground* (New York: Knopf, 1985).

31Henry Giroux, *Ideology, Culture and the Process of Schooling* (Philadelphia: Temple University Press, 1981); Ivan Illich, *Deschooling Society* (New York: Harper & Row, 1970); and Sarason.

32Cremin, *American Education*.

33Robert Dreeben, *On What Is Learned in Schools* (Reading, Mass.: Addison-Wesley, 1968); Jackson, *The Practice of Teaching*; and Philip Jackson, *Life in Classrooms* (New York: Holt, Rinehart & Winston, 1968).

34Hofstadter.

35Diane Ravitch, *The Troubled Crusade* (New York: Basic Books, 1983); and Diane Ravitch, *The Schools We Deserve* (New York: Basic Books, 1985).

36Howard Gardner, "An Individual-Centered Curriculum," in *The Schools We've Got, The Schools We Need* (Washington, D.C.: Council of Chief State School Officers and the American Association of Colleges of Teacher Education, 1987); Gardner, *To Open Minds*; and Howard Gardner, "The School of the Future," in *Ways of Knowing* (Englewood Cliffs, N.J.: Prentice Hall, 1991).

37Carnegie Foundation for the Advancement of Teaching, *The Condition of Teaching: A State-by-State Analysis, 1988* (Princeton, N.J.: Princeton University Press, 1988).

38John J. Cannell, *Nationally Normed Elementary Achievement Testing in America's Public Schools: How All Fifty States Are Above the National Average* (Daniels, W.Va.: Friends for Education, 1987).

39Raymond Callahan, *Education and the Cult of Efficiency: A Study of the Social Forces that Have Shaped Administration of the Public Schools* (Chicago: University of Chicago Press, 1963).

40Ernest Boyer, *High School: A Report on Secondary Education in America* (New York: Harper & Row, 1983); John I. Goodlad, *A Place Called School* (New

York: McGraw-Hill, 1984); Albert Shanker, "The Making of a Profession," *American Educator* 9 (3) (Fall 1985): 10–17, 46–48; Lee Shulman, "On Assessment of Teaching: A Conversation with Lee Shulman," *Educational Leadership* 46 (3) (November 1988): 42–46; and Theodore Sizer, *Horace's Compromise* (Boston: Houghton Mifflin, 1984).

⁴¹Berryman; and Richard Murnane, "Education and the Productivity of the Workforce: Looking Ahead," in Robert Litan, Robert Z. Lawrence, and Charles Schultze, eds., *American Living Standards: Threats and Challenges* (Washington, D.C.: Brookings Institution, 1988).

⁴²Israel Scheffler, *Of Human Potential: An Essay in the Philosophy of Education* (London: Routledge & Kegan Paul, 1985).

⁴³C. Emily Feistritzer, *Profiles of Teachers in the United States* (Washington, D.C.: National Center for Education Information, 1986), 61.

⁴⁴Hodgkinson.

⁴⁵Shirley Brice Heath, *Ways with Words* (New York: Cambridge University Press, 1983); and Stephen Arons, *Compelling Belief: The Culture of American Schooling* (New York: McGraw-Hill, 1983).

⁴⁶James M. Fallows, *More Like Us: Making America Great Again* (Boston: Houghton Mifflin, 1989).

⁴⁷Arthur G. Powell, Eleanor Farrar, and David K. Cohen, *The Shopping Mall High School: Winners and Losers in the Educational Marketplace* (Boston: Houghton Mifflin, 1985).

⁴⁸Gardner, "An Individual-Centered Curriculum"; Gardner, *To Open Minds*; Gardner, "The School of the Future"; Howard Gardner, "Balancing Specialized and Comprehensive Knowledge: The Growing Education Challenge," in T. Sergiovanni, ed., *Schooling for Tomorrow: Directing Reform to Issues that Count* (Boston: Allyn and Bacon, 1989). See also Lynn Olson, "Children Flourish Here: Eight Teachers and a Theory Changed a School World," *Education Week* 7 (18) (27 January 1988): 1, 18–20, and "In Pittsburgh: New Approaches to Testing Track Arts 'Footprints,' " *Education Week* 8 (11) (1988): 1, 22–23.

⁴⁹Linda McNeil, *The Contradictions of Control: School Structure and School Nature* (New York: Methuen, 1986).

⁵⁰Theodore Sizer, "The Coalition of Essential Schools," in *Horace's Compromise*, 1–5, passim.

⁵¹Howard Gardner, "Assessment in Context: The Alternative to Standardized Testing," in E. R. Gifford and M. C. O'Connor, eds., *Future Assessments: Changing Views of Aptitude, Achievement, and Instruction* (Boston: Kluwer Academic Publishers, 1991); and Howard Gardner and Thomas Hatch, "Multiple Intelligences Go to School," *Educational Researcher* 18 (8) (1989): 4–10.

⁵²For efforts to develop such systematic evidence see Mara Krechevsky and Howard Gardner, "The Emergence and Nurturance of Multiple Intelligences," in Michael J. A. Howe, ed., *Encouraging the Development of Exceptional Skills and Talents* (Leicester, England: British Psychological Society, 1990); and Gina

Kolata, "Project Spectrum Explores Many-Sided Minds," *New York Times Educational Supplement* (9 April 1989): 61.

53 Joseph Walters and Howard Gardner, "The Crystallizing Experience," in Robert Steinberg, ed., *Conceptions of Giftedness* (New York: Cambridge University Press, 1986).

54 Frank Oppenheimer, "Everyone Is You . . . or Me," *Technology Review* 78 (7) (June 1976).

55 Comer; and M. Rutter and D. Garmezy, "Developmental Psychopathology," in P. Mussen, ed., *Handbook of Child Psychology*, vol. 4 (New York: Wiley, 1983).

56 Eleanor Duckworth, *The Having of Wonderful Ideas and Other Essays* (New York: Teachers College Press, 1987).

57 Csikszentmihalyi and Csikszentmihalyi.

58 David N. Perkins and G. Salomon, "Teaching for Transfer," *Educational Leadership* 46 (1) (September 1988): 22–32; and D. N. Perkins and R. Simmons, "Patterns of Misunderstanding: An Integrative Model of Misconceptions in Science, Mathematics, and Programming," *Review of Educational Research* 58 (3) (1988): 303–26.

59 Howard Gardner, "Zero-Based Arts Education: An Introduction to Arts PROPEL," *Studies in Art Education* 30 (2) (Winter 1989): 71–83; Gardner, "The School of the Future"; Lynn Olson, "Children Flourish Here: Eight Teachers and a Theory Changed a School World," and "In Pittsburgh: New Approaches to Testing Track Arts 'Footprints.' "

60 Gene Maeroff, *The Empowerment of Teachers* (New York: Teachers College Press, 1988); Paul T. Hill, Arthur E. Wise, and Leslie Shapiro, *Educational Progress: Cities Mobilize to Improve Their Schools* (Washington, D.C.: Rand Corporation, 1989); Sizer.

The problem of educational illiteracy and its antidote have their roots in the preschool stages of development. Early childhood is probably the time when normal children are most sensitive and responsive to their environment. One need only observe that young children begin to understand and communicate in the language of their social environment, that this verbal facility increases within the support of the family and is reinforced by interaction in the first school experience, to see the importance of this early stage.

The development of language usually occurs through auditory stimulation, and does not in itself require visual stimulation. The visual stimuli involved in learning to read need not be so difficult to learn. Yet, such a variety of theories exists on the matter, often generating self-fulfilling prophecies to explain the failure to accomplish the desired end, that one can only express surprise. If such controversies existed also with respect to verbal communication, there would be a need for a plethora of remedial oral language skills courses to supplement those that now exist for remedial reading. An embarrassingly simple approach to the remedy of illiteracy among children and adults would be to teach them to read with the natural ease and flair that is common when they learn to speak and communicate orally. Learning to use visual stimuli, essential to reading, is not an unattainable goal in the struggle against illiteracy.

Kenneth B. Clark
President
Kenneth B. Clark & Associates, Inc.
Hastings-on-Hudson, New York

Literacy and Intrinsic Motivation
Mihaly Csikszentmihalyi

T*he chief impediments to learning are not cognitive. It is not that students cannot learn; it is that they do not wish to. If educators invested a fraction of the energy they now spend trying to transmit information in trying to stimulate the students' enjoyment of learning, we could achieve much better results.*

It has turned out that mass literacy is not as easy to achieve as educational reformers had anticipated. To close the gap between the rather dismal reality and the golden future envisaged, researchers and practitioners are investing their energies in teaching methods modeled on computers and other rational means for processing information—which in turn were modeled on industrial production techniques and on military human systems design. The implicit hope is that if we discover more and more rational ways of selecting, organizing, and conveying knowledge, children will learn more effectively.

Yet it seems increasingly clear that the chief impediments to literacy are not cognitive in nature. It is not that students cannot learn; it is that they do not wish to. Computers do not suffer from motivational problems, whereas human beings do. We have not found ways as yet to program children so that they will learn the information we present to them, as computers do. Unfortunately, cognitive science has not taken adequate notice of this fact, and hence the current cognitive emphasis on teaching is missing out on an essential component of what learning is about.

This essay will raise some motivational issues involved in achieving literacy, in the hope of reminding educators of the importance of this

Mihaly Csikszentmihalyi is Professor of Psychology and of Education at the University of Chicago.

dimension of learning. Of the two main forms of motivation—extrinsic and intrinsic—we shall focus primarily on the second kind. Both are needed to induce people to invest energy in learning. Intrinsic motivation, which is operative when we learn something primarily because we find the task enjoyable and not because it is useful, will be examined more closely because it is claimed to be a more effective and more satisfying way to learn.

The claim is that if educators invested a fraction of the energy they now spend trying to transmit information in trying to stimulate the students' enjoyment of learning, we could achieve much better results. Literacy, numeracy, or indeed any other subject matter will be mastered more readily and more thoroughly when the student becomes able to derive intrinsic rewards from learning. At present, however, lamentably few students recognize the idea that learning can be enjoyable.

THE PROBLEM

In the past few generations we have become used to the idea that every person on the planet ought to know how to read and write and be versed in arithmetics. Even the least developed countries strive to achieve 100 percent literacy in the three Rs. In technologically advanced societies, beyond these basic skills, we expect people to achieve all sorts of additional ones: visual, numeric, computer, geographical, cultural, and moral literacies have all been singled out as being essential. These expectations imply a view of the human mind as a bottomless vessel that will retain whatever information is poured into it.

Despite great expectations, the evidence suggests that, at least in the United States, a point of diminishing returns in educational achievements has been reached. Ignorance has proved to be more stubborn than anyone had expected. It is not my intention to document this claim, since anyone even mildly involved with educational issues is already quite aware of the extent of the problem and has his or her favorite horror statistics to back it up. I will, however, give some brief examples so that we might start from the same factual starting point in terms of what follows.

For instance, when the Educational Testing Service (ETS) in 1984 completed its assessment of the writing achievement of American schoolchildren, based on a sample of about 55,000 fourth-, eighth-, and eleventh-grade students, it found, among other things, that when requested to "write a convincing letter to get a summer job helping out at a swimming pool," 24 percent of the seventeen-year-olds wrote something on the order of:

> I want to work in the pool.

(This being their idea of how detailed a "convincing letter" should be.) An additional 56 percent wrote more elaborate letters of the following type:

> ⸗ I have been experience at cleaning house. Ive also work at a pool be for. I love keeping things neat organized and clean. Im very social I'll get to know peopl really fast. I never forget to do things.

Only 20 percent of the seventeen-year-olds wrote letters rated at a level of sophistication higher than the example above. And it should be noted that the survey included only *students*. By 1982, 15 percent of the white youth and 31 percent of the Hispanics in this age group had dropped out of school.[1] Just about the only silver lining this comprehensive report contains is that seventeen-year-olds tend to write somewhat more correctly and compellingly than ten-year-olds. But even by the very generous definition of adequacy the study employs, the conclusion was that "even at grade 11, fewer than one-fourth of the students performed adequately on writing tasks involving skills required for academic studies."[2]

A similar situation holds for numerical literacy. The 1986 ETS survey was again based on a representative national sample of over 50,000 students in grades three, seven, and eleven.[3] It found, among other things, that half of the seventeen-year-olds could not correctly answer multiple-choice questions on the order of: "Which of the following is true about 87% of 10?" with the choices being: "It is greater than 10," "It is less than 10," "It is equal to 10," "Can't tell," "I don't know." Another question that half of the seventeen-year-old students could not answer was: "What is the area of a rectangle with sides of 4 cm and 6 cm?" The possible answers ranged from 4 to 24 square cm.

Getting to the most difficult mathematical problems used in the survey—which still seem ridiculously easy—94 percent of the eleventh graders could not answer questions of the type: "Christine borrowed $850 for one year from the Friendly Finance Company. If she paid 12% simple interest on the loan, what was the total amount she repaid?" Educators in other countries complain at the mathematical backwardness of their students. But in most technologically advanced countries, the lowest level of performance tends to be above the American average. The Japanese average is higher than that of the top 5 percent of American students enrolled in college preparatory courses.[4] Given such results, it is difficult to comprehend how the majority of young Americans can ever find jobs, and how they can figure out whether they are making or losing money.

To counteract these alarming trends, educational researchers and cognitive psychologists have been devising new models of the learning process, new methods of instruction, new teaching technologies. Textbooks are getting revised so that the information they contain is more clearly presented (in terms of the currently fashionable theories); the latest advances in computers, data processing, and audiovisual equipment are harnessed to the task of delivering information to the recalcitrant students. This apotheosis of educational innovation, however, seems to make few inroads into the inertia of learning. The shining knights who ride forth equipped with the latest weapons of cognitive technology return blackened and bruised, while the dragon of ignorance goes on peacefully slumbering in its cave.

The problem is that educational methods that work well under laboratory conditions often fail dismally in real life. It is dangerous to generalize from experimental performance of humans—of children especially—to what they will do when they go home. Confined in a psychologist's lab, children may learn a new way of doing math very fast just to impress the tester, or because they want to get out of there as soon as possible. But they may completely ignore the same material when it is presented to them in school. Inferences about how children learn based on computer heuristics tend to be equally flawed. People are not like thinking machines in one important respect: whereas computers are built so that they will follow logical steps as long as they are plugged into the wall and the appropriate software gets booted up, people will think logically only when they feel like it.

The major impediments to literacy—and to learning in general—have little to do with the *logic* of packaging information; if anything, the *aesthetics* of it are more important. This is because the obstacles that stand in the way of learning are primarily motivational, not cognitive in nature. Who would doubt that students in 1990 could be learning to write and use numbers much better than they are, even if we used teaching methods prevalent in 1890—provided the students wanted to learn? So why are we exhausting our energies trying to improve the teaching of English and math, when the real problem is to stimulate the desire for learning? The only answer to this question seems to be that, just as the drunk who lost his keys kept looking for them under the streetlight even though that's not where he had dropped them, because at least near the lamp it was light and he could see, so we keep looking for the solution to our educational problems under the bright light of reason, even though the evidence suggests that that's not where the answer lies.

It is time, therefore, to seek solutions to our educational impasse that take motivation into account more seriously. Before doing so, however, we should begin at the beginning, and reflect on what literacy is, and how it came about. This excursion into historical origins might make it easier to think about the issues in their proper context.

WHAT IS LITERACY?

In the debates surrounding this issue, it often seems that the parties involved think of illiteracy as some sort of disease, as a natural scourge like a viral infection that debilitates an otherwise healthy organism. It takes only a little thought, however, to remind us that it is nothing of the sort. Illiteracy is a social phenomenon, not a natural one. It exists only as the shadow of literacy—as long as no one could read, there could be no illiterates. And the more forms of literacy are invented, the more the chances increase that a person will be illiterate in some way or another. Thirty years ago I was illiterate as far as the FORTRAN computer language is concerned. Today I am illiterate not only in FORTRAN, but also in Pascal, LISP, and the many other new idioms developed since.

Literacy presupposes the existence of a shared symbol system that mediates information between the individual's mind and external events. The earliest systems were probably pictorial—although it is likely that songs and ritual incantations provided the same purpose even earlier, but left no trace. In the fertility figurines carved 30,000 years ago, in the pictorial representation of hunts on the walls of caves, in the calendars scratched on bone, our ancestors condensed information they considered essential to keep before their eyes and to pass on to others. In this sense, humans had learned to extend the capacity of their minds outside their heads. They had learned to store information extrasomatically.

Before the invention of the first symbol systems, the limit on how much information we could process and remember was set by the biological capacity of the central nervous system. When a person died, his or her laboriously acquired knowledge also disappeared. Whatever useful knowledge a person learned had to be passed on by word of mouth, thus garbling the content and creating bottlenecks in communication. By removing knowledge from the fragile network of nerves, and carving it in bone and stone instead, our ancestors made it much more permanent and accessible.

The ability to code and to decode information preserved in such extrasomatic memory systems is what we call literacy. A person who is literate has access to the knowledge stored in a particular system. A person may be the greatest genius, and may have learned from experience more than any other person knows, yet still be an illiterate if the only knowledge he or she has access to is the one stored inside his or her brain. Thus, illiterates are not necessarily less knowledgeable, less smart, or less able than their literate counterparts. But they are excluded from the network of information mediated by symbols. Whether this is a great handicap or not depends on the extent to which one must rely on such mediated knowledge to function well in a particular society.

The first "true" literacy begins with the invention of writing. As far as we know, letters were first carved in clay to record transactions of taxes and tributes between lords of increasing power: the transfer of so many pigs, so many jars of oil, so many bushels of grain from one potentate to another.[5] "L'écriture," notes Maurice Lambert, "est née du besoin d'enrégistrer et de cataloguer les richesses des marchands et des grands."[6] In addition, letters were used to expedite the will of kings who had their commands written down and delivered to far-off provinces.[7] It is very clear that as soon as knowledge became externalized, it was immediately appropriated by those in control of social forces. The rulers of the temples and of the armies were the only ones who could afford to own scribes, and with their help the rulers were able to extend information-processing capacities beyond the thickness of their skulls. Their memory was expanded, and the reach of their will extended. Others who benefited from reading and writing were the young men who became the literary tools of the rulers and who were able to exchange a hard life in the fields for a much more comfortable existence in the library. But it is difficult to see literacy as liberating for the masses of people; for them, rather, it constituted another means by which oppression was made more complete.

Thus, from its very beginnings, literacy has raised two questions that recur through history and that are still baffling us today: What purpose does literacy serve? And, who benefits from it? To ask such questions may seem to introduce a political dimension into the discussion, but that is not the intent here. The reason for asking them is that unless we consider the *qui bono* question, it will be difficult to address motivational issues adequately.

The history of literacy is too intricate for even a short summary in this context. But a few selected highlights of how learning became institutionalized in Europe are useful in pointing out similarities with the current situation. After the decline of Rome, when the territories of the former empire were invaded by illiterate warrior tribes, the newly established Christian church maintained its supremacy by specializing in literacy—a career that was certainly not easily predictable from its anti-intellectual beginnings. For many centuries in Europe the only schools were located in monasteries and in the residences of bishops.[8] They trained the clerics whose skills provided the extended memory needed by the barbarian lords to rule their newly occupied territories. The clergy recorded the laws, kept up genealogies and histories, wrote contracts and decrees, and passed on medical and scientific knowledge.

The hierarchical and organic structure of medieval society precluded the notion of universal literacy. Extrasomatic information simply had no relevance to the majority of people. Why should a peasant read Augustine's philosophy, Roman law, or the Bible? It would do no good to him, and certainly would not benefit his betters. It made much more sense to let everyone follow his or her calling. The lord's burden was to rule; to do so efficiently, he needed to extend his control over information coded extrasomatically; for this he employed a small cadre of specialists who updated and kept his records. The organic analogy was compelling: just as in the body the brain does the thinking, and the rest of the organs do their job without bothering to speculate or remember, so in the body politic the majority were to limit themselves to toil within the confines of their biological destiny. Culture—the cumulating knowledge recorded in the various systems of literacy—was to be accessible only to a few.

This view began to break down only as the flow of energy in society became increasingly dependent on coded information that was widely disseminated and easily accessible. For example, when the wealth of Florentine merchants began to depend more on transactions carried out by salesmen in distant markets, with different currencies, on delicately carved margins of profit, based on complex credit structures rather than on straightforward barter or on local sales, the merchants began to realize that they needed an increasing supply of clerics who could write and do sums. Thus, by the early Renaissance the guild of merchants in Florence decided to start its own school, to supplement the teaching provided by the Church.[9]

After five centuries, history repeats itself neatly: in the past decade more and more businessmen in the United States are taking action to improve basic education, knowing that the survival of their enterprises depends on a work force more literate than the present one. As a research analyst for the American Enterprise Institute said a few years ago, "Businesses are beginning to look at school assistance as an investment that they can collect on in the future. They believe that helping education now will better enable them to meet their own needs later on."[10] The CEO of the Xerox Corporation is less optimistic. He figures that it will cost American industry $25 billion a year just to teach prospective employees how to read, write, and count.

But despite the endless rhetoric about how the jobs of the year 2000 will need employees with much higher levels of literacy, it is not at all clear whether that is indeed the case. It is true that most forecasts see computer system analysis and programming as the fastest growing occupations in the near future. But numerically such high-tech jobs are dwarfed by the much more numerous openings anticipated in a variety of jobs that require fewer skills than those farmers and skilled factory workers used to have a few generations ago. The greatest future demand in the labor market appears to be for armed guards, fast-food preparation personnel, truck drivers, sanitation workers, nurses' aides, and other relatively unspecialized tasks. For some reason our sophisticated economy still needs an underclass, and if we can't produce it domestically, we shall import it from abroad.

If this is true, and a substantial proportion of the youth in our country does not expect to benefit from acquiring high levels of literacy beyond what is needed to get a driver's license or to read the sports pages, then a very strong incentive for learning is not operating. And this situation will not be remedied by improved teaching methods and by new educational technology.

Although illiteracy will be an increasing problem for employers who need a skilled work force to run its more and more complex operations, for a great proportion of the work force this will not be a problem at all, since its members never planned to participate in that segment of the economy in the first place. As long as disadvantaged youth perceive that the greatest financial rewards accrue to drug dealers, athletes, and entertainers among their midst, none of whom made it good on the strength of their academic records, and as long as the unemployed can count on a social safety net to take care of their needs, why should they worry about not performing up to our expectations on abstract and meaningless intellectual tasks?

In other words, we may have in terms of literacy an educational parallel to the so-called "tragedy of the commons." In that classic ecological paradigm, if say fifty families each have a cow grazing on a common pasture, it makes sense for a family to invest everything they have in buying another cow, thereby doubling their capital while increasing the pressure on the common supply of fodder by only a tiny fraction. The problem is that if every family acts rationally, soon there will be 100 cows grazing, the pasture will be exhausted, the cattle will die, and the farmers will be ruined. The relevant analogy is that many young people nowadays think it isn't sensible for them to learn too much because the social system will not reward their knowledge anyway and they can live very well without it. Let others worry about stuffing their heads with esoteric facts. Yet if this attitude continues to spread, productivity will decrease to the point that the entire economy may collapse. If we don't want this to happen, it seems imperative that we find ways to provide realistic motives for the acquisition of literacy to more young people.

The problem is that neither teachers nor the educational system in general can change the way in which economic rewards are distributed in society. To that extent, we can do little to increase students' motivation and thus raise the level of literacy. Fortunately, there is one more string to the educator's bow, and that is the one we need to use if we wish to improve the situation.

So far, we have considered motivation to learn as if it were exclusively a response to *extrinsic* rewards. In fact, the historical record shows quite convincingly that reading, writing, and computation developed because they provided economic and power advantages to whoever knew how to use such information. To that extent a deterministic, materialist explanation is correct. However, it is not the entire story. As is often the case in human affairs, when a new discovery prompted by material needs takes place, the opportunity to have entirely new experiences also becomes possible. At that point the old extrinsic rewards may become less relevant and a new set of *intrinsic* rewards become operative instead.[11]

In the case of writing, for instance, the ancient scribes did not limit themselves to recording pigs and bales of hay forever. After a few millennia, they discovered that writing made it possible to record events that may have happened in the distant past, where the memory of men had become vague. They discovered that the cadences of sound and the rhythm of rhymes could also be preserved outside the telling of the bards. With time, literature emerged out of literacy, and for many writers and readers it became an end in itself. Writing was no longer motivated only extrinsically, by economic and by political need; it was now possible to enjoy it for its own sake. This transition from literacy as a tool to literature as an end in itself seems to have taken place in similar ways in several cultures that had developed writing more or less autonomously, such as in the Near East, the Indus valley, China, and Japan.

This emergence of a more complex motive out of a more primitive requirement is not a rare event; in fact, it constitutes a constant trend in the cultural evolution of humankind. The basic need to eat and drink have generated elaborate cuisines and intricate libations in every culture—and more often than not, what people enjoy now is not the satiation of hunger, which is a need programmed in the genes, but the satisfaction of taste, which is a pleasure made possible by the discovery of good cooking. Similarly, sexual pleasure, built into our nervous system by the need to reproduce, has made it possible to enjoy the refinements of romantic love in all its colorful cultural variations. Hunting, determined by the need to survive, has become a sport rewarding in itself. Music, once a mechanism for engendering religious fervor, is now enjoyed for its own sake. And so forth down the line: many things we once did because we had to do them, now we do because we like to do them.

More often than not, discoveries are initially motivated by old, well-entrenched human needs—by greed, fear, the need to keep one's head above water. But many discoveries, once they are made, open up previously unimaginable possibilities for action. At first the only reason to use geometry may have been to measure the extent of fields, and figure out how much water it took to irrigate them.[12] But after a long time the likes of Pythagoras discovered that quantitative ratios and relationships inhabited a beautifully ordered world of their own, a world where the mind could journey in awe. It was not something even the most brilliant genius could have imagined before geometry had served its humble apprenticeship as a farmers' tool. But when the domain had developed far enough, it unlocked its startling potentialities, and at that point it became possible to enjoy geometry for its own sake.

When a person realizes that a symbol system has an autonomous existence, related to but not homologous with the "paramount reality" of the everyday world, then a whole new set of rewards becomes available, the rewards of operating within the system itself. The writer who discovers the possibility of creating a fictional world more intriguing than the world of actual experience, and the reader who discovers that world, will seek out literacy for its own sake, whether it provides them with jobs in the long run or not.

Children are not interested in the rules and procedures for becoming literate that teachers spend so much time trying to hammer into their heads. If the pressure from parents and other adults is strong enough—as it is in Japan, or Germany, or many Third World countries where education promises the only avenue of advancement—children will reluctantly learn. But there is another way. If educators, instead of treating literacy as a tool, focused on the rewards intrinsic to literacy, they might get students interested enough in exploring the various domains of learning for the sake of what they can find there. When that happens, the teacher's task is done. Intrigued by the opportunities of the domain, most students will make sure to develop the skills they need to operate within it.

Not that the relationship between learning and extrinsic rewards should be ignored. At this point, the quickest way to increase literacy would still be to tie it more closely to better prospects for worldly success and advancement. To provide material rewards commensurate with knowledge is a sociopolitical goal to which people of goodwill may want to dedicate themselves. But educators as such have little say on this matter. Only as citizens or activists can they influence the recognition literacy will receive. They can, however, directly influence the intrinsic rewards students get from learning. For this reason, the next section will be devoted to a brief survey of what makes people want to do things for their own sake. Applying a model of intrinsic motivation to learning may make it possible to advance the cause of literacy beyond the point where technology and a mechanical rationality cease to be useful.

THE ANATOMY OF ENJOYMENT

Almost anything people do can either produce a sense of boredom or frustration in the doer or be so enjoyable that the doing itself becomes its own reward. This is easy to see when the activity is what we call "play" or "leisure"; these things people do for their own sake, even when they are as painstakingly tedious as building a ship in a bottle or as exhausting and dangerous as climbing a Himalayan peak. But leisurely play is not the only activity that is intrinsically rewarding. For some people, work becomes the most enjoyable part of life; they become "workaholics" who feel lost without the stimulation of their jobs. In many cultures women enjoy their traditional roles, especially childcare, cooking, and weaving, more than anything else. And of the almost infinite number of activities that people find so enjoyable that they will do them even without extrinsic reasons, the exercise of literacy stands out as one of the most important.

In a series of studies based on in-depth interviews in various cultures of the world, including India, Thailand, the American Southwest, and various European countries, a team of psychologists from the University of Milan concluded that reading was one of the most ubiquitous and widespread activities people did for sheer enjoyment.[13] Especially for people whose life circumstances restrict the range of alternative leisure activities—such as traveling, doing active sports, or participating in social or cultural events—reading provides an opportunity to experience novel states of being and a way of temporarily changing the outlines of the accustomed world. Reading alters the contents of a person's consciousness, and therefore the content of reality.

But how can reading (or writing, or doing sums), which all too often are experienced as boring nuisances, be turned into enjoyable, intrinsically rewarding, activities? I shall try to answer this question first at a general level, one that applies to every human activity regardless of content; then I shall endeavor to answer it with specific reference to the various literacies—reading, writing, and arithmetic.

When people enjoy whatever they are doing, they report some characteristic experiential state that distinguishes the enjoyable moment from the rest of life. The same dimensions are reported in the context of enjoying chess, climbing mountains, playing with babies, reading books, or writing poems. These dimensions are the same for young and old, male and female, American and Japanese, rich and poor. In other words, the phenomenology of enjoyment seems to be a panhuman constant. When all the characteristics are present, we call this state of consciousness *a flow experience,* because many of the respondents said that when what they were doing was especially enjoyable it felt like being carried away by a current, like being in a flow. Consequently, we have called the theoretical model that describes intrinsically rewarding experiences *the flow model.*[14]

The first phenomenological condition that separates a flow experience from everyday consciousness is the merging of action and awareness. The mind slips into the activity as if actor and action had become one. The duality of consciousness which is typical of ordinary life disappears: we no longer look at what we are doing from the outside; we become what we do. The climber feels he is part of the rock, the sky, and the wind; the chess player merges with the field of forces on the board; the dancer cannot be told from the dance; the mathematician is so involved in her calculations that she forgets sleep and hunger; reading a good book ". . . you are the patient pool or cataract of concepts which the author has constructed. . . . The will is at rest amid that moving like a gull asleep on the sea."[15]

This intense involvement is only possible when a person feels that the opportunities for action in the given activity (or challenges) are more or less in balance with the person's ability to respond to the opportunities (or skills). When the challenges are relatively greater than the skills, there is a sense of frustration that eventually results in worry and then anxiety; in the opposite case, when one's skills are greater than what is possible to do, one feels progressively more bored. But when a person feels that skills are fully engaged by challenges, one enters the state of flow, even if only temporarily—as the tennis player knows when a close volley is exchanged, or when the singer hears her voice following the ideal notes envisioned by the composer, or the student feels when he thinks he has found the solution to a difficult problem.

But what constitutes a challenge? This question raises the most profound issue in the theory of motivation, and points to the *pons asinorum* where so many well-intentioned educational programs fall. The problem is that the same thing will be an attractive challenge to one person and a bothersome nuisance to another. Imagine leaving a copy of Livy's *Histories* among the magazines in a doctor's waiting room, and then observing the reaction of the patients. Most people will look puzzled as they start thumbing through the pages, and quickly replace the book on the table with a faint air of having been insulted. Perhaps one person in a hundred—or a thousand?—after the initial puzzlement will start reading, and eventually get immersed in the book. Why would this imaginary person find Livy challenging, while everyone else did not?

In the most abstract sense, a challenge is a stimulus that attracts our attention, and demands some response on our part. A great number of challenges are programmed in our genes: to find food, shelter, a mate, and so on. These are generally shared by all human beings. Then there are physiological differences among people that make some of us more sensitive to visual stimuli, others to auditory or to kinesthetic ones. Early on, some children's attention is particularly attracted to sounds, and they try to reproduce variations in it. Some children respond more to social situations, and find challenges in getting along with others, or in exercising power over them.

Finally, there are social and cultural conditions that prompt people to pay attention to a certain range of stimuli, and ignore others. In some ethnic contexts, it is considered foolish to be interested in "book learning" for its own sake. On the other hand the Jews have been rightly called "the people of the book" in that even under very poor material conditions, in isolated rural communities, immersion in sacred texts was considered a privilege and a passion.

In other words, challenges are not such in virtue of objective reason, but because of the way they are interpreted. Although we are all programmed biologically to find food when hungry, it is possible for people to define hunger as an illusion that must be ignored, and then the challenge becomes to learn how to fast. Or to use another example, the Swiss cursed the Alps for centuries because they stood in the way of industrious farming. Nobody thought of the peaks as constituting a challenge. Only a little over a hundred years ago, thanks to the efforts of romantic Englishmen—mostly clerics repelled by urban industrial life—were the Alps reinterpreted as challenges fit for sturdy souls. Now, of course, many Swiss find mountaineering a perfectly enjoyable activity.

This flexibility in turning the same stimulus either into a challenge or into an obstacle is both a blessing and a bane to educators. It is a blessing because any information, no matter how difficult or abstruse, can be transmitted if the teacher is able to make it seem challenging to the student. It is a bane because, when children are bombarded with so many messages to the effect that studying is boring and unseemly, it is difficult to present learning as a worthwhile challenge. In any case, unless a person sees learning as a meaningful challenge, the activity will not become intrinsically rewarding.

A second and related characteristic of flow experiences is that people describe them as having clear goals. In everyday life we are often unclear why we are doing what we do, what is it exactly that we are trying to accomplish, whereas when we really enjoy what we do the goal is clear. It may be something obvious like winning a game, reaching the top of a mountain, or completing a poem; or it may be an ad hoc goal that the person formulates on the spur of the moment, like mowing the lawn in a certain way, or ironing a shirt in a determined sequence of moves. A goal is necessary so that we may get feedback on our actions, so that at any given moment we know how well we are doing in terms of the goal. Without a goal, there cannot be meaningful feedback, and without knowing whether we are doing well or not, it is very difficult to maintain involvement. It is important to realize, however, that the goal is not sought for itself; it is sought only because it makes the activity possible. A climber does not climb in order to reach the top; he reaches the top in order to climb. Poets do not write so that they will have poems; they seek to create poems so that they can write.

Typically, one starts to do an activity for extrinsic reasons, and only with time will the goal become intrinsic to the activity itself. A person usually learns the rudiments of reading and writing under compulsion. The goal is to avoid punishment, to get the praise of adults who are significant in our lives. But eventually, if the learning process has been successful, we begin to enjoy our ability to read. At that point the goal becomes intrinsic to the task itself—the anticipation of reading a book or solving a problem is enough to motivate the activity. If you have ever traveled in a car with a child who has just learned to read, you know what I mean: she will read aloud every sign along the way, delighting in the ability to turn abstract signs into words, concepts, and ideas. The task of the educator is to keep that delight alive by presenting goals that involve increasingly more complex challenges matched to the student's developing skills.

When a person finds a goal which presents a range of opportunities for action that matches his or her skills, attention becomes so concentrated on the activity that all irrelevant concerns tend to be excluded from awareness. The past and the future fade away, elbowed out by the urgency of the present. The usual hobgoblins of the mind—the anxieties of everyday life: insecurity, guilt, jealousy, financial worries—disappear. The reason for this clarity is simple. Consciousness cannot process more than a limited range of information at the same time.[16] When all the attention is needed to meet the challenges of an activity, there is simply not enough left to notice anything else. Hence, the perfect attentional focus of the athlete, the religious mystic, the artist, the climber hanging over the precipice from his fingertips, or the reader completely taken by the characters and the plot of a novel.

When one of my students recently asked some classes of fifth- and sixth-grade children to describe what they liked doing most, and why, I was struck by how important this characteristic of the flow experience is even at such an early age. One after the other, these children described what they enjoyed most about playing the piano, or swimming, or acting in the school plays. One said that while doing these things, "I can forget my problems." Another said, "I can keep the things that bother me out of my mind." And so on. In class, they claimed, they could seldom achieve such concentration—and so their minds were usually dwelling on arguments with parents, fights with siblings, injuries suffered at the hands of peers. Thus a vicious circle is set up: because they do not concentrate enough, extraneous thoughts enter consciousness, further undermining their concentration. Not surprisingly, little learning takes place under such conditions.

When concentration is intense, one consequence is that we lose the sense of self-consciousness that always shadows our actions in everyday life. Attention is so completely absorbed in the task that there is not enough left over to contemplate the self. This adds to the liberating feeling flow provides; no longer restricted to the confines of one's self-image, it is possible to transcend the boundaries of one's being. The puny individuality of the climber merges with the majestic environment of sky and stone. The musician's self expands to embrace the harmony of the spheres. The reader's identity grows as she roams the world created by the writer.

A related outcome is that flow provides a sense of control even when the person is involved in dangerous activities such as spelunking, sky diving, or rock climbing. Because these activities are clearly demarcated, and appropriate rules are identified, the participant is able to anticipate risks and minimize the unexpected. Besides, there is just too much to do to worry about failure. Those individuals who cannot keep their attention concentrated on the task at hand start worrying about the possibility of losing control. They do not enjoy the activity and eventually drop out of it. Singers who as they sing fret about not hitting the high C, or tennis players who anticipate missing the shot, cannot enter the flow state, and therefore stop progressing. Children who feel that learning to read well is beyond their grasp begin to feel anxious and try to avoid chances to test their reading skill.

A matching of challenges and skills, clear goals, and immediate feedback, resulting in a deep concentration that prevents worry and the intrusion of unwanted thoughts into consciousness, and in a transcendence of the self, are the universal characteristics associated with enjoyable activities. When these dimensions of experience are present, the activity becomes *autotelic*, or rewarding in itself. Even though initially one may have been forced to do it, or did it for some extrinsic reason like the promise of a good grade, a useful diploma, or a paycheck, if during the activity one starts to experience flow, the activity becomes autotelic, or worth doing for its own sake. That is how reading, writing, or doing sums can turn from a bore to something one eagerly wants to do.

It is important to note that what people enjoy the most in their lives is almost never something passive, like watching television or being entertained. When reading is enjoyed, it is active reading, which involves choosing the book, identifying with the characters, trying to recreate visually the places and the events described, anticipating turns of the plot, and responding with empathy, yet critically, to the writer's craft. Nor is enjoyment the same as pleasure. Flow requires the use of skills and depends on gradual increments of challenges and skills so that boredom or anxiety will not take over. Pleasure, on the other hand, is homeostatic: pleasurable experiences like resting when tired, drinking when thirsty, or having sex when aroused do not require complex skills and can be repeated over and over without losing their rewarding quality. For this very reason, pleasure does not drive us to develop new potentialities and thus does not lead to personal growth.

Of course, some activities are built to provide enjoyment. This is true of games, sports, music, literature and the other arts, religious ceremonies, and innumerable social customs such as gossiping or eating elaborate meals. The quality of life depends more on these opportunities to experience flow than on the size of the gross national product. But it would be a mistake to think that only playful activities can do this. Over the course of time we have separated work and leisure to the extent that now we think only unproductive leisure can be enjoyable, and productive work must necessarily be unpleasant. Nothing is further from the truth. Leisure becomes the sole source of enjoyment only when a culture loses its capacity to make everyday life enjoyable. The ideal condition is one where work, family life, politics, friendship, and community interaction provide most of the optimal experiences.

ENJOYMENT AND LITERACY

A teacher who understands the conditions that make people want to be literate—want to read, to write, and do sums—is in a position to turn these activities into flow experiences, and thereby set students on a course of autotelic learning. When the experience becomes intrinsically rewarding, students' motivation is engaged, and they are on their way to a lifetime of self-propelled acquisition of knowledge.

In this respect it is interesting to note that when teenagers are asked whether any of their teachers have been influential in making them the kind of persons they are now, and if so, to describe such influential teachers, one of the most important traits mentioned—second only to the teachers' caring for and supporting the students—is the quality of involvement, interest, and enjoyment they showed for what they taught.[17] How smart, knowledgeable, powerful, or well-trained they were mattered much less. Basically, young people are influenced by adults who appear to enjoy what they do, and who promise to make youth's life more enjoyable too. This is not such a bad yardstick to use—why should youth choose models who seem miserable, and who strive to impoverish their future? Especially if we remember that enjoyment is not a hedonistic goal, but the energy that propels a person to higher levels of performance.

But how can literacy—reading, for instance—be turned into an enjoyable activity? Applying the general categories of the flow model to the activity of reading yields several concrete suggestions. Some of these have already been advanced by scholars who have studied the motivation of students, and all of them have been known to good teachers. What the model of autotelic experience adds is a theoretical framework that makes it possible to order systematically the general knowledge on the topic, and to generate new alternatives that purely empirical know-how would not be able to identify.

Reading cannot be enjoyable unless the student can imagine, at least in principle, that the symbol system of letters is worth mastering for its own sake. If the child knows adults he respects who read, he will take it for granted that reading is worthwhile. People who grow up to believe that books are valuable have usually been read to as children, or have at least been told elaborate stories by their caretakers.[18] Unless children can form some positive expectations about reading, why should they choose to embark on that difficult journey?

This condition seems to imply that youth from disadvantaged backgrounds who lack literate adult models cannot get started enjoying books. It is true that early exposure to the rewards of literacy gives a great motivational advantage. But once we face up to the importance of this fact, the lack can be remedied. When a student of mine completed his Ph.D. and was offered a job at a university in Saudi Arabia, he wrote to his future department head to ask how much of his teaching should include lectures, how much discussion. Not to worry, came the answer. Part of his teaching could consist in just sitting in front of the class immersed in silent reading. That way the students would learn how to be scholars. I doubt this would work in our culture, but the point is not trivial: if we want them to want to read, we must find ways of showing young people that the effort is worth it.

Flow cannot be experienced if there is a large discrepancy between challenges and skills. This means that one of the most important tasks for a teacher is to make sure that students are neither too over-whelmed nor too bored by the material they must master. Standard reading texts and uniform curricula make life easier for teachers and administrators, but they make it very difficult for students to get involved with the material at the level that is right for them, and therefore to find intrinsic rewards in learning. Howard Gardner has recently explored various ways to customize learning and avoid the waste of mental energy that results when students are faced with challenges that are either meaningless to them, or that are inappro-priate to their levels of skill.[19] Clearly, we need to investigate these alternatives much further.

In our studies of classroom experience, we find that even in very good schools students actually pay attention to what is supposed to go on quite rarely. Science and mathematics are generally over-whelming, and students tend to feel anxious when these subjects are being taught. Humanities and social sciences, on the other hand, are more likely to be experienced as boring. In a series of studies teachers were given electronic pagers, and both they and their students were asked to fill out a short questionnaire whenever the pagers signaled (the signal was set to beep at random moments during the fifty-minute periods). In a typical high school history class, the pager went off as the teacher was describing how Genghis Khan had invaded China in 1234. At the same moment, of the twenty-seven students only two were thinking about something even remotely related to China. One of these two students was remembering a dinner she had had recently with her family at a Chinese restaurant; the other was wondering why Chinese men used to wear their hair in ponytails.

Learning involves processing information. Complex information processing requires the allocation of attention to the task. There cannot be any learning unless a person is willing to invest attention in a symbolic system. Human behavior is determined in all sorts of ways, but in one sense, for better or worse, we are relatively free: short of torture or other drastic means, no one can force us to pay attention to something unless we want to. The old saying "You can lead a horse to water, but you can't make him drink" is really a metaphor for the human ability to "tune out" at will. And that is what students usually do when the material fails to interest them— which is what invariably happens when the challenges are either much too high, or much too low, relative to their skills.

Even talented students in mathematics and science (who score in the upper 5 percent of national norms in these subjects) generally report overwhelming challenges when involved with math and science, and only rarely report matching challenges and skills. As a result, their self-ratings of intrinsic motivation are very significantly below baseline when involved in the area of their talent. (Conversely, students talented in the arts or in music—that is, in fields which notoriously lack extrinsic rewards such as status or monetary incentives—show an opposite trend: challenges and skills are usually in balance when students do art or music in school, and consequently their level of intrinsic motivation is much above baseline when involved with their talent. These findings help flesh out the distinction between the "hard" sciences and the arts.)

It is not only the lack of balance between skills and challenges that detracts from intrinsic motivation in learning. The second condition that makes flow possible is the clarity of goals and the immediacy of feedback. Both of these are usually lacking in formal learning settings. To many children, even if they are dimly aware of the long-term goals of education, the purpose of specific drills and lessons remains opaque. For instance, they tend to have little choice about what they have to read, and the content of the books is usually alien to their past experiences or future concerns. Textbooks are usually chosen because they illustrate abstract principles, in conformity with the theoretical orientations of the curriculum designers, not because they relate to students' interests, goals, and abilities. Not surprisingly, students feel estranged from such books, and the only reason they may read them is because of external coercion, not intrinsic interest.

At the Key School in Indianapolis, where teachers have tried innovative attempts to make education more intrinsically rewarding, first graders are interviewed on videotape before they start school. One of the questions they are asked is why they want to learn to read and write. The answers are often touchingly eloquent: one boy wants to be able to read the paper in the morning to know "what's going on in the world," as his father does; another wants to keep up with his favorite football team in the sport pages; a girl wants to learn to read so she can be a doctor and make children well. Compared with these concerns, the usual diet of Dick and Jane pabulum must seem depressingly trivial.

If literacy is for the sake of the children, how come we so rarely bother to find out what they want to use it for? The standard answer is "Because they don't know what's good for them, or at least they don't know what will be good for them in the future." Children are like the grasshopper in Aesop's fable; they would dance all summer long if left to their own devices. There is much truth in this rationale. Yet it is also true that it does not make sense to expect children to get interested in learning subjects for which they don't see any likely use. The task of educators is *educare*, "to lead out"—which implies meeting youth wherever they are and taking into account their goals, interests, and skills. Only after the contact is made and attention engaged is there hope that they shall willingly follow our lead.

The nature of the feedback teachers give students also determines how easy or how difficult it will be for the latter to experience flow while learning. Many of the students who participate in our studies end up filling sheet after sheet in their response booklets with imprecations addressed to teachers who have just embarrassed them in front of the class. One episode like that may divert the attention of a child for an entire day, making it impossible for him or her to focus on the subject matter. Students need feedback to keep on track. But the feedback should be "informational" rather than "controlling"[20]— it should focus on why a performance is not up to par, and how it could be improved, rather than on the students' shortcomings. Nothing destroys focused involvement as quickly as being made self-conscious.

Teresa Amabile, who has researched the matter extensively, concludes that there are four main ways the spontaneous interest of the child can be destroyed. One is for adults to attempt to control the child's performance as much as possible, by imposing strict rules, procedures, time constraints, and so forth. The more the child's attention is drawn to external rules, the more difficult it becomes to experience the intrinsic rewards of flow. The second way to kill interest is through emphasizing evaluation. Excessive concern for rewards—or punishment—distracts from the task at hand and disrupts the concentration necessary for sustaining flow. Too much emphasis on competition has the same effect. The Latin roots of this word, *con petire,* or "to seek together," point to the idea that people can best find out the limits of their ability by matching performance against other persons'. But when attention shifts to winning rather than doing one's best, competition also endangers flow. The last prescription Amabile gives for disrupting intrinsic rewards is to make the person self-conscious. Because everyone's priority is to keep the self safe, whenever danger or ridicule threatens it, we lose concentration and focus attention on defending ourselves rather than on getting involved with the task.[21]

Schools follow very closely Amabile's prescription of how to disrupt enjoyment. Formal education thrives on external controls, evaluation, competition, and self-consciousness. Yet as long as this is so, it will be difficult for children to be motivated to learn spontaneously for the sake of learning.

Fortunately, many teachers intuitively know that the best way to achieve their goals is to enlist students' interest on their side. They do this by being sensitive to students' goals and desires, and thus are able to articulate the pedagogical goals as meaningful challenges. They empower students to take control of their learning; they provide clear feedback to the students' efforts without threatening their egos and without making them self-conscious. They help students concentrate and get immersed in the symbolic world of the subject matter. As a result, good teachers still turn out children who enjoy learning, and who will continue to face the world with curiosity and interest.

And a few researchers are beginning to explore the intrinsic rewards of learning, including the basic literacies. For example, Nell describes "ludic reading" in great detail, and explores why people over the world enjoy pulp fiction as well as the classics.[22] Elbow gives concrete instructions about "free writing," or the ways to make the task of writing more enjoyable and successful.[23] Larson has shown that schoolchildren overwhelmed by their topics write essays that readers find confusing; when students are bored by the topic they write essays that are boring; but when they are excited by what they write, their stories are also exciting to read. The poet Kenneth Koch has eloquently shown that illiterate ghetto children and semiliterate nursing home residents can create moving poetry when the task is related to their personal goals and they are shown how enjoyable writing can be.[24]

It is to be hoped that with time the realization that children are not miniature computing machines will take root in educational circles, and more attention will be paid to motivational issues. Unless this comes to pass, the current problems with literacy are not likely to go away.

There are two main ways that children's motivation to master symbolic systems can be enhanced. The first is by a realistic reassessment of the extrinsic rewards attendant to literacy. This would involve a much clearer communication of the advantages and disadvantages one might expect as a result of being able to read, write, and do sums. Of course, these consequences must be real, and not just a matter of educational propaganda. Hypocrisy is easy to detect, and nothing turns motivation off more effectively than the realization that one has been had.

The second way to enhance motivation is to make children aware of how much fun literacy can be. This strategy is preferable on many counts. In the first place, it is something teachers can do something about. Second, it should be easier to implement—it does not require expensive technology, although it does require sensitivity and intelligence, which, some may argue, is harder to come by than the fruits of technology are. Third, it is a more efficient and permanent way to empower children with the tools of knowledge. And finally, this strategy is preferable because it adds immensely to the enjoyment learners will take in the use of their abilities, and hence also to the quality of their lives.

ENDNOTES

[1]A. N. Applebee, J. A. Langer, and I. V. S. Mullis, *The Writing Report Card* (Princeton, N.J.: Educational Testing Service, 1986), 46.

[2]Ibid., 9.

[3]J. A. Dossey, I. V. S. Mullis, M. M. Lindquist, and D. L. Chambers, *The Mathematics Report Card* (Princeton, N.J.: Educational Testing Service, 1988).

[4]C. McKnight et al., *The Underachieving Curriculum: Assessing U.S. Mathematics from an International Perspective* (Champaign, Ill.: International Association for the Evaluation of Educational Achievement, 1987).

[5]D. Schmandt-Basserat, "The Envelopes that Bear the First Writing," *Technology and Culture* 21 (3) (1980): 357–85.

[6]M. Lambert, "La Naissance de la bureaucratie," *Révue Historique* 224 (1960): 1–26.

[7]L. A. Oppenheim, *Ancient Mesopotamia* (Chicago: University of Chicago Press, 1964).

[8]P. Ariès, *Centuries of Childhood* (New York: Vintage Press, 1965).

[9]F. Braudel, *The Wheels of Commerce* (New York: Harper & Row, 1982).

[10]J. Gallagher, "Business 'Invests' in Quality Education," *The Chicago Tribune*, 27 July 1983.

[11]M. Csikszentmihalyi, "Emergent Motivation and the Evolution of the Self," in D. Kleiber and M. Maehr, eds., *Motivation of Adulthood* (Greenwich, Conn.: JAI Press, 1985), 93–113.

[12]K. Wittfogel, *Oriental Despotism* (New Haven: Yale University Press, 1957).

[13]P. Inghilleri, "L'Importanza dei processi psicologici quotidiani nell'evoluzione culturale: uno studio in Thailandia," in F. Massimini and P. Inghilleri, eds., *L'Esperienza quotidiana: Teoria e metodo d'analisi* (Milan: F. Angeli Editore, 1986), 251–72; and F. Massimini, M. Csikszentmihalyi, and A. Delle Fave, "Flow and Biocultural Evolution," in M. Csikszentmihalyi and I. Csikszentmihalyi, eds., *Optimal Experience: Psychological Studies of Flow in Consciousness* (New York: Cambridge University Press, 1988), 60–84.

[14]For a full description of the flow experience and how it can be identified, see M. Csikszentmihalyi, *Beyond Boredom and Anxiety* (San Francisco: Jossey-Bass, 1975); and M. Csikszentmihalyi and I. Csikszentmihalyi, *Optimal Experience*.

[15]W. H. Gass, *Fiction and the Figures of Life* (New York: Viking, 1972).

[16]M. Csikszentmihalyi, "Attention and the Wholistic Approach to Behavior," in K. S. Pope and J. S. Singer, eds., *The Stream of Consciousness* (New York: Plenum, 1978), 335–58; M. W. Eysenck, *Attention and Arousal* (Berlin: Springer Verlag, 1982); L. Hasher and R. T. Zacks, "Automatic and Effortful Processes in Memory," in *Journal of Experimental Psychology* 108 (3) (1979): 356–88; and D. Kahneman, *Attention and Effort* (Englewood Cliffs, N.J.: Prentice-Hall, 1973).

[17]M. Csikszentmihalyi and J. McCormack, "The Influence of Teachers," *Phi Delta Kappan* (February 1986): 415–19.

[18]R. C. Anderson et al., *Becoming a Nation of Readers: The Report of the Commission on Reading* (Urbana, Ill.: University of Illinois, Center for the Study of Reading, 1985); O. Beattie Emory and M. Csikszentmihalyi, "On the Socialization Influence of Books," *Child Psychology* 2 (1) (1981): 3–18; M.

Csikszentmihalyi and O. Beattie, "Life Themes: A Theoretical and Empirical Investigation of Their Origins and Effects," *Journal of Humanistic Psychology* 19 (1) (1979): 45–63; and U.S. Department of Education, *What Works: Research about Teaching and Learning* (Washington, D.C.: U. S. Dept. of Education, Office of Educational Research and Improvement, 1986).

[19]H. Gardner, "An Individual-Centered Curriculum," in *The Schools We've Got, the Schools We Need* (Washington, D.C.: Council of Chief State School Officers and the American Association of Colleges of Teacher Education, 1987); and H. Gardner, "Balancing Specialized and Comprehensive Knowledge: The Growing Education Challenge," in T. Sergiovanni, ed., *Schooling for Tomorrow: Directing Reform to Issues that Count* (Boston: Allyn and Bacon, 1989).

[20]E. L. Deci and R. M. Ryan, *Intrinsic Motivation and Self-Determination in Human Behavior* (New York: Plenum Press, 1985).

[21]Teresa Amabile, *The Social Psychology of Creativity* (New York: Springer Verlag, 1983).

[22]V. Nell, *Lost in a Book: The Psychology of Reading for Pleasure* (New Haven: Yale University Press, 1988).

[23]P. Elbow, *Writing without Teachers* (London: Oxford University Press, 1973).

[24]K. Koch, *Wishes, Lies, and Dreams: Teaching Children to Write Poetry* (New York: Chelsea House, 1970), and *I Never Told Anybody: Teaching Poetry Writing in a Nursing Home* (New York: Random House, 1977).

Minority Status and Literacy in Comparative Perspective

John U. Ogbu

*S*ome *minority groups are more successful than others at becoming literate and numerate. "Voluntary" minorities do better because they came to the United States expecting to improve their status through participation in such American institutions as the education system. "Involuntary" minorities have less success because they were incorporated into American society against their will and had no such expectation. The two minority types perceive and respond differently to educational institutions and to those who control them.*

In many contemporary plural societies racial and ethnic minorities lag behind members of the dominant groups in acquisition of literacy and numeracy, that is, in school performance. It is well known that in the United States many minorities do not perform as well as the dominant white Americans. Similar gaps in school performance between minorities and the dominant groups are also found in Britain, Japan, and New Zealand, to mention only a few.[1] At the same time, however, some other minorities perform as well as the dominant groups or even surpass them.[2] In this essay I seek to explain why certain minority groups do not do particularly well in school while certain other minority groups do relatively better.

Most studies of minority schooling in the United States focus on what goes on inside the school, inside the home, or in the biology of

John Ogbu is Distinguished Alumni Professor of Anthropology at the University of California in Berkeley.

the individual child. To take the last first, proponents of differential mental ability theory claim that children do well academically in school because they possess certain mental abilities defined as IQ, the amount and type of which can be determined by IQ tests. When such tests are administered, minority children score lower than their white peers; minorities do not do as well either on those parts of the test believed to indicate potential for school success. Some attribute these lower IQ test scores to inadequate genetic endowment.[3] Others find the cause in inadequate home environment and early childhood experience.[4] Both groups agree, however, that minority children's school failure is caused by an inadequate IQ or mental ability.

To raise minority children's IQ through preschool programs, compensatory education programs for older children and training of minority parents to raise children as white middle-class parents do have become common. Though minority children who participate in such programs may score higher on IQ tests while they are in the programs, later tests generally show that such higher scores tend to "fade out" after these children leave the programs or while they are in the middle years of elementary school.[5]

If some insist that lower-class children generally do less well in school because they lack ability as measured by IQ tests, others stress the failure of their families to prepare them for school adjustment and academic success. Using socioeconomic status as a measure of class membership, most black youths are generally classified as belonging to the lower class; their school-adjustment problems and lower academic performance are attributed to this lower-class status.[*6]

Such correlational studies fail, however, to explain why black students do not perform as well as their white peers of similar social class background. In a study of black and white candidates who took the Scholastic Aptitude Tests in 1980–1981, candidates from black families with annual average incomes of $50,000 or more had median verbal scores of about the same level as candidates from

---

*I want to emphasize the fact that this essay is about minority groups qua minority groups, not about lower-class minorities. The problem of lower school performance is not limited to lower-class members of minority groups. The cases described in this section should make that clear in the case of black Americans: middle-class black children perform less well than middle-class white children; and lower-class black children perform less well than lower-class white children. The question is, Why do blacks as a minority group perform less well than whites and less well than some other minorities?

white families with average annual incomes of $13,000 to $18,000. Black candidates from homes with average annual incomes of $50,000 or more had median math scores slightly below the median math scores of white candidates from homes with average annual incomes of $6,000 or less.[7] Why? Other studies show similar results.

While there is a clear pattern for white students, with their academic performance tending to rise as their parents' education (and socioeconomic status) goes up, there is no such clear pattern for blacks. In a study of the performance of eighth-grade students in California on the California Assessment Program Survey of Basic Skills, it was found (a) that the gap between black students whose parents were highly educated and those whose parents had little formal education was only about half as great as the gap between such groups among white students; (b) that black students whose parents had advanced degrees scored, on the average, below white students whose parents had completed only high school education; and (c) that black students whose parents had completed only some college education consistently outperformed other black students whose parents had actually completed college.[8]

The issue is clearly not whether minority children from middle-class backgrounds do better than minority children from lower-class or underclass backgrounds. The issue is whether minority children do as well as their white counterparts. They do not.[9]

Anthropologists, less concerned about the effects of social class differences on minority education, have concentrated on the effects of cultural differences, broadly defined, in the belief that the problem is caused by cultural differences and cultural conflicts. Where children receive their education in a learning environment different from the one familiar to them at home, they have difficulty acquiring the content and style of learning presupposed by the curriculum and the teaching methods.[10] Cultural conflicts occur when non-Western children attend Western-type schools and also when immigrant children, minority children, and lower-class children attend schools controlled by middle-class members of the dominant group in an urban industrial society like the United States.[11]

The conflict may be in language and communication, cognition, cognitive style, social interaction, values, or teaching and learning techniques. For example, it has been claimed that Puerto Rican children living on the mainland experience learning difficulties because they do not interpret eye contacts as their white middle-class teachers do.[12] The Oglala Sioux Indian children's learning difficulties seem also to stem from cultural miscommunication with white teachers. The Indians, it is said, resist the teachers' attempts to teach them because they are not used to a situation in which adults control child-adult communication.[13] Warm Springs Indian children in Oregon fail to learn under white teachers because they require the use of rules of speech in the classroom different from those with which the children are familiar in their community.[14] Similar situations exist among black children.[15]

While I agree that cultural differences and cultural conflicts cause real difficulties for non-Western children in Western-type schools and for minority children in the U.S. public schools,[16] studies suggest that the persistent disproportionate school failure rates of blacks and similar minorities are not caused simply by conflicts in cognitive, communication, social interaction, teaching, and learning styles. In any case, such theories fail to explain why certain minorities cross cultural boundaries, why others seem to have greater difficulties in crossing them. All three theories fail to take account of the incentive motivation in a minority's pursuit of education.

In our attempt to understand the school performance of minority children, the field is dominated by what may be called "improvement research," or "applied research," studies designed to search for "what works" or "does not work" in minority education. These studies focus on the microsetting events of classroom, school, or home and sometimes on the biographies of minority children. Such events are rarely analyzed in the context of the minority group's history or its structural position in society. My view is that what goes on inside the classroom and school is greatly affected by the minority group's perceptions of and responses to schooling, and that is related to its historical and structural experience in the larger society.*

---

*Commenting on an earlier draft of this essay, some colleagues said that it lacked "any real historical dimension." For example, in the case of black Americans the essay failed to note that after the Reconstruction in the nineteenth century, blacks in the South had achieved a higher rate of literacy than poor whites in some cities in Scotland, Italy, and elsewhere in Europe. This kind of information is interesting but not necessary for the theme of the essay.

The task of the essay is to explain differences in the school performance of different types of minorities as well as differences between the minorities and the dominant group of their society. The historical dimension relevant to this task includes the following: (a) an account of the history of the incorporation of the minority groups into their respective societies; (b) an account

In my research on minority education I have found it useful to classify specific groups as autonomous minorities, immigrant or voluntary minorities, and castelike or involuntary minorities.[†]

Autonomous minorities, represented in the United States by Jews and Mormons, for example, are found also in most developing nations in Africa and Asia. While these minorities may be victims of prejudice or pillory, stratification does not define their position. Their separate existence is rarely based on a special economic, ritual, or political role; they generally employ a cultural frame of reference which encourages success.

Immigrant or *voluntary minorities* are those who have more or less chosen to move to the United States or to some other society, in the belief that this change will lead to an improvement in their economic well-being or to greater political freedom. These expectations influence the way they perceive and respond to white Americans and to institutions controlled by whites. The Chinese in Stockton, California, and the Punjabi in Valleyside, California, are representative examples.[‡][17]

Castelike or *involuntary minorities* are people initially brought into the United States through slavery, conquest, or colonization. Resenting the loss of their former freedom and perceiving the social, political, and economic barriers against them as part of an undeserved oppression, American Indians, black Americans, Mexican Americans, and native Hawaiians are characteristic American exam-

---

of how the minorities were subsequently treated by the dominant group, including their treatment in education; and (c) an account of the responses of the minorities to their treatment, including their responses in the field of education. The central point of the essay is that all these historical events impact on minorities' perceptions of and responses to schooling and should help to account for the variability in minority school performance.

[†]Internal or external forces may cause a minority group to change from one type to another (see my book, *Minority Education and Caste: The American System in Cross-Cultural Perspective* [New York: Academic Press, 1978]). On the other hand, there are minorities that do not seem to change and seem to maintain the same status for centuries. These have been called "persistent peoples" or "cultural enclaves" (see G. P. Castile and G. Kushner, eds., *Persistent Peoples: Cultural Enclaves in Perspective* [Tucson: University of Arizona Press, 1981]).

[‡]I classify a minority group as "voluntary" if its members have chosen to come to the United States and have not been forced by the United States to become part of the country through conquest, slavery, or colonization. The fact that some immigrants were "forced" to leave their homeland by war, famine, political upheaval, and the like is not relevant to my typology. What matters is that members of the minority group do not *perceive their presence as forced on them* by white Americans.

ples.* Similar minorities exist in Japan—the Buraku outcastes and the Koreans—and in New Zealand—the Maoris.[18]

By comparing the historical, structural, and psychological factors influencing school-adjustment problems of immigrants (i.e., voluntary minorities) with those of nonimmigrants (i.e., involuntary minorities) one can show why the latter are plagued by persistent poor academic performance while the former are not.

The cultural and language differences of various minorities vis-à-vis white American culture and language are not qualitatively the same. Such differences can be a significant factor in school adjustment, in the academic performance of a specific minority group. One must distinguish between primary and secondary cultural differences.[19] _Primary cultural differences_ are those that existed before two specific populations came into continuous contact. For example, before Punjabis emigrated from the Punjab to California, they spoke Punjabi, often wore turbans, accepted arranged marriages, and practiced the Sikh, Hindu, or Muslim religion. They also had their distinctive child-rearing practices. In California these immigrants maintained these beliefs and practices to some degree.[20]

---

*There are differences among the groups included in the category of involuntary minorities, both in the way they were incorporated and in the way they were subsequently treated by the dominant groups.

Some people will question the inclusion of Mexican Americans as well as Puerto Ricans among involuntary minorities and the exclusion of West Indians from the category. Mexican Americans are classified as an involuntary minority group because they were initially incorporated by conquest: the "Anglos" conquered and annexed the Mexican territory where the Chicanos were living in the Southwest, acts that were completed by the Treaty of Guadalupe Hildago in 1848. (See R. Acuna, _Occupied America: The Chicano's Struggle Toward Liberation_ [San Francisco: Canfield Press, 1981]; C. Knowlton, "Neglected Chapters in Mexican American History," in G. Taylor, ed., _Mexican Americans Tomorrow: Educational and Economic Perspectives_ [Albuquerque: New Mexico University Press, 1975]; and my article with M. E. Matute-Bianchi, "Understanding Sociocultural Factors: Knowledge, Identity, and School Adjustment," in _Beyond Language: Social and Cultural Factors in Schooling Language Minority Students_ [Sacramento: Bilingual Education Office, State Department of Education, 1986].) Other Mexicans who later immigrated both legally and illegally were usually defined and treated by the Anglos in terms of the status of the conquered group. And the immigrants were often forced to live and work among members of the conquered group, with whom they developed and shared the same sense of peoplehood or group identity in the course of time. (See my book _Minority Education and Caste_.)

Puerto Ricans are classified as an involuntary minority because they are more or less "a colonized people." The United States conquered or colonized Cuba, the Philippines, and Puerto Rico in 1898. Both Cuba and the Philippines have since then achieved independence, so that Cubans and Filipinos coming to the United States come more or less as immigrants or refugees. The status of Puerto Rico is, however, ambiguous—it is neither a state within the U.S. polity nor an independent nation in the real sense. To many Puerto Ricans, their "country" is still a U.S. colony. (See my book _Minority Education and Caste_.)

A better understanding of the nature of primary cultural differences may be gained by studying the situation of non-Western children introduced to Western-type education in their own societies. The Kpelle of Liberia, who attend schools established by Americans on an American model, were studied by John Gay and Michael Cole, who were interested in finding out how Kpelle culture and language affected the learning of the American mathematical system. The study focused on the kinds of mathematical knowledge, concepts, and activities found in Kpelle culture: indigenous arithmetical concepts, knowledge of geometry, systems of measurement, and Kpelle logic or reasoning all figured.[21]

While the arithmetical concepts were similar in some ways, they were different in others. For example, like Americans, the Kpelle classify; unlike Americans, they do not carry out such classificatory activities explicitly or consciously. The Kpelle counting system does not include the concepts of "zero" or "number." Nor do the Kpelle recognize such abstract operations as addition, subtraction, multiplication, and division, though they do add, subtract, multiply, and divide. Lacking any terms for such operations, Kpelle culture has few geometrical concepts, which are generally used imprecisely. For example, when they were asked to name circular things, a pot, pan, frog, sledge hammer, tortoise, water turtle, and rice fanner were all mentioned. For the shape of a triangle, a tortoise shell, arrowhead, monkey's elbow, drum, and bow seemed relevant. The Kpelle measure length, time, volume, and money; but they lack measurements for weight, area, speed, and temperature. Such differences between American and Kpelle culture in mathematical knowledge and concepts existed before the Kpelle were introduced to American-type education.

Such primary cultural differences are found among many immigrant minorities. Immigrant minority children confront problems because of such primary cultural differences. The problems may range from interpersonal relations with teachers and other students, to academic work. Under favorable conditions, immigrant children are generally able to overcome such problems in the course of time.

Secondary cultural and *language differences* are those which arise after two populations have come into contact, or after members of one population have begun to participate in an institution controlled by members of another. Secondary cultural and language differences develop as a response to such contact, often involving the domination of one group by another.

In the beginning, the minorities and the dominant group will usually show primary cultural and language differences. In the course of time, a new type of cultural and language difference may emerge, reflecting the way the minorities are treated by the dominant group and the way they have come to perceive, interpret, and respond to that treatment. For example, when slavery was common, white Americans used legal and extralegal means to discourage black Americans from acquiring literacy and the associated behaviors and benefits. After the abolition of slavery, whites created barriers in employment and in other areas of life, effectively denying blacks certain social and economic benefits, but also the incentives associated with the education whites made available to them. Such barriers extended to places of residence, public accommodations, and political and legal rights. Blacks, like other involuntary minorities, developed new or "secondary" cultural ways of coping, perceiving, and feeling in relating to whites and to the public schools controlled by whites.

Most descriptions of cultural differences between involuntary minorities and white Americans emphasize differences in the style of cognition,[22] communication,[23] interaction,[24] and learning.[25] In contrast, descriptions of primary cultural differences emphasize differences in the content of cognition, communication, and so on.[26] A further distinguishing feature of a secondary cultural system is *cultural inversion,* the tendency for members of one population, in this case a minority group, to regard certain forms of behavior, events, symbols, and meanings as inappropriate, precisely because they are characteristic of members of another population, for example, white Americans. These minorities may claim other forms of behavior, events, symbols, and meanings as more appropriate precisely because they are not characteristic of members of the dominant group.

Involuntary minorities use cultural inversion to repudiate negative stereotypes or derogatory images attributed to them by members of the dominant group. Cultural inversion is also used as a strategy to manipulate whites, to get even with whites, or, as one observer says, in the case of black Americans, "to turn the table against whites."[27] Because secondary cultural differences are developed in opposition to and in response to perceived unjustified treatment by the dominant group, such cultural differences are intimately tied to the minorities' sense of group identity.

Because researchers, policymakers, and educators in the field of minority education tend to idealize educational pursuit, they forget that schooling in the United States has generally been structured on the commonsense notion of training in marketable skills, credentialing for labor-force entry, remuneration, advancement. Thus, whatever other functions schooling may serve, the most important function, as perceived by most Americans, is economic; children go to school to secure the credentials for employment, remuneration, and advancement.[28]

Schools, however, do not succeed uniformly in credentialing members of society by content or method of teaching. The labor-force experience of members of a given group, and their perceptions of and responses to schooling as a consequence of their overall status in U.S. society, are significant factors.*[29]

In a plural society like the United States, the various segments of the society—the dominant whites and the minority groups—tend to have specific cultural models, understandings of their status, of how American society works and their place in that working order. The cultural model of white Americans, like that of a specific minority group, is never right or wrong, better or worse. As Bohannan puts it, "The folk systems [i.e., cultural models] are *never* right nor wrong. They exist to guide behavior, to interpret behavior and events."[30]

The cultural models of minorities are shaped by the initial terms of their incorporation in American society, and their subsequent treatment by white Americans. The formative influence that differentiates the cultural model of immigrants from that of nonimmigrants or involuntary minorities is the initial term of incorporation—voluntary

---

*It seems strange to be asked, as I have been sometimes, why involuntary minorities like black Americans want to succeed like the dominant group, whites. American society qua society preaches equality and equal opportunity through education, presumably for everyone. Involuntary minorities are expected to "buy into" this ideology and mode of social mobility; they are expected to strive to succeed like whites through education. The trouble is that for generations the minorities were denied equal rewards given to whites for their educational accomplishments: equal employment opportunities, wages, advancement, and the like, commensurate with their education and ability. In this essay, it is suggested that such discriminatory treatment must have some adverse effects on the *incentive motivation* of the minorities to pursue education or school credentials.

incorporation in the case of the immigrants, involuntary incorporation in the case of nonimmigrants.

What does it mean to be a minority in the United States? Voluntary
and involuntary minorities answer this question differently. Immigrants generally regard themselves as "foreigners," "strangers" who
came to America with expectation of certain economic, political, and
social benefits. While anticipating that such benefits might come at
some cost—involving discrimination and other hardships—the immigrants did not measure their success or failure primarily by the
standards of other white Americans, but by the standards of their
homelands. Such minorities, at least during the first generation, did
not internalize the effects of such discrimination, of cultural and
intellectual denigration. Their effects were not ingrained in their
culture. Even when they were restricted to menial labor, they did not
consider themselves to be occupying the lowest rung of the American
status system, and partly because they did not fully understand that
system, and partly because they did not consider themselves as
belonging to it, they saw their situation as temporary.

For involuntary minorities, there were no expectations of economic, political, and social benefits. Resenting their initial incorporation by force, regarding their past as a "golden age," and seeing
their future as grim in the absence of collective struggle,[31] they
understood that the American system was based on social class and
minority conditions. Resenting exclusion from a status system available to whites, based on achieved criteria, they felt the power of white
domination in almost every domain. While refusing to accept white
denigration, the common white belief that they were biologically,
culturally, and intellectually inferior to whites, their own thoughts
and behaviors were not entirely free from the influence of such
denigration and belief. Involuntary minorities tended to develop
other explanations for their persistent menial status; they used these
explanations to rationalize their responses.

Both voluntary and involuntary minorities face discrimination in
various spheres of American life. Discriminated against in employment, usually through job ceilings, minorities are often relegated to
menial jobs and low wages. Also, political barriers may exist,
exacerbated by social and residential segregation. Their children,
often channeled into inferior, segregated schools, discover as adults

that they are denied employment and wages commensurate with their school credentials.³²

Immigrant and involuntary minorities suffer, in addition, expressive or symbolic discrimination. White Americans tend to denigrate such minorities, culturally and intellectually, stereotyping them, characterizing them by specific undesirable traits. Minorities are used as scapegoats, often subjected to violent treatment in times of economic and political crisis.³³ They are denied assimilation, admission into mainstream American society.

Immigrant and involuntary minorities, while resenting such treatment, perceive and interpret it differently, and appear to work out different collective solutions to their common collective problems. (In the case of blacks the problem is made more complicated by race and color.)

The coping responses are of three types: instrumental, relational, and expressive. *Instrumental responses* include: (1) a dual-status frame of comparison, a comparison that minorities make of their status and opportunities in the United States with the status and opportunities of their peers "back home," in the case of immigrants, or with the status and opportunities of white Americans, especially in the case of the nonimmigrants; (2) a folk theory or folk theories of "making it" in America; (3) collective efforts to change those rules of "getting ahead" that do not work well for minorities; (4) alternative survival strategies, developed by minorities to compensate for barriers encountered in the opportunity structure; and (5) role models. *Relational responses* have to do with the degree of trust that the minorities have for white Americans and the institutions they control. *Expressive, or symbolic, responses* reflect the minority-group members' sense of group identity, their cultural frames of reference, and their ideal ways of behaving.

On the instrumental side, immigrants appear to interpret the economic, political, and social barriers set against them as a more or less temporary problem that they can (and will) overcome with time through hard work and/or education.

Immigrants will often compare their situation in the United States with what they have known or what their peers are experiencing "back home." When making such comparisons, they find encouraging evidence to believe that they will enjoy greater opportunities in the United States for themselves or for their children. Even if they are permitted only marginal jobs, they see themselves as better off than they would be in their homelands. They believe the United States to be a land of opportunity where success comes with hard work. They rationalize discrimination in employment and other things by attributing this to their status as "foreigners," to the fact that they do not speak the English language well, that they lack "an American education." Given these perceptions, immigrant minorities tend to adopt what they understand to be the folk theory of getting ahead among white Americans; they try to behave accordingly. Among such immigrants, schooling, knowledge, and individual effort emerge as the primary avenues for getting ahead. Contrast this with the situation that obtains in their countries of origin, where advancement occurs through a network of friends, nepotism, or *"por apellido"* (because of one's last name, in the case of a Latino immigrant), and not necessarily because of one's effort, knowledge, or educational credentials.[34]

Voluntary minorities also develop survival or alternative strategies to cope with their problems. The survival strategies include the option of returning to their former homelands or emigrating to yet another place. They recognize also the possibility of exploiting economic resources not desired by white Americans and involuntary minorities.

In the relational domain, voluntary minorities have a greater degree of trust for white Americans, for the societal institutions controlled by whites, than do involuntary minorities. Such immigrants acquiesce and rationalize the prejudice and discrimination against them by saying, in effect, that they are "strangers in a foreign land [and] have no choice but to tolerate prejudice and discrimination."[35] In relating to the public schools, they rationalize their accommodation by saying that they came to America to give their children the opportunity to secure an American education. Indeed, they find their relationship with the public schools to be "better" than what they knew in their homelands, and speak favorably of conditions where their children are given free textbooks and other supplies.[36]

In the expressive or symbolic domain, the immigrants' response to cultural and language differences is also influenced by expectations. The immigrants, such as the Punjabis, for example, interpret certain of the cultural and language differences as barriers to be overcome.

Never imagining that this requires them to abandon their own minority culture and language, they selectively learn the language and cultural features of the mainstream. There is no perceived threat to cultural or language identity. As for social or collective identity, voluntary minorities bring with them a keen sense of who they were before they emigrated. They perceive their social identities as different from rather than as opposed to the identity of white Americans. They appear to retain this social identity, at least during the first generation, all the time they are learning the English language and adapting other aspects of mainstream American culture.

The instrumental responses of involuntary minorities are different. They do not interpret the economic, social, and political barriers against them as temporary. Their reference group is different. Because they do not have a "homeland" to compare with the situation in the United States, they do not find solace in their menial jobs and low wages. Recognizing that they belong to a subordinate, indeed a disparaged, minority, they compare their situation with that of their white American peers. The prejudice against them seems permanent, indeed institutionalized.

In their folk theory of "making it," involuntary minorities often wish they could advance through education and ability as white Americans do, but know they cannot. They come to realize that it requires more than education and effort to overcome the barriers set up against them. Consequently, they develop a folk theory of getting ahead which differs from that of white Americans; it emphasizes collective effort as providing the best chances for overcoming barriers in those areas controlled by white Americans.*

Since involuntary minorities do not believe that the societal rules for self-advancement work for them, they try to change the rules. They may, for example, seek to alter the criteria for school credentialing, for employment. One strategy effectively used by black Americans is to change the rules through "collective struggle," one of

---

*In any given minority group there are likely to be competing "folk theories" of making it or at least some variants of the dominant theory. Thus, among black Americans some people emphasize making it through education; others emphasize making it through alternative strategies. However, even among those who emphasize using education as a way of achieving success, there is also the understanding that their minority status is a factor to be taken into account. Public statements by candidates for public office about the "traditional American way" of making it cannot be taken at face value, however.

several survival strategies developed to eliminate, lower, or circumvent specific barriers in securing desirable jobs and in advancing in other ways. Collective struggle includes what white Americans regard as legitimate "civil rights activities"; for the minorities, these include rioting and other forms of collective action that promise to increase the opportunities or the pool of resources available to them.

Patron-client relationships, or "Uncle Tomming" ("Tio Tacoing," etc.), is another survival strategy, more common in the past. Other survival strategies include opting for certain activities—sports, entertainment, hustling, pimping, and, nowadays, drug dealing.

In the relational domain, involuntary minorities distrust white Americans and their institutions. White Americans have a record that merits such mistrust. The public schools, for example, cannot be relied on to provide minority children with "the right education." Involuntary minorities find no justification for the prejudice and discrimination they find in school and society, which appears to be institutionalized, and enduring.

On the expressive side, involuntary minorities are characterized by secondary cultural systems, in which cultural differences arise or are reinterpreted after the groups have become involuntary minorities. They develop certain beliefs and practices, including particular ways of communicating or speaking, as coping mechanisms in conditions of subordination. These may be new creations or simply reinterpretations of old ones. The secondary cultural system, on the whole, constitutes a new cultural frame of reference, an ideal way of believing and acting which affirms one as a bona fide member of a group. Involuntary minorities perceive their cultural frames of reference not merely as different from but as opposed to the cultural frames of reference of their white "oppressors." The cultural and language differences emerging under these conditions serve as boundary-making mechanisms. Involuntary minorities do not interpret language and cultural differences encountered in school or society as barriers to overcome; they interpret such differences as symbols of their identity. Their culture provides a frame of reference that gives them a sense of collective or social identity, a sense of self-worth.

Involuntary minorities develop a new sense of peoplehood or social identity after their forced incorporation into American society, because of the ways they interpret the discrimination they are obliged to endure. In some instances, involuntary minorities may develop a new sense of peoplehood because of their forced integration into mainstream society.[37] Many appear to believe that they cannot expect to be treated as white Americans, whatever' their ability, training or education; whatever their place of origin, residence, economic status, or physical appearance.[38] These involuntary minorities know that they cannot escape from their birth-ascribed membership in subordinate and disparaged groups by "passing" or returning to their "homelands."[39] They do not see their social identity as different from that of their white "oppressors," but as opposed to the social identity of white Americans. This oppositional identity, combined with their oppositional or ambivalent cultural frames of reference, make cross-cultural learning, the "crossing of cultural boundaries," very problematic. Crossing cultural boundaries, behaving in a manner regarded as falling under the white American cultural frames of reference, is threatening to their minority identity and security, but also to their solidarity. Individuals seeking to behave like whites are discouraged by peer group pressures and by "affective dissonance."[40]

Factors affecting minority children's acquisition of literacy and numeracy came from "the system" and from "the minority community." In American folk terminology, "the system" is made up of the public schools, of the powers-that-be in the wider society. Before 1960, the United States, like other urban industrial societies, did not provide equal educational opportunity for minorities.[41] Even today, minorities do not enjoy equal educational opportunity, partly because vestiges of past discriminatory educational policies and practices survive. However, in some instances, significant improvements have been made to equalize the education provided minorities with that of the dominant group.

Denial of equal educational opportunity shows up in the denial of equal access to desirable jobs, to positions in adult life that require good education, where education clearly pays off. Generations of black Americans were regularly denied equal employment opportunity through a job ceiling.[42] Blacks with school credentials comparable to those of their white peers were not hired for similar jobs, were not paid equal wages, were not permitted to advance on the basis of education and ability. By denying minorities the opportunity to enter the labor force, by denying them equal rewards, American society discouraged whole generations, especially involuntary minorities (blacks and Indians, for example), from investing time and effort in education to maximize their educational accomplishments. The experience may have discouraged such minorities from developing a strong tradition of striving for academic achievement.

Minorities were also denied equal access to good education. Before 1960, blacks were channeled into inferior schools by formal statutes in the South, and by informal practices in the North. Such schools, characterized by inadequately trained and overworked teachers, a different and inferior curriculum, inadequate funding, insufficient facilities and services, were conspicuous in the South, where black school terms were shorter than those of white schools. Although formal aspects of unequal educational opportunity have been abolished by law, recent desegregation cases continue to reveal that minority and majority education in the United States remain unequal. Inferior education guarantees that blacks and other minorities will not qualify as whites do for desirable jobs and other positions in adult life that require good education. More importantly, minority children receiving inferior education cannot learn as much or test as well as white children do who have access to better education.

Minority children receive inferior education also through what occurs inside the schools, inside individual classrooms. Among the mechanisms discovered to affect minority education adversely, none is more important than teachers' low expectations. So, also, too many minority children are treated as having educational "handicaps." A disproportionate number are channeled into "special education," a pseudonym for inferior education. Problems that arise from cultural and language differences are inadequately attended to. The failure of school personnel to understand the cultural behaviors of minority children often results in conflicts that affect the children's capacity to adjust and learn. While minority children have an obligation to understand and relate to the culture and language of the schools, this is a two-way thoroughfare.

As is obvious from what has already been said, complex and interlocking forces affect the social adjustment and academic performance of minority children. These forces are not limited to those of the wider society, of the schools and classrooms already described. They also derive from minority communities themselves. These, again, are different for voluntary and involuntary minorities. Among voluntary minorities, the interaction of community forces with societal and school factors does not necessarily discourage the striving for academic success. Among involuntary minorities, this interaction appears to discourage such striving.

Immigrant parents tend to stress education for their children and generally take steps to ensure that their children behave in a manner conducive to school success. For their part, the children, whether they are Chinese, Central or South American Latinos, Cubans, Koreans, Punjabi Indians, or West Indians, appear to share their parents' attitudes toward American education. They take their schoolwork seriously, and persevere. Immigrant minority parents do not care to have their children look upon them as role models; they expect their children to be different, to succeed according to the American mainstream system of status mobility. Nor do the children care to resemble their parents, who are often doing menial work.[43]

Symbolic responses work also to promote a striving for school success among voluntary minorities. Their nonoppositional group identity and their nonoppositional cultural frames of reference facilitate their children's ability to cross cultural and language boundaries in school. Such immigrants learn to distinguish what they need to know in order to achieve their goals for immigration—including learning the English language and adjusting to the standard practices of school and workplace—from other aspects of mainstream American culture which might threaten their minority language, culture, or identity. These children do not go to school to be taught their native languages or cultures. Rather, they expect to learn the English language, are anxious to do so, along with the standard practices of the school. This does not imply that certain of these children do not experience language and cultural difficulties; it is simply that they and their parents, together with their communities, perceive the language and cultural conflicts to be problems that have to be overcome, with appropriate help from the schools.

The *relational responses* of the immigrants serve also to enhance their school success. The immigrants' acquiescing and trusting relationship with teachers and other school personnel promotes such success. These immigrants consider schools in the United States to be better than those of their homelands; they think of the schools they left behind, not of the schools as they exist in the white suburbs of North America. The immigrants see themselves as being better treated by the public school personnel in their new homes than in their original homelands.[44] Even where they experience prejudice and discrimination, which they resent, they rationalize such treatment so as not to be discouraged from striving for school success.[45] Ethnographic studies suggest that immigrant minority parents teach their children to trust school officials and to accept, internalize, and follow school rules and standard practices for academic success, and that the children more or less do follow these instructions.

The instrumental responses of involuntary minorities are not equally encouraging for school success. Comparing themselves unfavorably with white Americans, these minorities tend to conclude that they are worse off, whatever their education or ability. The role of education, the worth of a school credential is uncertain.

While the folk theory of involuntary minorities emphasizes the importance of education in getting ahead, such verbal endorsement is not generally accompanied by the appropriate and necessary effort partly because historically involuntary minorities have never been given the chance to get the sorts of jobs and wages available to whites of comparable education. These minorities have never had a "back home" situation with which to compare their new situation. Inevitably, they come to see their treatment as part of institutionalized discrimination, never entirely eliminated by securing an education.[46] Such minorities, never developing "effort optimism" toward academic work,[47] have had no incentive to fashion a strong tradition of cultural know-how, emphasizing hard work and perseverance in academic tasks.

Given this circumstance, such minority parents have tended to teach their children contradictory things about getting ahead through schooling. In my own ethnographic research among blacks and Mexican Americans in Stockton, California, I have observed parents telling their children to get a good education, encouraging them verbally to do well in school, while the actual texture of their own lives, with their low-level jobs, underemployment, and unemployment have provided a different kind of message, contradicting all their verbal exhortations. Unavoidably, such minority parents discuss their problems with "the system," with their relatives, friends, and neighbors in the presence of their children. The result, inevitably, is that such children become increasingly disillusioned about their ability to succeed in adult life through the mainstream strategy of schooling.

The folk theory of involuntary minorities stresses other means of getting ahead, survival strategies both within and beyond the mainstream. Such strategies tend to generate attitudes and behaviors in students that are not conducive to good classroom teaching or learning. Sometimes they convey contradictory messages about schooling itself. For example, when survival strategies are used, such as the collective struggle among black Americans to succeed in increasing the pool of jobs and other resources, they may indeed encourage certain minority youths to work hard in school. They may also lead such youths to blame "the system," even to rationalize their lack of serious school effort.

Clientship, or Uncle Tomming (Tio Tacoing), does not create role models for school success through good study habits and hard work. Instead, clientship teaches minority children manipulative attitudes and trains them in the knowledge and skills used by their parents to deal with white people and white institutions. As the children become familiar with other survival strategies, including hustling and pimping as well as drug dealing, their attitudes toward schooling are adversely affected. For example, in the norms that support such survival strategies, like hustling, the work ethic is reversed by the insistence that one ought to be able to make it without working, especially without "doing the white man's thing," which includes doing schoolwork. Furthermore, for students who are engaged in hustling, social interactions in the classroom are seen as opportunities to exploit, opportunities to gain prestige by putting others down.

Because survival strategies can become serious competitors with schooling as ways of getting ahead, leading young people to channel their time and efforts into nonacademic activities, particularly as minority children become older, more aware of how certain adults in their communities "make it" without mainstream school credentials and employment, this shift is dangerous.[48] There is evidence, for example, that among young black Americans, many see sports and entertainment, rather than education, as the way to get ahead. Their perceptions are reinforced by the realities they observe in the community, in society at large, as represented by the media. Blacks, for example, are overrepresented in such lucrative sports as baseball, basketball, and football. The average annual salary in the National Basketball Association is over $300,000; in the National Football League, it is over $90,000. Many of the superstars who earn between

$1 million and $2 million a year are black; many have had little education. While the number of such highly paid athletes is low, the media make them, together with black entertainers, more visible than black lawyers, doctors, engineers, or scientists. There is preliminary evidence to suggest that black parents, imagining that such activities will lead to careers in professional sports, encourage their children's athletic activities.[49]

To summarize, while such children, like their parents, may verbally express interest in doing well in school, in obtaining school credentials for future employment in the mainstream economy, they do not necessarily match their wishes and aspirations with effort. Black and Mexican-American students in Stockton, California, for example, correctly explained that Chinese, Japanese, and white students are more academically successful because they expend more time and effort in their schoolwork, both at school and at home. The lack of serious academic attitudes, of substantial effort, appears to increase as these students grow older, become more aware of their own social reality, and accept the prevailing beliefs that as members of disparaged minority groups they have limited opportunities to get good jobs, even with a superior education. They increasingly divert their time and effort from schoolwork into nonacademic activities.

The symbolic or expressive responses of involuntary minorities contribute greatly to their school-adjustment and performance problems. Because they appear to interpret cultural and language differences as markers or symbols of group identity to be maintained, not as barriers to be overcome, they do not appear to make a clear distinction, as immigrants do, between what they have to learn or do to enhance their school success (such as learning and using standard English and standard behavior practices) and what they must do to maintain a cultural frame of reference distinct from that of their "oppressors."

Involuntary minorities perceive or interpret learning certain aspects of white American culture, behaving according to white American cultural standards, as detrimental to their own cultures, languages, and identities. The equating of standard English and standard school practices with white American culture and white identity often results in conscious or unconscious opposition, showing itself in ambivalence toward learning. Those minority students who adopt the attitudes and behaviors conducive to school success, who use standard English and behave according to standard school practices, are accused by their peers of "acting white" or, in the case of black students, of being Uncle Toms.[50] They are said to be disloyal to the cause of their groups; they risk being isolated from their peers.

Furthermore, as one authority has noted, even in the absence of peer pressures, such minority students appear to avoid adopting serious academic attitudes, persevering in their academic tasks.[51] They have internalized their groups' interpretations of such attitudes and behaviors; also, they are uncertain, even if they succeed in learning to "act white," whether they will be accepted by whites. Minorities are afraid to lose the support of their own groups.

The dilemma of such students, as one observer has pointed out, is that they are compelled to choose between academic success and maintaining their minority identity and cultural frame of reference, a choice that does not arise for the children of immigrants.[52] Those who wish to achieve academic success are compelled to adopt strategies that will shield them from peer criticism and ostracism.

Involuntary minorities tend to compare their schools with white schools, especially schools in the white suburbs; they usually end up with the negative judgment that they are being provided with an inferior education for which there is no justification. Since they mistrust the public schools and the whites who control them, the minorities are generally skeptical that the schools can educate their children well. This skepticism of parents, together with that of other members of the minority communities, is communicated to the children through family and community discussions, but also in public debates over minority education in general and debates on particular issues, such as school desegregation.

Another factor discouraging academic effort is that such minorities—parents as well as students—tend to question the schools' rules for behavior and their standard practices, the perception being that they represent the imposition of a white cultural frame of reference which does not necessarily meet their real educational needs.

The problems are only exacerbated by the tendency of schools to approach the educational issues defensively. In these circumstances, parents would have great difficulty teaching their children to accept and follow standard school rules of behavior, this being true particularly of the older ones.[53]

I have described what appears to be the dominant patterns of academic orientation and adaptation for two types of minorities. Within each type, obviously, there are several culturally patterned strategies that enhance school success. However, in each, the degree of support—especially peer support—for the individual utilizing certain strategies to enhance school success is markedly different. Among immigrant minority youths, the collective orientation appears to be toward making good grades; social pressures from the community, family, and peer groups support this. Individuals threatened with criticism and peer isolation are those who do not achieve academically.[54] Partly to avoid ridicule, criticism, and isolation, which may extend to their families, immigrant minority youths tend to use strategies that are commonly known in the community to enhance their chances of success in school.[55]

Among involuntary minorities the situation is different, as are the responses of individual youths. Here, while making good grades is given lip service, there is less community and family pressure to achieve that goal. There is, for example, no stigma that attaches to youths who do not make good grades. As for peer groups, their collective orientation is almost precisely the opposite of what it is among immigrants; the orientation of involuntary minorities militates against academic success. Peer pressures among these students discourage the use of strategies to enhance individual success in school. Those subjected to peer criticism and isolation are those perceived to be behaving as if they wished to succeed academically, and those who actually do succeed. Under these circumstances, those who want to succeed academically often consciously choose from a variety of secondary strategies to enable themselves to succeed, and shield themselves from peer pressures and other forces. These secondary strategies go beyond the conventional strategies of correct academic attitudes, hard work, perseverance. They are strategies that allow such minority youths to practice a more conventional strategy.

Employing black Americans as an example, to indicate certain of the secondary strategies used, ethnographic studies suggest that one secondary strategy that promotes school success is assimilation, the emulation of whites. Black youths who choose this strategy seek to dissociate themselves from their black peers, from black cultural identity. They appear to prefer white norms and values, clearly in conflict with those of blacks. They reason that in order to succeed they must repudiate their black peers, black identity, and black cultural frames of reference.[56] Such minority youths are often academically successful; the price paid is peer criticism and isolation.

Camouflage is another secondary strategy used by black youths. Some consciously choose gender-appropriate specific strategies to camouflage their real academic attitudes and efforts.[57] These students adopt camouflaging techniques to escape adverse peer influences on their schoolwork. One technique is to become heavily involved in athletic or other team-oriented activities. This appears to reassure others that they are not simply pursuing their own interests and trying to get ahead of others.

Another camouflage technique is to assume the role of comedian or jester.[58] By acting foolishly, the black youth satisfies the peer expectation that he or she is not very serious about school. The jester, however, takes schoolwork seriously when he is away from his peers and often does well in school. Jesters conceal their school achievement and never brag about their school success. Some who are good at camouflaging, and are indeed academically successful, are regarded by their peers as being "naturally smart." Academically successful black males are the ones who very often play the role of class clown.

Some black youths adopt what may be regarded as the immigrants' strategy of accommodation without assimilation.[59] While not rejecting their minority or black identity and cultural frames of reference, they elect to play by the rules of the system. Their stance appears to be "When in Rome, do as the Romans do."

Other secondary strategies include the security of mentors, attending private schools to get away from black peers, becoming involved in church activities where there are support groups for academic striving, getting a bully to protect oneself from one's peers in exchange for helping the bully with his homework, participating in mainstreaming or intervention programs.

Some black youths obviously become more or less imprisoned in peer orientation and activity that are hostile to academic striving. These youths not only equate school learning with "acting white," but make no attempt to "act white." They refuse to learn, to conform to school rules of behavior and standard practices; these are defined as being within the white American cultural frame of reference.[60]

To promote a greater degree of school success among the less academically successful minorities, it is essential to recognize and remove certain obstacles from the larger society, but also from within the schools. The obstacles within the minority communities need also to be acknowledged, which manifest themselves in specific perceptions and strategies of schooling.

ACKNOWLEDGMENTS

The preparation of this essay was made possible by grants to Minority Education Project from the Carnegie Corporation, Exxon Educational Foundation, W. T. Grant Foundation, John D. and Catherine T. MacArthur Foundation, Rockefeller Foundation, Russell Sage Foundation, and California State Department of Education. The data presented, the statements made, and the views expressed are solely the responsibility of the author.

ENDNOTES

[1] J. U. Ogbu, *Minority Education and Caste: The American System in Cross-Cultural Perspective* (New York: Academic Press, 1978).

[2] B. M. Bullivant, *The Ethnic Encounters in the Secondary Schools: Ethnocultural Reproduction and Resistance, Theory and Case Studies* (London: Falmer Press, 1987); M. Taylor and S. Hegarty, *The Best of Both Worlds. . . ? A Review of Research into the Education of Pupils of South Asian Origin* (Windsor: NFER-Nelson, 1985); and Ogbu, *Minority Education and Caste*.

[3] A. R. Jensen, "How Much Can We Boost IQ and Scholastic Achievement?" *Harvard Educational Review* 39 (1) (1969): 1–123.

[4] C. T. Ramey and J. J. Gallagher, "The Nature of Cultural Deprivation: Theoretical Issues and Suggested Research Strategies," *North Carolina Journal of Mental Health* (1975): 41–47; and S. H. White et al., *Goals and Standards of Public Programs for Children*, vol. 1, *Federal Programs for Young Children, Review and Recommendations* (Washington, D.C.: U.S. Government Printing Office, 1973).

[5] M. L. Goldberg, "Socio-Psychological Issues in the Education of the Disadvantaged," in *Urban Education in the 1970s*, ed. A. Harry Passow (New York: Teachers College Press, 1971); C. T. Ramey and F. A. Campbell, "The Carolina Abecedarian Project: An Educational Experiment Concerning Human Malleability," in *The Malleability of Children*, ed. J. J. Gallagher and C. T. Ramey (Baltimore: Paul H. Brooks, 1987); and Ogbu, *Minority Education and Caste*.

[6] J. S. Coleman et al., *Equality of Educational Opportunity* (Washington, D.C.: U.S. Government Printing Office, 1966).

[7] M. Slade, "Aptitude, Intelligence or What," *New York Times*, 24 October 1981.

[8]K. Haycock and M. S. Navarro, *Unfinished Business: Report from the Achievement Council* (Oakland, Calif.: The Achievement Council, 1988).

[9]S. Fordham and J. U. Ogbu, "Black Students' School Success: Coping with the Burden of 'Acting White,'" *The Urban Review* 18 (3) (1986): 176–206; and M. L. Oliver, C. Rodriguez, and R. A. Mickelson, "Brown and Black in White: The Social Adjustment and Academic Performance of Chicano and Black Students in a Predominantly White University," *The Urban Review* 17 (2) (1985): 3–24.

[10]S. U. Philips, "Commentary: Access to Power and Maintenance of Ethnic Identity as Goals of Multi-Cultural Education," *Anthropology and Education Quarterly* 7 (4) (1976): 30–32.

[11]T. J. LaBelle, "Anthropological Framework for Studying Education," in *Schooling in the Cultural Context: Anthropological Studies of Education,* ed. J. I. Roberts and S. Akinsanya (New York: David McKay, 1976).

[12]P. Byers and H. Byers, "Non-Verbal Communication and the Education of Children," in *Functions of Language in the Classroom,* ed. C. B. Cazden et al. (New York: Teachers College Press, 1972).

[13]R. V. Dumont, Jr., "Learning English and How to be Silent: Studies in Sioux and Cherokee Classrooms," in *Functions of Language in the Classroom,* ed. C. B. Cazden et al. (New York: Teachers College Press, 1972).

[14]S. U. Philips, *The Invisible Culture: Communication in Classroom and Community on the Warm Springs Indian Reservation* (New York: Longman, 1983).

[15]A. W. Boykin, "Reading Achievement and the Social Cultural Frame of Afro-American Children," a paper presented at the National Institute of Education roundtable discussion on issues in urban reading, Washington, D.C., 19–20 November 1980, and "The Triple Quandary and the Schooling of Afro-American Children," in *The School Achievement of Minority Children: New Perspectives,* ed. U. Neisser (Hillsdale, N.J.: Erlbaum, 1986), 57–92; and B. J. Shade, "Afro-American Patterns of Cognition," unpublished manuscript (Madison: Wisconsin Center for Educational Research, 1982).

[16]J. Gay and M. Cole, *The New Mathematics and an Old Culture: A Study of Learning among the Kpelle of Liberia* (New York: Holt, 1967); D. F. Lancy, *Cross-Cultural Studies in Cognition and Mathematics* (New York: Academic Press, 1983); F. Musgrove, "Education and the Culture Concept," *Africa* 23 (2) (1953): 110–26; and LaBelle.

[17]M. A. Gibson, *Accommodation without Assimilation: Punjabi Sikh Immigrants in an American High School and Community* (Ithaca: Cornell University Press, 1988); and J. U. Ogbu, *The Next Generation: An Ethnography of Education in an Urban Neighborhood* (New York: Academic Press, 1974).

[18]Ogbu, *Minority Education and Caste.*

[19]J. U. Ogbu, "Cultural Discontinuities and Schooling," *Anthropology and Education Quarterly* 13 (4) (1982): 290–307.

[20]Gibson, *Accommodation without Assimilation.*

[21]Gay and Cole.

[22]M. Ramirez and A. Castenada, *Cultural Democracy, Bicognitive Development and Education* (New York: Academic Press, 1974); and Shade.

[23]J. J. Gumperz, "Conversational Inferences and Classroom Learning," in *Ethnographic Approach to Face-to-Face Interaction,* ed. J. Green and C. Wallat (Norwood, N.J.: ABLEX, 1981); T. Kochman, *Black and White Styles in Conflict* (Chicago: University of Chicago Press, 1982); and Philips, *The Invisible Culture.*

[24]F. Erickson and J. Mohartt, "Cultural Organization of Participant Structure in Two Classrooms of Indian Students," in *Doing the Ethnography of Schooling: Educational Anthropology in Action,* ed. G. D. Spindler (New York: Holt, 1982).

[25]K. H. Au, "Participant Structure in a Reading Lesson with Hawaiian Children: Analysis of a Culturally Appropriate Instructional Event," *Anthropology and Education Quarterly* 10 (2) (1981): 91–115; Boykin, *Reading Achievement*; and Philips, "Commentary."

[26]Gay and Cole; Gibson, *Accommodation without Assimilation.*

[27]G. S. Holt, " 'Inversion' in Black Communication," in *Rappin' and Stylin' Out: Communication in Urban Black America* (Chicago: University of Illinois Press, 1972).

[28]W. L. Warner, R. J. Havighurst, and M. B. Loeb, *Who Shall Be Educated? The Challenge of Equal Opportunity* (New York: Harper, 1944); and Ogbu, *The Next Generation* and *Minority Education and Caste.*

[29]J. U. Ogbu, "The Consequences of the American Caste System," in *The School Achievement of Minority Children: New Perspectives,* ed. U. Neisser (Hillsdale, N.J.: Erlbaum, 1986); and J. U. Ogbu and M. E. Matute-Bianchi, "Understanding Sociocultural Factors: Knowledge, Identity, and School Adjustment," in *Beyond Language: Social and Cultural Factors in Schooling Language Minority Students* (Sacramento: Bilingual Education Office, Calif. State Department of Education, 1986).

[30]P. Bohannan, *Justice and Judgment among the Tiv* (London: Oxford University Press, 1957), 5.

[31]W. A. Shack, "On Black American Values in White America: Some Perspectives on the Cultural Aspects of Learning Behavior and Compensatory Education," unpublished manuscript, Social Science Research Council, Subcommittee on Values and Compensatory Education, 1970–1971.

[32] J. U. Ogbu, "Minority Status and Schooling in Plural Societies," *Comparative Education Review* 27 (2) (1983): 168–90, and *Minority Education and Caste*; See also P. M. Blair, *Job Discrimination and Education: An Investment Analysis* (New York: Praeger, 1972); and Gibson, *Accommodation without Assimilation.*

[33]M. Wallace, "The Uses of Violence in American History," *American Scholar* 40 (1) (Winter 1970–1971): 81–102.

[34]M. M. Suarez-Orozco, *Central American Refugees and U.S. High Schools: A Psychological Study of Motivation and Achievement* (Stanford: Stanford University Press, 1989).

[35]Gibson, *Accommodation without Assimilation.*

36Suarez-Orozco, *Central American Refugees.*

37See G. P. Castile and G. Kushner, eds., *Persistent Peoples: Cultural Enclaves in Perspective* (Tucson: University of Arizona Press, 1981); G. A. DeVos, "Ethnic Persistence and Role Degradation: An Illustration from Japan," paper prepared for the American-Soviet Symposium on Contemporary Ethnic Processes in the U.S.A. and the U.S.S.R., New Orleans, April 1984, and "Essential Elements of Caste: Psychological Determinants in Structural Theory," in *Japan's Invisible Race: Caste in Culture and Personality,* ed. G. A. Devos and H. Wagatsuma (Berkeley: University of California Press, 1967); and E. H. Spicer, "The Process of Cultural Enclavement in Middle America," *36th Congress of International de Americanistas, Seville* 3 (1966): 267–79, and "Persistent Cultural Systems: A Comparative Study of Identity Systems that Can Adapt to Contrasting Environments," *Science* 174 (19 November 1971): 795–800.

38V. Green, "Blacks in the United States: The Creation of an Enduring People," in *Persistent Peoples: Cultural Enclaves in Perspective,* ed. G. P. Castile and G. Kushner (Tucson: University of Arizona Press, 1981).

39J. U. Ogbu, *Understanding Community Forces Affecting Minority Students' Academic Achievement Effort,* unpublished manuscript (Oakland, Calif.: The Achievement Council, 1984); and DeVos, "Essential Elements of Caste."

40DeVos, "Ethnic Persistence."

41Ogbu, *Minority Education and Caste.*

42Ibid.

43M. A. Gibson, "The School Performance of Immigrant Minorities: A Comparative View," *Anthropology and Education Quarterly* 18 (4) (1987): 262–75, and *Accommodation without Assimilation*; M. M. Suarez-Orozco, " 'Becoming Somebody': Central American Immigrants in U.S. Inner-City Schools," *Anthropology and Education Quarterly* 18 (4): 287–99, and *Central American Refugees.*

44Suarez-Orozco, " 'Becoming Somebody,' " and *Central American Refugees.*

45Gibson, *Accommodation without Assimilation.*

46Ogbu, "Cultural Discontinuities and Schooling."

47Shack.

48A. Bouie, *Student Perceptions of Behavior and Misbehavior in the School Setting: An Exploratory Study and Discussion* (San Francisco: Far West Laboratory for Educational Research and Development, 1981); and Ogbu, *The Next Generation.*

49M. L. Wong, "Education versus Sports," special project, University of California at Berkeley, 1987.

50F. A. Petroni, "Uncle Sams: White Stereotypes in the Black Movement," *Human Organization* 29 (4) (1970): 260–66; and Fordham and Ogbu.

51DeVos, "Essential Elements of Caste."

52Petroni.

[53]J. U. Ogbu, "Diversity and Equity in Public Education: Community Forces and Minority School Adjustment and Performance," in *Policies for America's Public Schools: Teachers, Equity, and Indicators,* ed. R. Haskins and D. MaCrae (Norwood, N.J.: ABLEX, 1988); "Variability in Minority School Performance: A Problem in Search of an Explanation," *Anthropology and Education Quarterly* 18 (4) (1987): 312–34; "Understanding Community Forces Affecting Minority Students' Academic Achievement Effort," unpublished manuscript (Oakland, Calif.: The Achievement Council, 1984); and *The Next Generation.*

[54]E. Yu, personal communication, 1987.

[55]Ogbu, "Variability in Minority School Performance."

[56]S. Fordham, "Restlessness as a Factor in Black Students' School Success: Pragmatic Strategy or Pyrrhic Victory?" *Harvard Education Review* 58 (1) (1988): 54–84.

[57]S. Fordham, *Black Student School Success as Related to Fictive Kinship,* final report to National Institute of Education (Washington, D.C.: National Institute of Education, 1985).

[58]J. U. Ogbu, "Cultural-Ecological Influences on Minority Education," *Language Arts* 62 (8) (1985): 860–69, and "Schooling in the Ghetto: An Ecological Perspective on Community and Home Influences," ERIC ED (1985): 252–70; and Fordham, *Black Student School Success.*

[59]Gibson, *Accommodation without Assimilation.*

[60]Fordham and Ogbu; and J. U. Ogbu, "Minority Youth and School Success," in *Teaching At-Risk Youth,* conference proceedings of Council of State Chief School Officers, Baltimore (Washington, D.C.: Council of State Chief School Officers, 1989).

Literacy In School and Out

Lauren B. Resnick

T o *understand the literacy crisis and imagine possible solutions, it is essential to examine the nature of literacy practice outside school as well as within. Schools are too isolated from everyday ways of using the written word to serve as the only source of literacy competence in society. Young people need to function as apprentices in communities where people use the written word for practical, informational, and pleasurable purposes. To change our general levels of literacy, efforts to provide such literacy apprenticeships in the community and at work, as well as in the schools, are needed.*

We are told there is a literacy crisis in the United States. Nearing the end of the twentieth century, we have still not succeeded in educating a fully literate citizenry, a goal that was articulated by our founding fathers and that motivated creation of what is probably the most inclusive public education system in the world. As the structure of the economy changes, America's declining ability to compete is attributed to workers' inadequate literacy and numeracy. All of this fuels demands for educational reform, mostly calling for tougher standards and higher rates of high school completion. It is assumed that school is the agency responsible for the nation's level of literacy, and that if schools just did their jobs more skillfully and resolutely, the literacy problem would be solved.

I will challenge that assumption in this essay. School is only one of many social forces, institutionalized and not, that determine the

Lauren Resnick is Professor of Psychology and Director of the Learning Research and Development Center at the University of Pittsburgh.

nature and extent of the nation's literacy. To understand the literacy crisis and imagine possible solutions, it is essential to examine the nature of literacy practice outside school as well as within. Continuing an earlier analysis of the relationship between mental work as it is performed outside school and the practices of the schools,[1] I examine here several different ways in which people engage with the written word. Since literacy practice outside school has been the object of very little systematic research, my analysis is suggestive rather than definitive. Nevertheless, it is possible to see that there are important discontinuities between school literacy practices and literacy outside school. These discontinuities make it doubtful that schools alone can successfully address the problem.

In most discussions of the literacy crisis, it is assumed that literacy is an acquired ability that characterizes individuals; people either possess literacy skills or they do not. The *practice* of literacy, the social conditions under which people actually engage in literate activities, is not examined. Although cognitive scientists and other students of literacy have done much to reveal the invisible mental processes involved in reading and making sense of written texts, most have worked on a widely shared assumption that these processes are, at most, only peripherally affected by the social contexts in which people read and write. It is assumed that individuals carry literacy skills in their heads. As a result, the nature of the situation in which people "do" literacy is not thought to alter the nature of the process.

I adopt here, as a heuristic for understanding literacy more deeply, a shift in epistemological perspective. Instead of asking what constitutes literacy *competency* or *ability*, terms that invite efforts to list the skills and knowledge possessed by individuals who are judged literate, I want to examine literacy as a set of cultural practices that people engage in. Taking this perspective does not deny that people engaging in literate activity must be knowledgeable and skillful in particular ways. However, examining literacy as a set of cultural practices rather than as skills or abilities leads to questions that are not often posed in discussions of the literacy crisis. These are questions about the kinds of situations in which literacy is practiced, that is, in which people engage with written texts. *Who* are the actors—both readers and writers—in these situations? How do they define themselves in relation to the texts they engage with, to each other, to other people who may also engage with those texts? *Why* are they reading and writing? What are they attempting to do with the written word? What kinds of institutional or broadly social invitations, permissions, and constraints influence their activities? *How* do people read and write? What are the processes, cognitive and social, that define literate practices? Finally, *what* do people read and write? What are the texts themselves like, and how do their characteristics facilitate particular forms of literate practice?

The shift in perspective from personal skill to cultural practice carries with it implications for a changed view of teaching and instruction. If literacy is viewed as a bundle of skills, then education for literacy is most naturally seen as a matter of organizing effective lessons: that is, diagnosing skill strengths and deficits, providing appropriate exercises in developmentally felicitous sequences, motivating students to engage in these exercises, giving clear explanations and directions. But if literacy is viewed as a set of cultural practices, then education for literacy is more naturally seen as a process of socialization, of induction into a community of literacy practic*ers*. The best model (*metaphor* is perhaps a more accurate term) we have for such induction into communities of practice is the ancient one of apprenticeship. *Apprenticeship* has largely dropped out of our educational vocabulary but warrants revival in new forms.

The heart of apprenticeship as a mode of learning is coached practice in actual tasks of production, with decreasing degrees of support from the master or more advanced colleagues. This practice takes place in the context of preparing a product that is socially valued. In traditional craft apprenticeships, there was far less direct instruction than we are used to in schools and relatively little decontextualized practice of component skills. Instead, by working collaboratively, often on tasks they could not yet accomplish entirely on their own, apprentices practiced in a context that both motivated work and gave it meaning. A series of increasingly complex production tasks through which apprentices progressed provided the equivalent of a curriculum. The conditions of work and learning made it possible to rely on considerable self-correction, with apprentices judging their own products against criteria established through extensive observation and discussion of the group's products. Several recent experimental programs have demonstrated possibilities for adapting elements of traditional apprenticeship forms to education in complex cognitive practices of literacy and mathematics.[2] These programs attempt to establish communities of literate practice in which children can participate under special forms of guidance. Such programs try to make usually hidden mental processes overt, and they encourage student observation and commentary. They also allow skills to build up bit by bit, yet permit participation in meaningful work even for the relatively unskilled, often as a result of sharing the tasks among several participants.

In this essay I consider briefly several different kinds of literacy practice and attempt to characterize each in ways that respond to the *who, why, how,* and *what* questions raised earlier. For each, I begin by sketching skilled adult practices as a way of setting a "developmental target"—a possible educational goal. I then try to imagine "beginner" forms of that practice, forms that might characterize the early stages of apprenticeship in literacy. This educational thought experiment provides a template for assessing school literacy practice. How much apprenticeship opportunity does the school typically provide? How might the school be organized to provide more such opportunity? How much of the job of educating a literate citizenry can the school alone be expected to do? In light of this analysis of literacy as situated activity, I then reexamine the nature of the literacy crisis and propose some institutional responses that may be necessary for change.

THREE FORMS OF LITERACY PRACTICE

Literacy is practiced in any situation in which people engage with written texts. The range of literacy situations is vast and varied. In earlier work,[3] we identified, without claiming to be exhaustive, six major categories of literacy activity: the sacred (using print in religious practice and instruction); the useful (using print to mediate practical activities); the informational (using print to convey or acquire knowledge; the pleasurable (reading for the fun of it); the persuasive (using print to influence the behavior or beliefs of others); and the personal-familial (using letters to stay in touch with family and friends). Here I consider three of these categories that are most frequently cited as literacy objectives of the school—the useful, the informational, and the pleasurable.

Useful Literacy

A common type of literacy practice is the use of written texts to mediate action in the world. Some everyday examples of such practical literacy include reading recipes, following instructions for assembling or manipulating equipment, and consulting bus or airline schedules. These are among the kinds of activities that appear on functional literacy tests such as the recent National Assessment of Educational Progress. The class of useful literacy practices would also include writing letters of inquiry, filling out job applications, and leaving notes for coworkers. Readers come to functional literacy practice of this kind with very immediate goals, usually assuming that the text is authoritative and can successfully guide action. They willingly follow the author's plan of action in order to accomplish a specific task.

This action-oriented stance shapes the nature of the reading process. Consider, for example, texts that provide instructions for action on physical systems. To engage successfully as a reader of such texts, one must relate each proposition in the text to a specific set of physical objects, infer relationships among those objects, and plan actions on them. In the simplest form of practical literacy, this is done with the objects present. Under these conditions, the physical objects substantially assist the reader in making sense of the text. Research on the processes of following directions shows that readers of such texts shift attention back and forth between the text and the physical display. Furthermore, there is evidence that diagrams, when available, are relied on to a great extent, and that readers often favor the information in diagrams when text and figures conflict. In this kind of literacy activity, the reader needs to construct only a limited mental representation of the situation described by the text, because the elements of the situation are physically present, and it is possible to act directly on them. Furthermore, the physical results of one's actions often provide continuous (if only partial) information about whether one has correctly interpreted the text and diagrams.

A more cognitively demanding form of practical literacy requires readers to make inferences about the state of a physical system from textual materials, without being able to see or interact with the physical system directly. In these situations, a more complete mental representation must be constructed by the reader, with less supportive help from the physical environment. This kind of processing is necessary, for example, when texts are read in anticipation of action—that is, preparing to do something without actually doing it. Some simple examples of anticipatory practical reading are using a bus schedule to decide when to go to the bus stop, and reading a recipe to determine if a shopping trip is needed before cooking can begin. More complex examples can be found in automated work situations in which the actual physical labor is done by machines, while workers monitor and adjust those machines on the basis of their readings of various indicators.[4] To perform such tasks, workers need a complex mental model of the physical system on which they are operating, a model whose immediate states can be updated on the basis of indicator readings. As such jobs proliferate, a new standard of technical literacy is developing. As in more "hands-on" practical literacy, the reader must be able to act on a physical environment, but a much greater effort of purely mental representation is required.

Practical literacy also includes uses of texts to help one act in and on social systems. Tax forms and job applications are of this type. Such forms are used much like instructions for physical systems—that is, in step-by-step fashion, reading a line, then immediately following the instructions given. To participate effectively in this form of literacy, one needs only to understand each line of the instructions and to be willing to persist through many steps. A more general mental model of a situation—of tax rules, for example, or of what a potential employer might be seeking—can help in this step-by-step interpretation but is not strictly necessary. Thus, in this kind of literacy, there is only a limited requirement for mental representation. There are also less formulaic texts that help people act in a social system. Such texts might, for example, guide one in using services of a health care system, initiating grievance proceedings against an employer, or choosing among insurance options. When using these texts, the reader needs to construct a mental model of the system as a whole before it becomes possible to decide how to act.

How do people learn to engage in practical literacy? It is not difficult to imagine an apprenticeship in the functional use of texts occurring within families. With a parent or other older person, a child as young as four or five can participate in an activity in which a text is used to guide physical acts (assembling a game or following a recipe, for example). Very young children cannot yet read the texts themselves, but they can observe important aspects of the practical literacy form such as the ways in which one alternates between reading the text and carrying out a physical act, or the fact that the text is used to verify accuracy of action. By eight or nine years of age, a child participating with an adult might do some or even all of the reading but would not be expected to figure out alone exactly what actions were prescribed. Later, the child might do most of the work alone, calling for occasional help in interpreting certain difficult words or steps. This kind of "scaffolded" learning has been well analyzed and described for a number of typical family activities as well as for learning in traditional craft apprenticeships. Regular engagement in such activities in the family or other extra-school settings probably helps children develop a generalized pattern of interacting with texts ("read-do, read-do") and a broad confidence that enables them to use texts to guide practical activity on their own.[5]

Such practical literacy apprenticeships, however, are largely absent from school. The reading done in school seldom mediates any practical action in the world, and there is hardly ever a chance to work side by side with a more skillful partner toward a shared goal. An exception may be found in the science laboratory. Science educators often complain that too much time is spent setting up experiments and too little on interpreting them. Yet students may learn something about a very basic form of practical literacy from these exercises—to the extent that they get to participate in them. Much elementary-level science instruction proceeds from textbooks rather than laboratories, and the students whose functional literacy is a source of public worry almost never take upper-level science courses. Vocational courses offer another potential site for functional literacy practice in school. Often, however, functional literacy skills are *prerequisite* to entering vocational courses, rather than what can be learned in them. A result is that the students most in need of this form of literacy practice are excluded from the opportunity for practice. Significant opportunities for functional literacy activity also occur in some extracurricular school activities. There is evidence, however, that, with the exception of sports, extracurricular participation in high school is largely limited to the more academically inclined and successful students and does not include those for whom functional literacy development is a concern.

These observations suggest that, if school were the only place in which people learned literate practices, we would probably observe far *less* functional literacy in the general population than we do. It seems likely that the many people who become competent at various forms of functional literacy develop their initial competence outside school, through participation with family members and friends. If functional literacy practices are learned mainly outside school, however, certain students—those from families who do not practice much literacy in the home or do not engage their children in such activities—can be expected not to learn them.

Informational Literacy

People also read to learn about the world when there is no immediate practical utility for the information acquired. In this kind of literacy activity, the only likely immediate activity after reading is discussion with others. The reader's main task is to build a mental representation of the situation presented in the text and to relate the new information to previously held knowledge. This process of text comprehension has been intensively studied by cognitive scientists. From their research, we know that building mental *situation models* on the basis of a text requires much more than an ability to recognize the words—a level of literacy ability that few people in this country lack. Rather, it depends crucially on the reader's prior knowledge, along with certain general linguistic abilities. It is also highly sensitive to aspects of the text structure, including rhetorical devices, signals about the relationships among sections of the text, and the extent to which suppositions and arguments are laid out explicitly.

One aspect of informational reading that has not been much studied is how the reader interprets the author's intention and what knowledge the reader attributes to the author—what we might call building an *author model*. Furthermore, cognitive science has paid almost no attention to what the reader expects to do with the information gained from the text, or to the social context of either the reading or subsequent information use. All of these can be expected to influence reading activity substantially.

A wide range of intentions, from personal interest and wanting to know what people are talking about to needing background knowledge for one's profession, can motivate informational reading. Some forms of informational reading can have eventual practical aims, even though immediate action is neither called for nor possible. For example, many advice and "how-to" texts—ranging from household hints and Ann Landers columns to books offering guidance in personal finance or business management—are geared not to individual situations, but to prototypical situations that many people encounter. When reading such texts, people have to imagine themselves in others' situations in order to find useful information for themselves. To do this, they must not only build a mental representation of the situation described in the text, but also relate the situation described to their own.

In everyday life, probably the most frequent kind of informational literacy activity is newspaper and magazine reading. For most people, reading the news is a matter of "keeping up"—finding out what is going on in the world, updating one's mental accounts of ongoing events. Although such reading appears to be a private activity, it is socially defined in two important senses. First, informational reading is often followed by discussion with others of like interests, and what one chooses to read in a newspaper probably depends to an important degree on what kinds of conversations one anticipates. People may keep up with sports, for example, in order to join the talk at work or follow local news because that is discussed at parties or while attending to business in town. What we find it necessary to "keep up with" is determined partly by the people with whom we associate and the conversational habits of that group. If one is not in a social circle that discusses national and international political events, those parts of the newspaper will probably not receive attention. Thus, everyday informational reading is a function of the social groups with whom one interacts.

A second sense in which reading is socially defined is that the kind of mental representation constructed from the reading depends on the kinds of intentions one ascribes to the authors. American newspaper readers expect journalists to be both knowledgeable and neutral, to convey the facts fully and without bias. Except when reading signed columns and editorials, readers do not devote much attention to determining the newswriters' persuasive intentions, what political positions are represented, or what might have been left out of the communication. In contrast, continental European newspaper readers do not assume neutrality; newspapers and newswriters have known political positions, and readers interpret their articles in this light. People trying to get the whole picture of some important event are likely to read several different news reports because they expect an interpretive slant in each report. In countries with active press censorship, readers must go even further to read between the lines in order to learn what is happening in the world. These different social assumptions can cause differences in the cognitive processes involved in reading. The American assumption of a neutral press, together with a relative absence of political discussion in everyday life, probably has the effect of providing our people with minimal practice in critical textual interpretation. Americans have little experience in looking for authors' intentions or hidden meanings or tracking down missing parts of an argument. Although many become fluent at constructing text and situation models, they have little practice at building author models.

Imagined author-reader relations also play a role in the process of writing informational texts. In actual literacy practice, authors writing informational texts have, in the best cases, a lively sense of their audience. They are used to crafting their communications to appeal to imagined readers. Definitions of what constitutes a well-crafted text vary among social communities of readers and writers. Broad distinctions between popular and scholarly writing do not do justice to the variety and distinctiveness of what have come to be called "discourse communities." The readers of different segments of the popular press expect different forms of writing. In recent years a lively analysis of the varied ways in which different scholarly disciplines shape their written discourse has emerged, and students of literacy have begun to speak of processes of initiation into these discourse communities, referring both to practices of interpretive reading and to those of authoring.

Informal, family-based opportunities for apprenticeship in these informational literacy practices are probably less available than are practical literacy apprenticeship opportunities. Not all families regularly read and discuss the information in newspapers or magazines, and most such reading is limited to particular narrow segments of the press. Reading of informational books occurs in only a limited number of families. And even among children growing up in our most literate families, few ever get to observe—much less participate in—the process of actually creating an extended informational text for an interested audience.

More than for practical literacy, it seems, we depend on the school as the place in which informational literacy will be cultivated. School is the time and place in most people's lives when they are most intensively engaged in reading for information. Indeed, other than newspapers, textbooks provide most Americans' only practice of informational literacy. A populace with the capacity and taste for engaging in informational literacy activities, particularly as they bear on public and civic issues, is part of the Jeffersonian vision of democracy. It is a major reason for treating universal public education as a requirement for a democratic society. But as education has developed, very little literacy practice in school engages students in activities from which they might learn the habits and skills of using texts to understand public issues and participate in public decision making. A consideration of the actual activity of textbook reading in school shows that it is a very different form of literacy practice from the informational reading that might be envisioned as part of the Jeffersonian ideal. Differences can be found in the intentions that people bring to school text reading as opposed to other kinds of informational texts, in the nature of the texts themselves, in the kinds of background knowledge they bring to the reading, and in the rhythm of the activity itself.

When texts are assigned in school, they are almost always on topics new to students, for which the students must build initial mental representations. Textbook reading thus provides little experience in updating mental models, as occurs when keeping up with the news. Worse still, school textbooks are often badly written, a jumble of bits of information without the coherence needed to support this initial building of a representation.[6] Finally, and perhaps most important, students in school read textbooks because of an assignment or a test to be passed, not because they are personally interested in the topic or expect lively conversation about it with others. In many classrooms, there is a catechetical flavor to the way that texts are assigned and used. Small sections are read, and students are expected to give specific, generally noninterpretive answers to questions posed by the teacher. Informational writing experience is, if anything, more restricted. For the most part, if students write informational or analytical texts at all, it is to show teachers that they have done the required reading and absorbed the canonical interpretation. The normal relationship between author (as someone who knows something of interest) and reader (as someone who would like to learn about that something) is absent or seriously attenuated. The typical audience for student writing is only the teacher, who already knows (or is thought to know) all the information conveyed. For the large majority of students, then, no place—neither home nor school—provides an extended opportunity to engage in high levels of authentic informational literacy practice.

Pleasurable Literacy

Being literate can also mean reading for pleasure, a form of literacy practice in which reading is its own end. The kinds of texts that people read for the fun of reading are diverse, and the cognitive and social processes engaged are equally different. Narratives—texts with a story line, whether fictional or based in reality—are generally considered to be the material of pleasurable reading, although some people read expository texts that might be classed as information just for the fun of it. Engagement with the text is the primary requisite for pleasurable literacy, and many kinds of texts—from pulp crime stories and Gothic romances to high literature—are capable of providing that engagement. Different kinds of texts, of course, require differing degrees and types of interpretive activity; what is engaging for some may be too difficult or too simple to engage others.

Cognitive scientists have given substantially less attention to the processes involved in pleasurable reading than to the processes of informational and practical literacy, although some psychologists with more interest in motivation and consciousness (including Mihaly Csikszentmihalyi in this volume)[7] have tried to understand the nature of psychological engagement with a story. The nature of fiction reading is also, of course, a major concern of literary theory and criticism. Proponents of a recent literary theory are now exploring the many personal goals served by pleasurable reading—from escape and imagining oneself in more satisfying conditions (as in reading romance stories)[8] to stimulating and resolving curiosity (as in reading mysteries) to penetrating cultures and life situations to which one does not have personal access. Psychologists and literary scholars seem to agree that readers of popular stories—mysteries, romances, and the like—focus all energies on understanding the situation described and perhaps on imagining themselves in that situation. This engagement with the story contrasts with what some would reserve as truly "literary" reading, which involves deliberate attention to language and expressive device. This aspect of literary reading distinguishes it from more popular forms of pleasurable literacy in which language is "transparent," unattended to in its own right, just a vehicle for conveying a story.

At first look, pleasurable literacy seems to fare better than informational literacy in terms of apprenticeship opportunities. For many children, pleasurable literacy practice begins in being read to by parents. The process by which children who are regularly read to gradually "appropriate" the reading act for themselves is often used as a model of how apprenticeship in cultural practice might work for literacy. Encouragement of parents to read to and with their children and extensive reading aloud to children in preschools and kindergartens represent efforts to extend these forms of apprenticeship opportunity to more children.

Similar efforts are made throughout the elementary grades in many schools. Finding pleasure in reading is frequently stressed as a goal of reading instruction. In support of this goal, books of interest to children are made available, and children are encouraged to read them. Time is allowed in the school week for free-choice reading programs and reading for which children are not formally accountable, although they are encouraged to discuss or even write about their reading. Many civic programs aimed at supporting literacy development in schools also stress the pleasurable aspects of literacy. Such programs, which include bookmobiles and other community access programs organized by public libraries, programs that distribute children's books to families at no or low cost, and programs in which volunteers either read to schoolchildren or listen to the children read, focus either implicitly or explicitly on the pleasures of reading.

The motivation for such emphasis on reading for pleasure is partly based on sound pedagogy. We know that reading skill develops best when there is massive practice in reading, and children (like adults) are more likely to read a lot when they enjoy the process of reading as well as its possible practical or informational outcomes. But educators and civic organizations also stress reading for pleasure because they recognize it as an authentic form of literacy practice; a more literate nation would engage in more reading for its own sake. With respect to pleasurable literacy, then, more than for the useful or the informational, many schools and surrounding institutions seem to be reaching for authentic forms of practice.

Yet the programs that seem to provide some pleasurable literacy apprenticeship opportunities represent a very limited part of the school experience of most students. For most Americans, the only extended discussion of literature they are likely to encounter is in school. But even a brief consideration of the ways in which literature reading is organized in school suggests a fundamental discontinuity with the features of pleasurable reading as we engage in it outside school.

A key—perhaps the defining—feature of pleasurable reading is that one picks up and puts down a book or a story at will. There is no need to prove to others that one has read, although sharing opinions about books is not uncommon among those who read for pleasure. In schooling, by contrast, literature is usually doled out in daily assignments. Not only what one is to read, but also the pace of the reading is imposed. Reading ahead if one is captivated and engaged by the story is not encouraged and may be subtly punished. Proving that one has read the assigned material by answering questions about it or writing book reports is central to school literacy. Not infrequently, literature study is turned into a kind of catechism—a canonic set of readings, standard questions, and expected answers. These activities implicitly carry a message that reading is not a pleasure in its own right. As a result, students who have not acquired a sense of the pleasures of reading elsewhere may not easily acquire it through standard schooling practice, especially after the primary grades.

LITERACY APPRENTICESHIPS

The preceding analyses suggest that the schools are not the only—or perhaps even the primary—source of literacy competence. As we have seen, dominant school practice is so mismatched to the ways in which practical, informational, and pleasurable literacy activities take place in everyday life that it seems highly unlikely that schools alone are responsible for the levels of literacy practice we observe in society. We must understand the nation's literacy—or lack of it—in terms of the kinds of literacy apprenticeships that are available to young people. For many, these apprenticeship opportunities are severely limited. In order to substantially change literacy practices in the nation, we cannot simply call for raising school standards. Without a broad cultural shift in the direction of more interpretive literacy activity in all segments of adult society, we cannot expect young people to acquire the skills and habits of literacy practice.

Schools could become sites for true literacy apprenticeship, but fundamental shifts in school practice would be required. What is called for are school activities in which students have extensive reason to use written texts in the ways that characterize out-of-school practical, informational, and pleasurable literacy. A number of experimental programs now in use point to the possibilities. These programs share features of apprenticeship environments: children work to produce a product that will be used by others (e.g., they produce a book on a history topic that is then used to teach others, or they collect data that are used to produce a scientific report); they work collaboratively, but under conditions in which individuals are held responsible for their work; they use tools and apparatus appropriate to the problem; they read and critique each other's writing; they are called upon to elaborate and defend their own work until it reaches a community standard. We know considerably more about how to design and manage such environments than we do about how to get schools to adopt and maintain them. Educational programs are often adopted enthusiastically by a few schools during an experimental phase and then abandoned in favor of conventional school literacy forms, often in the wake of calls for a return to "the basics" and the practices that adult citizens recall from their own school days. Apparently, the school system cannot move far ahead of the general culture.

To "bootstrap" ourselves into new levels of literacy participation, I believe we must actively develop other institutions for literacy practice. These can function jointly with schools in the best circumstances or independently when necessary. We need multiple apprenticeship sites where children and youth can spend significant amounts of time working among people who are using the written word for practical, informational, and pleasurable purposes. For younger children, community centers, churches, and other agencies could play this role. Many children now attend after-school and weekend programs at such centers, and there is some evidence that participation in community programs is positively related to school and later work performance. For the most part, however, these agencies offer child care and recreational programs but make no attempt to provide literacy-related activities. When after-school or summer programs are offered with the intention of improving school performance, they usually mimic school conditions rather than provide truly alternative occasions for literacy practice. We need new forms of community programs aimed at developing literacy through apprenticeship. For older students—at least from the beginning of high school—participating (preferably with pay) at real work sites is probably the best way to experience literacy practice, along with training in a variety of social skills and habits that are essential to work performance. Such on-the-job participation would not only provide natural apprenticeships for literacy, but might also solve important motivational problems resulting from some students' belief that even good school performance will not assure them access to jobs and other forms of economic participation.

These proposals follow from the shift in perspective with which I began this essay. When we stop thinking about literacy as a collection of skills and begin to view it as a form of cultural practice, we are led to consider the multiple ways in which young people are socialized into the practices of their societies. Although there is room for improvement, schools appear to be doing reasonably well at teaching the basic skills of literacy. But, at least as currently organized, schools are too isolated from everyday ways of using the written word to serve as the only sites for learning literacy practice. For some young people, family, community life, and, eventually, work provide informal apprenticeship opportunities for various literacy practices. For many others, though, these apprenticeship opportunities are unavailable. Unless organized efforts are made to provide literacy apprenticeship environments for these young people, there seems to be little hope of change in our general levels of literacy participation. There is historical precedent for looking outside schools for major changes in literacy levels in a population. Europe's earliest literacy drives took place in homes and churches. Recent literacy campaigns, for example in Cuba and China, have looked to institutions such as citizen armies for literacy education. In past efforts of this kind, only very basic forms of literacy were sought. Today's challenge is greater, and the relatively simple forms of literacy activity that sufficed for basic literacy campaigns cannot be expected to succeed. But with imagination and perseverance, we should be able to develop places and forms for apprenticeship that can effectively reshape literacy practice in our society.

ENDNOTES

1Lauren B. Resnick, "Learning In School and Out," *Educational Researcher* 16 (9) (December 1987): 13–20.

2Allan Collins, John Seely Brown, and Susan E. Newman, "Cognitive Apprenticeship: Teaching the Crafts of Reading, Writing, and Mathematics," in Lauren B. Resnick, ed., *Knowing, Learning, and Instruction: Essays in Honor of Robert Glaser* (Hillsdale, N.J.: Erlbaum, 1989).

3Daniel P. Resnick and Lauren B. Resnick, "Varieties of Literacy," in A. E. Barnes and P. N. Stearnes, eds., *Social History and Issues in Human Consciousness: Interdisciplinary Connections* (New York: New York University Press, 1990).

4Shoshana Zuboff, *In the Age of the Smart Machine: The Future of Work and Power* (New York: Basic Books, 1988).

5Jean Lave, *The Culture of Acquisition and the Practice of Understanding*, Report No. IRL 88–0007 (Palo Alto: Institute for Research on Learning, 1988); and Barbara Rogoff, *Apprentices in Thinking: Children's Guided Participation in Culture* (New York: Oxford University Press, 1990).

6Isabel L. Beck, Margaret G. McKeown, and Erika W. Gromoll, "Learning from Social Studies Texts," *Cognition and Instruction* 6 (2) (1989): 99–158; and Harriet Tyson-Bernstein, *America's Textbook Fiasco: A Crisis of Good Intentions* (Washington, D.C.: The Council for Basic Education, 1988).

7Mihaly Csikszentmihalyi, "Literacy and Intrinsic Motivation," *Dædalus* 119 (2) (Spring 1990): 115–40.

8Janice A. Radway, *Reading the Romance: Women, Patriarchy and Popular Literature* (Chapel Hill: University of North Carolina Press, 1984).

Adult literacy has never had a powerful voice at the federal or the state level, so it is not surprising that many are suspicious of the notion of work-force literacy. It seems to imply the compression of literacy into literacy solely for economic ends, literacy to prepare people for the job market, instead of literacy as a tool to enable people to do exactly what they want to do.

But work-force literacy is a concept that embraces the full range of adult basic skills, starting with the solid foundation necessary before people can go on to qualify for job training or work. The publication of *Workforce 2000: Work and Workers for the Twenty-first Century* in 1987 provided the impetus for this new conceptualization. A major policy paper prepared by the Hudson Institute for the U.S. Department of Labor, it made the case for the importance of educating adults in basic skills.

A panoply of books and reports since the early 1970s, from *Crisis in the Classroom* to *Horace's Compromise* and *A Nation at Risk*, concerns the crisis in public school education. *Workforce 2000* was the first major report asserting that the crisis could not be solved simply by preparing the next generation. Given the demographics of the work force of the coming decades, educating our current adult population was the only way, according to this report, for the United States to have the flexible, skilled work force it needed. While we cannot ignore the problems of our public schools, we must concentrate our resources on creating greater access to adult literacy education.

Sondra Gayle Stein
Director
The Commonwealth of Massachusetts
Literacy Campaign

Improving the Education of Reading Teachers

*Richard C. Anderson,
Bonnie B. Armbruster, and Mary Roe*

T *he usual preservice teacher-education program suffers from several shortcomings. Notably, it tries to transmit knowledge and skills in the abstract, decontextualized from their uses in classrooms. Such classroom experience as preservice teachers are able to get is difficult for them to interpret and only loosely related to teaching-methods courses. This report offers several principles for developing expertise that could improve preservice teacher education. These principles could be incorporated into teacher training with the use of videotechnology. Preservice teachers could videotape each other teaching several times a semester. Close analysis and discussion of the tapes could be made the centerpiece of university teacher education courses.*

Common sense and educational research converge on the conclusion that the quality of teaching that children receive is a major determinant of their progress in reading, writing, and the other language arts. It is an easy step to the further conclusion that improving teacher

Richard Anderson is Director of the Center for the Study of Reading and Professor of Education and Psychology at the University of Illinois.

Bonnie Armbruster is Associate Professor in the Department of Curriculum and Instruction and at the Center for the Study of Reading at the University of Illinois.

Mary Roe is Assistant Professor of Education at Eastern Washington University.

education is a major lever for raising the level of literacy. In the words of *Becoming a Nation of Readers,* "the knowledge is now available to make worthwhile improvements in reading throughout the United States. If the practices seen in the classrooms of the best teachers in the best schools could be introduced everywhere, the improvements would be dramatic."[1]

The "best teachers" have an expert understanding of the complex ecological habitat, the dynamic ecosystem that is the classroom. This understanding enables them to make rapid-fire decisions about complex, ill-structured situations as they struggle to achieve balance in the classroom system. Expert teachers solve multiple problems efficiently and effectively.

What does it mean to have an expert's understanding? For example, what does an experienced physician know about diagnosing a medical problem that a beginning medical student does not know? What does an expert reader know about acquiring information from a textbook that is still mysterious to a novice reader? What does an expert teacher know about managing the classroom ecosystem that a beginning teacher does not know?

The general form of the answer to these questions appears to be that experts in any domain have not only good problem-solving strategies but also a rich store of knowledge about the domain. Experts have had so much experience with problems that they can rapidly recognize the type of problem and select an appropriate strategy to solve it. They have learned to integrate artfully "knowing that" with "knowing how." The knowledge of experts is organized in large units; they perceive order and pattern in what seems chaos to novices. Experts have a wide repertoire of routines that they perform automatically and fluently, which frees their mental resources for more complicated problem-solving strategies.

What do expert teachers know? They possess a rich body of knowledge, including knowledge of curriculum and content, of learners and their characteristics, of the ends, purposes, and values of education, and of educational contexts.[2] In addition, expert teachers have organized problem-solving strategies and routines at various levels of generality. For example, teachers may have a global routine for conducting reading lessons, with specific routines for correcting errors, managing independent seatwork, and handling disruptions. Expert teachers negotiate "knowing that" and "knowing how" as they plan, predict, anticipate, and solve problems, estimate what students know and don't know, revise teaching plans, and make the most of unexpected opportunities.

Typical "preservice" education (the training that prospective teachers receive prior to becoming certified teachers) falls short of preparing teachers to be expert problem solvers. Teachers frequently assert that education courses have contributed little to their development as teachers. Generation after generation of teachers have complained that so-called foundation courses in psychology and philosophy, which are supposed to transmit "knowing that," and even teaching-methods courses that disseminate "knowing how," have been woefully inadequate in preparing them to cope with the complex problems of real classrooms. Teachers who excel in all their university courses and score high on credentialing exams may still flounder in real classrooms. Why is this the case?

We believe that the usual preservice education is ill suited to training experts because knowledge and skills are taught in the abstract, decontextualized from their uses in the classroom. The medium of preservice instruction is the spoken and written word. We submit that there are inherent limits on the value of verbal formulations of knowledge about expertise. Few people would try to become expert chess or bridge players by studying a thick book on the subject. It is the rare person whose first step in attempting to master a new computer program would be to read the technical manual from cover to cover. No basketball coach begins preparing players by offering a six-hour lecture-discussion course.

The way to expertise in chess, computers, basketball, or any other domain is to intermingle spoken or written advice with actual attempts by the student to perform in authentic settings. Typically, the only opportunity for performance in an authentic setting for teacher trainees is during student teaching, when prospective teachers go out into the schools for field experience. Student teaching is universally rated as the most valuable part of teacher preparation. As one first-year teacher maintained, "I learned more in the first month of student teaching than in all my coursework combined." Student teaching is essential to giving would-be teachers a taste of reality and an opportunity to practice knowledge and skills.

However, there are still several problems with student teaching as it is typically practiced. First, it is too little, too late. It is often the culminating experience of preservice training. It usually lasts a few short months and takes place in only one classroom. The amount of actual practice a teacher trainee receives varies widely, depending on school policy, whether the regular classroom teacher will relinquish control, the amount and quality of supervision, and so on.

Second, prospective teachers may not see models of good teaching. If they do see good teaching, they may not be able to determine what makes it good. Since only one or two members of a class will see a given lesson, they have no common experience to discuss with their instructor and classmates. Furthermore, student teachers receive infrequent feedback of indifferent quality. They are preoccupied with mastering unfamiliar routines, maintaining attention and discipline, and above all, presenting themselves well. Inevitably, there is neither the time nor the inclination for reflection about the fine points of pedagogy.

Thus, the training of prospective teachers often leads to knowledge that is inert and inaccessible. Beginning teachers are frequently unable to translate this knowledge into practice or to develop it into expertise. That abstractly stated advice may be an uncertain guide for action is best appreciated in the context of particular cases. Consider, for example, children's oral reading mistakes. Prospective teachers will be told that research shows (as it does) that children's year-to-year growth in reading is greater when oral reading errors are followed with "sustaining feedback" rather than "terminal feedback." Sustaining feedback, the aspiring teachers will be further told, means giving the child a hint; terminal feedback means telling the child the correct word.

The foregoing advice will enable the prospective teacher to pass a multiple-choice item, such as "Usually, the best practice when a child makes an oral reading mistake is to (a) ignore the mistake, (b) provide the word, (c) give a hint, (d) ask another child." But it is too impoverished to enable the teacher to deal skillfully with oral reading errors in actual practice. What counts as a mistake? Should a teacher deal with every mistake? What sorts of hints are most effective? With which sorts of children? Under what conditions? For instance, should there be a different tactic for handling the substitution of *house* for *home, house* for *horse, growed* for *grew,* and *blake* for *black*? Should a teacher pause before giving a hint or jump in immediately? Should other children be encouraged or discouraged from offering help?

Comparably difficult questions arise when a child's answer to a question suggests a comprehension problem. Does the student lack relevant background knowledge? Are individual words the problem, or is it their meaningful integration? Does the answer really reflect a lack of comprehension, or does the child understand but fail to remember the appropriate information? And so on. The answers to these questions are not straightforward, yet a practicing primary school teacher must answer them many times a day within a time frame calibrated in seconds.

Whereas formal training often has embarrassingly little influence on how teachers teach, there is no doubting the influence of teachers' prior personal experience as students. According to Lortie, "Teachers start their professional preparation early in life; their entire school experience contributes to their work socialization."[3] Notice that the amount of prior experience prospective teachers have with teachers and teaching is a couple of orders of magnitude greater than the amount that, say, prospective doctors have with doctors and doctoring. By the time young people have graduated from high school, they have clocked more than 10,000 hours of class time. Inevitably this experience makes a deep impression. Getting new teachers to seriously entertain alternative approaches to teaching requires freeing them from the "hand of the past."[4]

The inadequacies of formal training and the heavy hand of the past are no doubt major reasons why teachers are slow to change, and why in the nation's classrooms text-bound recitation is more common than genuine discussion, and drill and practice more common than opportunities for discovery. Observation in classrooms suggests instruction seldom does much to promote reasoning about texts as a whole or reasoning beyond the given. For example, in a series of observations completed in the mid-1970s, reading and social studies teachers were seen to devote just one-quarter of 1 percent of instructional time to comprehension instruction that went beyond the meanings of individual words.[5] In another well-known study done a decade earlier, 70 percent of the questions elementary teachers were observed to ask during classroom discussions required no more than literal recall or recognition of the information in textbooks.[6] A study done in the mid-1980s, however, found that only 43 percent of teachers' questions could be satisfied with literal answers, while the rest required at least some reasoning.[7] Thus, there may be a trend toward instruction that demands more thinking from students, although there is still plenty of room for further improvement.

So far we have tried to portray the shortcomings of the current method of educating reading teachers, and explain why this is one reason classrooms are often not very intellectually stimulating. What do we propose as an alternative? We begin with some effective principles for training experts, borrowed from analyses of apprenticeship.[8] An underlying principle is that learning and acting are intimately related. Learning results from acting in authentic situations. Therefore, practice *in situ* is essential to becoming an expert. Collins, Brown, and Newman[9] discuss the following specific principles for fostering expertise:

Modeling. Apprenticeship begins with the observation of a master or an expert, who models the process. By reflectively "thinking aloud," the model makes explicit invisible mental processes that might otherwise remain mysterious to novices. Observation helps the learner develop a conceptual model of the task before attempting to execute it.

Coaching. Coaching involves observing and helping students as they attempt to execute the process. The coach directs the student to particular aspects of the task, reminds students about a part of the task they may have overlooked, provides hints and feedback, and designs and sequences new tasks aimed at bringing the students' performance close to expert performance.

Scaffolding. Scaffolding consists of the support the coach provides as the students continue practice. Scaffolding may be in the form of hints or suggestions. Or, the coach may perform parts of the task students cannot yet manage on their own. Appropriate scaffolding requires accurate diagnosis of the students' skill levels and the ability to provide just the right amount of support to enable the students to perform the target task. The gradual removal of scaffolding as students assume greater independence is known as fading.

Articulation. Articulation refers to getting students to articulate their knowledge, reasoning, or problem-solving strategies. Articulation helps students gain consciousness of and control over basic conceptual and procedural knowledge.

Reflection. Reflection involves comparing one's own conceptual and procedural understandings with those of an expert, or another student, and eventually an internalized model of expertise. The goal is to develop reflective thinkers who can monitor their own performance and, if necessary, bring it more in line with expert performance. Technology such as video- and audiotapes or computers can be employed to provide a medium for reflection. For example, the "think aloud" protocols of experts and novices as they perform a common task might be compared.

The foregoing principles are exemplified in several powerful teaching programs involving reading. Three of these programs are described in the following sections. All three programs teach reading, but in our discussion of successful programs we shall emphasize, respectively, the education of the children, the education of the teachers, and the education of the teachers of the teachers.

RECIPROCAL TEACHING

A notable example of a method for successfully teaching children to read with comprehension is Palincsar and Brown's reciprocal teaching.[10] The method centers on modeling and coaching students in four basic reading comprehension strategies: formulating questions based on the text, summarizing the text, making predictions about what will come next, and clarifying difficulties in understanding the text. The name *reciprocal teaching* comes from the fact that the teacher and students take turns playing the role of the teacher.

In reciprocal teaching, the teacher begins by modeling the strategies. After she and the students have read a paragraph silently, she asks a "main idea" question based on the paragraph, formulates a summary, makes a prediction about what the next bit of text will be about, and clarifies any confusing or obscure ideas. As the students begin to learn the process, the teacher provides scaffolding by coaching them on how to construct good questions and summaries, prompting, encouraging, and offering feedback on their efforts. As the students become more proficient, the teacher gradually withdraws the support. She assumes the role of monitor, occasionally providing prompts or feedback.

The following example of reciprocal teaching[11] shows dramatic improvement over two weeks of instruction for a seventh-grade minority student, Charles, who is a weak reader:

Day 1:

TEXT: The water moccasin, somewhat longer than the copperhead, is found in the southeastern states. It lives in swampy regions. It belongs, as do also the copperhead and the rattlesnakes, to a group of poisonous snakes called pit vipers. They have pits between their eyes and their nostrils which, because they are sensitive to heat, help the snakes tell when they are near a warm-blooded animal. Another name for the water moccasin is "cottonmouth." This name comes from the white lining of the snake's mouth.

Charles: What is found in the southeastern snakes, also the copperhead, rattlesnakes, vipers—they have. I'm not doing this right.

Teacher: All right. Do you want to know about the pit vipers?

Charles: Yeah.

Teacher: What would be a good question about the pit vipers that starts with the word "why?"

Charles: (No response.)

Teacher: How about, "Why are the snakes called pit vipers?"

Charles: Why do they want to know that they are called pit vipers?

Teacher: Try it again.

Charles: Why do they, pit vipers in a pit?

Teacher: How about, "Why do they call the snakes pit vipers?"

Charles: Why do they call the snakes pit vipers?

Teacher: There you go! Good for you.

Day 4:

TEXT: Spinner's mate is much smaller than she, and his body is dull brown. He spends most of his time sitting at one side of her web.

Teacher [to Charles, who remains silent, with no question]: What's this paragraph about?

Charles: Spinner's mate. How do spinner's mate. . .

Teacher: That's good. Keep going.

Charles: How do spinner's mate is smaller than. . . How am I going to say that?

Teacher: Take your time with it. You want to ask a question about spinner's mate and what he does, beginning with the word "how."

Charles: How do they spend most of his time sitting?

Teacher: You're very close. The question would be, "How does spinner's mate spend most of his time?" Now, you ask it.

Charles: How does spinner's mate spend most of his time?

Day 7:

TEXT: Perhaps you are wondering where the lava and other volcanic products come from. Deep within our earth there are pockets of molten rock called magma. Forced upward in part by gas pressure, this molten rock continually tries to reach the surface. Eventually—by means of cracks in the crustal rocks or some similar zone of weakness—the magma may break out of the ground. It then flows from the vent as lava, or spews skyward as dense clouds of lava particles.

Charles: How does the pressure from below push the mass of hot rock against the opening? Is that it?

Teacher: Not quite. Start your question with, "What happens when?"

Charles: What happens when the pressure from below pushes the mass of hot rock against the opening?

Teacher: Good for you! Good job.

Day 11:

TEXT: One of the most interesting of the insect-eating plants is the Venus's flytrap. This plant lives in only one small area of the world—the coastal marshes of North and South Carolina. The Venus's flytrap doesn't look unusual. Its habits, however, make it truly a plant wonder.

Charles: What is the most interesting of the insect-eating plants, and where do the plants live at?

Teacher: Two excellent questions! They are both clear and important questions. Ask us one at a time now.

Day 15:

TEXT: Scientists also come to the South Pole to study the strange lights that glow overhead during the Antarctic night. (It's a cold and lonely world for the few hardy people who "winter over" the polar night.) These "southern lights" are caused by the Earth acting like a magnet on electrical particles in the air. They are clues that may help us understand the Earth's core and the upper edges of its blanket of air.

Charles: Why do scientists come to the South Pole to study?

Teacher: Excellent question! That is what this paragraph is all about.

At the beginning of instruction, Charles is unable to formulate a question. The teacher coaches Charles by stating the main idea (Statement 2), providing a clue about how to begin the question (4), and finally resorting to forming the question for him (6). But Charles even has difficulty imitating the teacher's question (7, 9). On Day 4, the teacher waits longer for Charles to try to formulate an adequate answer, providing encouragement (16), and prompting (14, 18), before again suggesting a question for him (20). As Charles improves, the teacher "fades" her direct help and demands greater participation from him. Finally, by Day 15, Charles can form good questions independently.

Reciprocal teaching is a very successful method. It has proven effective with poorer readers at several grade levels, and in both small-group and whole-class settings.

READING RECOVERY

Reading Recovery is another highly successful program that makes integral use of coaching, in this case in both the education of the children and in the training of the teachers themselves. Pioneered in New Zealand, the program was first introduced in this country in Ohio by Ohio State University, the Columbus Public Schools, and the Ohio Department of Education. The program has now been introduced throughout Ohio and is beginning to spread to other states. The Center for the Study of Reading is sponsoring the program in Illinois.

The goal of Reading Recovery is to help the very poorest readers make accelerated progress, until they read as well or better than the average child in their class. When properly implemented, the program appears to achieve this ambitious goal. It is reported that after an average of twelve weeks of instruction, more than 95 percent of New Zealand children who receive the program make normal progress in reading thereafter.[12] The success rate in Ohio is currently reported to be 85 percent.[13] It should be stressed that the available data suggest that the gains produced by Reading Recovery persist over a period of years.

As implemented in this country, Reading Recovery provides a second chance for children who are failing to learn to read in the first grade. Children who fall into the lowest 20 percent in reading within a class are provided one-on-one thirty-minute lessons every day by a teacher trained in the strategies and techniques of Reading Recovery. The typical lesson includes rereading of books introduced in previous lessons, reading a new book at what is supposed to be just the right level of challenge, composing and writing a brief story, and word study and analysis. The teacher employs special techniques intended to help children develop fluency and use the strategies that are characteristic of successful readers.

Reading Recovery teachers are selected from among experienced elementary school teachers. They receive a year of intensive training in Reading Recovery methods and strategies. The goals are for teachers to become sensitive observers of children's reading and writing and to develop facility in making moment-by-moment diagnoses upon which to base instructional decisions. The creators of Reading Recovery say that the program "does not come in a box"; they claim the program depends upon carefully nurtured teacher expertise. A group of outside educators and scholars who evaluated Reading Recovery in Ohio concurred that the program would achieve uncertain results if teacher training were attenuated.

A notable feature of Reading Recovery training is supervised implementation of the program with at-risk children. Under the guidance of a trained teacher leader, teachers critique each other as they teach children behind a one-way window. At each session, two teachers bring children whom they tutor regularly and conduct lessons "behind the glass." On the other side of the glass, the rest of the trainees observe and engage in what is usually a vigorous discussion of all aspects of the lesson. The teacher leader provides scaffolding by prodding the group with rapid-fire, Socratic-style questions about the child's behavior and what may be inferred from the behavior about the child's reading strategies, the appropriateness of the books, the pacing of the lesson, the teacher's decisions at choice points, the teacher's control of key techniques, and whether opportunities were seized or lost. Trainees can be heard to applaud the teacher who has managed to convey a "powerful example." At other times, they can be heard to frankly challenge ill-considered decisions. A discussion exemplifying articulation and reflection continues when the two teachers who have taught behind the glass rejoin the group.

To reach a high proportion of first graders failing to learn to read had seemed an almost impossible dream before Reading Recovery. And, the consistent success the program is able to achieve would almost certainly be impossible without excellent teacher training.

KAMEHAMEHA EARLY EDUCATION PROGRAM

Another highly successful program, the Kamehameha Early Education Program (KEEP), makes integral use of modeling, coaching, and scaffolding for educating children, training their teachers, and training "consultants" who provide continuing training for the teachers. It is the education of this third layer of professionals that we will stress in the following discussion.

KEEP was developed to ameliorate the poor reading and high incidence of school failure among native Polynesian-Hawaiian children in Hawaii. Over a period of years, children who have participated in KEEP have averaged near the fiftieth percentile on standardized reading texts, whereas comparable children without the program have averaged near the twenty-fifth percentile.[14]

The KEEP program involves a scope and sequence chart detailing the specific skills that must be mastered and the best order for introducing them. Criterion-referenced tests matching the skills are administered at least once every two weeks. The program features lively, intellectually stimulating discussions of stories in which the teacher leads the children to see deeper themes that relate to their own background of experience. KEEP attempts to maximize the fit between the culture of the home and the culture of the school, building upon the skills and knowledge that children acquire in their home culture. One way this is done is through learning centers in which children cooperate to teach and learn from one another. Another way is through the "talk story," a pattern of interaction found in Hawaiian homes in which people cooperate in developing stories and in which more than one person may speak at once. KEEP teachers encourage talk-story-style discussions during reading lessons. The children may speak when they wish, without waiting for the teacher to call on them, and they collaborate in explicating the story and advancing their understanding of its meaning.

KEEP is a complicated, highly structured program that is demanding to teach and requires high levels of teacher expertise, preparation time, and energy. Yet the program is implemented with a fairly high degree of fidelity in a far-flung network of schools around the state of Hawaii. One key to KEEP's success is specially trained "consultants."[15] Working with four to six classroom teachers is a full-time job for a consultant. Consultants spend more time with beginning KEEP teachers than they do with experienced teachers, but they spend at least a half hour a week in the classrooms of every teacher, including veterans regarded as master teachers. The consultants provide the coaching, support, and feedback that inform and sustain the practicing teacher.

The consultant must have a broad background in the foundations of the KEEP program and a great deal of specific knowledge about how reading, writing, and language are handled within the program. Since the consultant's job is to train others, skills in classroom observation, a working knowledge of curriculum design and techniques of effective teaching, and abilities in troubleshooting and problem solving are essential. Also necessary are the interpersonal skills for working with others and the communication skills for delivering informative advice and feedback.

KEEP consultants receive a year of training that involves reading followed by discussion, guided observation of both live and videotaped lessons, and role playing.[16] Consultants-in-training observe and critique videotapes of exemplary and less exemplary illustrations of each teaching strategy. As part of their training for teaching strategies, each consultant trainee prepares and teaches a series of fifteen- to twenty-minute small-group reading lessons. These lessons are taught in real classrooms and are videotaped. Each trainee has multiple opportunities to observe his or her own lessons as well as those of the other trainees.

In short, it would appear that KEEP's success can be attributed to excellent teaching of children, excellent training of teachers, and excellent training of teachers of teachers. It is doubtful that the program could consistently achieve such good results without excellence at each of these levels.

The examples of reciprocal teaching, Reading Recovery, and KEEP illustrate how programs that embody the principles we espouse can succeed in developing expertise in children, teachers, and teachers of teachers. We believe that these same principles can and should be applied more broadly to the education of reading teachers.

The first principle that should be used more broadly is modeling: by observing an expert perform the task, the novice begins to form a conceptual model of the process. Because preservice education takes place mostly in colleges and universities rather than schools, observing experts in authentic situations can be problematic. We propose that one way prospective teachers can witness authentic practice is through the use of videotapes of real classrooms. We further propose that modeling include not only the models of expert practice, but also models of various stages of developing expertise. In the case of teaching reading, videotapes could capture both good and not-so-good reading lessons. The teachers whose lessons were taped could be encouraged to reflect about what they were thinking and doing during the lesson. Since such reflection would probably disrupt the lesson, the teacher models could delay sharing their reflections until immediately after the lesson.

Videotapes not only enable modeling, but also provide the medium for realizing the other principles of effective instruction. Practice in authentic situations with coaching and scaffolding is critical to becoming an expert. Would-be teachers need the opportunity to translate what they have learned in content and methods courses and what they have observed of teacher models into actual practice, with coaches to guide and support them. The best arrangement would be to have opportunities to "do" coached teaching distributed throughout the education of reading teachers rather than massed at the end of the program of study. Ideally, in other words, candidate teachers would participate in an iterative cycle of theory-observation-practice-coaching which more closely approximates the training of experts in many other fields.

We are by no means the first to believe that the best teacher training would involve modeling and practice with coaching and scaffolding. Yet these features have never been seriously tried in mass teacher education. One reason is that education courses are typically staffed by a single instructor who cannot possibly provide as much coaching as is really needed. The kind of teacher training we advocate would be prohibitively expensive under today's formulas for funding teacher education.

The foregoing analysis leads us to advance a modest proposal. Send prospective teachers out into the schools with inexpensive TV cameras and video recorders. Ask them to tape fellow teacher trainees and their pupils several times a semester during reading, writing, and language lessons. Make the close analysis and discussion of the tapes the centerpiece of university courses on methods of teaching reading and language arts.

This proposal is economically and logistically viable. A camcorder, extra microphones, tripod, and monitor can be purchased for $1,750 or less. Assuming that four to six teacher trainees could share one set of equipment, the basic capital outlay for a school of education graduating fifty elementary school teachers a year would be less than $20,000. Candidate teachers could tape themselves. An even better idea, we think, is for them to work in pairs. One week one teacher trainee prepares and teaches a lesson on camera. The other teacher trainee records the lesson and critiques it. The next week the two switch roles.

Videotechnology allows leveraged use of the time of instructors in education courses. Experience in the schools often is not even a part of reading and language-arts methods courses, because it is not perceived to be valuable enough to be worth the time and trouble. When field experience is included in a methods course, it usually happens without the direct involvement of the education professor. Traveling from school to school, chatting with principals, and so on makes inefficient use of the professor's time. We believe that employing videotechnology would increase the value of the classroom experience for the teacher trainee and decrease the time and energy the education professor would otherwise have to spend on ancillary matters. This time could be invested in scrutiny of the teacher trainees' videotaped lessons. However, in our plan, too much videotape would be recorded for education instructors to look at it all. Instead, they could train the prospective teachers to analyze each others' tapes. Continuing the coaching metaphor, the course instructor might be thought of as the "head coach."

We envision a semester-length, three-hour, lecture-discussion course. One hour would be spent providing information about the teaching of reading or language arts. This time should be rich in pedagogical principles, and should provide a sound, theoretical basis for teaching reading. The complement to verbalized theory would be the videotaped modeling of expert and not-so-expert practice. The instructor would bridge theory and modeling in two ways: by judiciously selecting tape segments that illustrate key points, and by focusing the discussion on important issues illustrated by the target segments. The instructor would need to ensure that students understand the critical attributes that differentiate better from poorer lessons. The instructor would also need to reconcile any discrepancies between theory and practice and between the explanation and rationale offered by the model teachers and the observed effects on the classroom.

On their own time, the teacher trainees would then engage in teaching and videotaping lessons in classrooms as previously described. The remaining two hours of university class time would be devoted primarily to critical analysis of videotapes of prospective teachers' lessons. Assuming ten enrollees per discussion section, there would be time for each student teacher to have about three lessons orally critiqued. The remaining lessons could be analyzed in writing by other teacher trainees and, occasionally, by the course instructor.

The key to the success of the practice teaching–videotaping sessions is how they are handled in these two-hour discussion-critique periods. These sessions provide the opportunity for coaching, scaffolding, articulation, and reflection. Coaching by the instructor is important, but we think the participation of peers in a collaborative learning enterprise is invaluable in developing articulation and reflection. By critiquing each others' lessons, students learn to articulate their knowledge and understanding; they also have an opportunity for reflection by comparing their own skills with those of others at varying levels of expertise. A videotape is probably even better suited than a real lesson to developing articulation and reflection. A videotape can be stopped for discussion; a live lesson goes on, and discussion while it is taking place may be distracting. Illuminating episodes captured on videotape can be viewed a second time; a live lesson does not permit instant replay. The following scenario illustrates how we think a discussion session might go.

The scenario begins with the professor addressing reading vocabulary. Her presentation includes a range of theoretical ideas, research-based information, and classroom lore about vocabulary growth and development, the role of vocabulary knowledge in reading comprehension, how to select words to preteach, the characteristics of effective vocabulary instruction, and specific suggestions about instructional activities. The professor uses key concepts from her presentation to demonstrate three recommended components of vocabulary instruction. Next, the class members and professor work together to design a vocabulary lesson based on the first chapter of *Charlotte's Web,* a book the prospective teachers read in a children's literature class. Finally, they review the information and analyze its usefulness.

This segment extends the typical lecture format in several ways. First, the professor intentionally models the abstractly presented ideas using vocabulary that might be new to the prospective teachers themselves. Second, the professor interacts with them about the techniques for applying the ideas. Finally, class members reflect upon the entire process. In essence, the professor attempts to incorporate the five principles for fostering expertise: modeling, coaching, scaffolding, articulation, and reflection.

Next, the prospective teachers design lessons that focus on vocabulary to implement with their students. All have their lessons videotaped by their partners. Some have their lessons formally critiqued in the discussion sessions. The scenario continues with a discussion session. This day, a discussion group reviews a lesson designed and taught by Kate, one of the students in the class. Prior to starting the tape, Kate shares her planning with her nine classmates:

Kate: I'm assigned to a third-grade class. I work with a group of five students. For this lesson I selected *The White Stallion,* a selection from their basal reader. I selected six words to preteach: *Conestoga wagon, mustang, mare, Guadaloupe River, stallion,* and *coyote.*

John: Why did you select those words?

Kate: Well, I read the story and selected words that were crucial to its plot and that I didn't think the students would know. From those, I selected the ones that lacked sufficient contextual information for their understanding.

Professor: Do the rest of you think she planned appropriately?

Mildred: I think she used reasonable criteria. You want to teach the necessary but unknown words that students can't figure out by themselves.

Susan: Yes, but you're supposed to teach words that have general value—you know, words that will have some value beyond this story. I don't think *Conestoga wagon* and *Guadaloupe River* qualify.

Professor: What do you say to that, Kate?

Kate: Well, maybe they don't have general value, but I was trying to use them to build up a feeling for the setting of the story, the historical context.

Professor: Do the rest of you think Kate has given a good justification for her choices?

Several in the class agree that she has.

This exchange began with one person's inquiry about Kate's decision. It forced Kate to explain her action and gave class members a chance to evaluate it. The professor intentionally turned the evaluation back to the class members. This exchange demonstrates the incorporation of articulation and reflection into the discussion. The remainder of this hypothetical discussion continues to exhibit these features.

The tape begins, showing Kate arriving early and, while her students work with their teacher, printing the list of words on the blackboard. Kate calls the students to her work area. They arrive and the lesson begins.

Kate first checks to see if students can pronounce the words. "Are there any words on the board that you're not sure how to say?" asks Kate. One student, Samantha, points to *Guadaloupe River*. Kate first asks about the word *river*. Samantha correctly pronounces it. Kate then says, "Well, whatever this is we know that it is the name of a river."

Tom: Do you think the students understood how you knew it was a river's name?

Kate: Gee, I should have further explained how I knew that. I'll remember that for the next time. I think I do a better job in a subsequent section.

The tape resumes. "This river is the Guadaloupe River," says Kate. Kate then asks the entire group to say the name of the river. They repeat in unison. Mark asks about *Conestoga wagon*. This time Kate says, "What do you know about this pair of words?" Mark shrugs his shoulders. "Well, let's see," says Kate. "What do you know about capital letters?" Mark answers, "They usually are names of things." "Right," says Kate. Is one of these words capitalized?" "Oh," says Mark. "It's probably the name of a type of wagon." "Good," answers Kate. "It's called a Conestoga wagon." She then gives some characteristics of Conestoga wagons. When the students' questions about pronunciation end, Kate begins providing information about their meaning:

Ted: How do you know the students can pronounce the remaining words?

Kate: (No response.)

Professor: What could you have done, Kate?

Kate and others in the class provide suggestions.

The lesson continues. Kate starts with *Conestoga wagon,* asking students to provide some of the characteristics she mentioned earlier. She then goes to *mustang,* the next word on the list:

Nancy: I was wondering if it would be a good idea to group the words *mustang, mare,* and *stallion.*

Mildred: Couldn't you have used a semantic feature analysis?

Susie: In that case, *coyote* could have been included, too.

Professor: What is the purpose of semantic feature analysis?

Mildred: It's to get children to pay attention to similarities and differences in meanings. It's not enough that they just vaguely know that *mare* and *stallion* are names for kinds of horses. They need to know specific distinctions.

Professor: Yes, good answer. We want children to learn to pay attention to fine distinctions in meanings. This is necessary for them to become good independent word learners. Kate, what about coming to the board and leading us through a feature analysis with these words?

In addition to further representing articulation and reflection about goals in relation to techniques, coaching and scaffolding appear in this section as Kate practices an activity initially suggested by a classmate.

When the tape resumes, Kate is asking questions. "What word is something you could ride?" "Mustang," says Eric. "Stallion," says

Samantha. "I could ride in a Conestoga wagon," adds George. "How are mustangs and stallions alike?" asks Kate. "They have four legs," says Tina. "They're both horses," adds Travis. "How are coyotes and mustangs alike?" continues Kate. "They're both wild," offers Eric. "How are they different?" queries Kate. "A coyote couldn't pull a Conestoga wagon," says Samantha. "I'd be afraid to see a coyote but not a mustang," says George.

> Kate: I was really pleased with the students' responses. They were creative and interesting to me. I think we were all having fun and learning the vocabulary.
>
> Susie: The pace was good.
>
> Tom: So were the questions.
>
> Professor: Why were they good, Tom?
>
> Tom: Well, they required some reasoning instead of just repeating a definition.

The tape starts again. "Four of the six words will appear again in the story you'll read tomorrow," says Kate.

> Professor: Kate, do you think this is the best time to share this information with your students?
>
> Kate: Didn't I tell them at the beginning of the lesson that the words were from their story?
>
> Class: (Several classmates and the professor shake their heads "no.")
>
> Kate: I was so concerned about remembering the vocabulary stuff, I forgot other things we've discussed.

Other students also comment about the amount of information that needs to be integrated for a quality lesson to result. From the questions about her lesson, Kate realizes an important omission. Again, the shared viewing permits addressing this oversight, another dimension of coaching.

The class members return to the tape and hear Kate telling her students to write their own stories using as many of the words as possible from their list. "We'll listen to some of your stories before reading *The White Stallion*," says Kate. Her students return to their desks as the tape ends.

This experience affords more than the implementation of a lesson containing good and improvable points. It provides a forum for prospective teachers to reflect on a teaching experience, share their ideas, support their suggestions, and gain insight into the nature of teaching. The professor's theoretical information comes to life as a result of its contextualization.

Using videotapes in the manner we have sketched incorporates the principles of effective instruction we have espoused—students see modeling of authentic practice, they receive coaching and scaffolding as they engage in the activity of teaching, and they have opportunities to develop articulation and reflection in videotape discussion-critique sessions. The use of videotapes would make possible an order of magnitude more authentic in practice than is typical in teacher education. Prospective teachers would also receive vastly better coaching and scaffolding than they generally do now. All in all, as a pedagogical tool, well-planned use of videotapes may be better than live lessons and is certainly better than the typical preservice teacher education.

We have stressed preservice teacher education in this paper. The approach applies equally well to *inservice* professional development of experienced teachers. Translating talk about teaching into practice is neither simple nor certain for them, either, particularly if the point is subtle, requires a change in beliefs, or entails a substantial modification of the teacher's usual ways of teaching. Moreover, veteran teachers can be jaded. They have received all kinds of advice, much of which may not have worked well, at least as they were able to understand and implement it. Thus, we argue that, like new teachers, experienced teachers, too, are best served by training that features authentic examples and opportunities for authentic practice with coaching and scaffolding.

To recapitulate, our thesis is that there is a gap between talk about teaching that is featured in most preservice teacher education and the working knowledge and problem-solving expertise that characterize skilled teaching. This gap exists, we believe, because typical teacher training does not embody the principles of modeling, coaching, scaffolding, articulation, and reflection. To foster these principles, we propose extensive use of videotapes in teacher education—videotapes of the authentic lessons of practicing teachers and videotapes of aspiring teachers as they struggle with their first real teaching experiences. Videotapes used in the ways we have recommended offer perhaps the most feasible avenue open to improve the quality of teacher education and thus assure higher returns on the nation's investment in literacy.

ENDNOTES

1R. C. Anderson, E. H. Hiebert, J. A. Scott, and I. Wilkinson, *Becoming a Nation of Readers* (Washington, D.C.: National Institute of Education, 1985), 3.

2L. S. Shulman, "Knowledge and Teaching: Foundations of the New Reform," *Harvard Educational Review* 57 (1) (1987): 1–22.

3D. C. Lortie, *Schoolteacher* (Chicago: University of Chicago Press, 1975).

4S. F. Nemser, "Learning to Teach," in *The Handbook of Teaching and Policy*, ed. L. S. Shulman and G. Sykes (New York: Longman, 1983).

5D. Durkin, "What Classroom Observations Reveal about Reading Comprehension Instruction," *Reading Research Quarterly* 14 (4) (1978–1979): 481–533.

6F. J. Guzak, "Teacher Questioning and Reading," *The Reading Teacher* 21 (3) (1967): 227–34.

7J. F. O'Flahavan, D. K. Hartman, and P. D. Pearson, "Teacher Questioning and Feedback Practices: A Twenty-Year Retrospective," in *Dialogues in Literacy Research, 37th Yearbook of the National Reading Conference*, ed. J. E. Readence et al. (Chicago: National Reading Conference, 1988).

8J. S. Brown, A. Collins, and P. Duguid, "Situated Cognition and the Culture of Learning," *Educational Researcher* 18 (1) (1989): 32–42.

9A. Collins, J. S. Brown, and S. E. Newman, "Cognitive Apprenticeship: Teaching the Crafts of Reading, Writing, and Mathematics," chap. 14 in *Knowing, Learning, and Instruction: Essays in Honor of Robert Glaser*, ed. Lauren B. Resnick (Hillsdale, N.J.: Erlbaum, 1989).

10A. S. Palincsar and A. L. Brown, "Reciprocal Teaching of Comprehension-Fostering and Comprehension-Monitoring Activities," *Cognition and Instruction* 1 (2) (1984): 117–75.

11Ibid. The dialogue here comes from this source.

12M. Clay, *The Early Detection of Reading Difficulties: A Diagnostic Survey with Recovery Procedures* (Auckland: Heinemann Educational Books, 1985).

[13]G. S. Pinnell, D. E. DeFord, and C. A. Lyons, *Reading Recovery: Early Intervention for At-Risk First Graders* (Arlington, Va.: Educational Research Service, 1988).

[14]Anderson et al.

[15]K. Bogert and M. Kent, *The KEEP Consultant Training Program* (Honolulu: Center for Development of Early Education, Kamehameha Schools, 1988).

[16]Ibid.

The joy of working in the field of adult literacy is the privilege of spending time with a group of courageous men and women. In the middle of the many other stresses in their lives, they have chosen to take time to tackle their literacy needs. These adults, often able—even gifted—in other areas, at home, work, and on the street, lack competence in the one area where society expects a high level of performance: literacy.

Many have been dealing all their lives with learning disabilities, often undiagnosed. Others have simply not had the opportunity to learn to read and write. The solution is to find good materials, teaching methods appropriate to individuals' needs, and as many hours of instruction per week as possible. In a setting where students receive both classroom instruction and one-on-one tutoring, volunteers can be of tremendous help to these adults. This program design assures continuing support for the volunteer tutors from the professional staff. Adult literacy instruction profits from having a strong group component. People working on their reading and writing are able to support each other. Their life stories, dictated to teachers or tutors, become some of the finest texts that they can share with each other.

Sylvia Greene
Adult Basic Education Reading Specialist
Community Learning Center
Cambridge, Massachusetts

Numeracy

Lynn Arthur Steen

I lliteracy and innumeracy are social ills created in part by increased demand for words and numbers. As printing brought words to the masses and made literacy a prerequisite for productive life, so now computing has made numeracy an essential feature of today's society. But it is innumeracy, not numeracy, that dominates the headlines: ignorance of basic quantitative tools is endemic in American society and is approaching epidemic levels among many subcultures of the American mosaic. Innumeracy thus leads to inequity in opportunity and threatens to undermine America's capacity for productive work. Today's schools must accept the daunting challenge of achieving appropriate levels of numeracy for all students.

Numeracy is to mathematics as literacy is to language. Each represents a distinctive means of communication that is indispensable to civilized life. Nevertheless, if persistent news reports are to be believed, both numeracy and literacy are in serious decline in contemporary U. S. society.

Despite great differences in structure and form, both mathematical language and natural language are powerful tools for description, communication, and representation. Numeracy is especially important for a nation expecting to compete in a global economy fueled by information technology. Whereas natural language is redundant,

Lynn Steen is Professor of Mathematics at St. Olaf College.

ambiguous, and concrete, mathematical language is concise, precise, and abstract. Full expression of our thoughts and visions requires the richness of both natural and mathematical language. Like the yin and the yang, numeracy and literacy are the entwined complements of human communication.

A RISING TIDE OF NUMBERS

The term *numeracy* (and its adjectival form *numerate*) is more widely used in England than in the United States. It was described in a report of an official British government committee of inquiry as comprising those mathematical skills that "enable an individual to cope with the practical demands of everyday life."[1] Literacy is often defined in similar terms, for example, as "using printed and written information to function in society."[2]

This tradition of practical purpose has had the effect of equating both literacy and numeracy with the scope of the elementary school curriculum. It is what is meant by "reading, 'riting, and 'rithmetic." Indeed, in countries all over the world, the principal purpose of primary education is to achieve a minimal acceptable level of literacy and numeracy. Yet it is only in the last century that this goal has become widely accepted. So whatever levels of literacy and numeracy we may have achieved are not standards steeped in ancient tradition. Today's vision of a literate and numerate society is a rather recent ideal.

Fifty years ago literacy was defined in the United States as fourth-grade education. Even today this standard is common in developing nations as a minimum goal for educational policy. But as society has become more complex, with global communication and worldwide markets penetrating local societies, minimal levels of both literacy and numeracy have risen relentlessly. Today we read regularly about "functional literacy," "cultural literacy," "scientific literacy," "quantitative literacy," and "environmental literacy." These terms, however defined, represent diverse attempts to express the higher demands of literacy imposed by contemporary society.

Expectations for numeracy have risen at least as fast as have the demands for literacy. Daily news is filled with statistics and graphs, with data and percentages. From home finance to sports, from tax policy to state lotteries, and from health insurance to new drug approvals, citizens are bombarded with information expressed in numbers, rates, and percentages.

A glance at any newspaper reveals how common numbers, graphs, and percentages have become. "Consumer prices rise 0.3 percent. But 5 of index's 7 components slowed rate of increase in November." This actual four-column headline in a typical daily newspaper assumes a reader who understands that 0.3 percent is a monthly (rather than an annual) increase, who can mentally translate 0.3 percent to the more common annual rate of 3.6 percent, who understands that the consumer price index is a weighted composite of several components, and who recognizes what a "slowed rate of increase" of the CPI might mean for the future. More sophisticated readers might be expected to understand the variability inherent in the single digit 0.3 percent (which could suggest anything between 3.0 percent and 4.2 percent annual rates, a 40 percent margin of error); or the impact of compounding on monthly rates (which in itself leads to a 4.3 percent annual rate, or to a range of 3.4 percent to 5.1 percent); or perhaps the relation between changing rates of increase and second derivatives.

In the workplace, numeracy has become the gatekeeper of many desirable jobs. According to one recent study, the fraction of new jobs needing mathematical skills that correspond to a full four-year high school curriculum will be 60 percent higher in the 1990s than in the 1970s, whereas the fraction of new jobs requiring the lowest levels of mathematics skills is projected to decline by 50 percent in the next fifteen to twenty years.[3] Already, three-fourths of all majors available at colleges and universities now require some college-level mathematics.

HISTORICAL PERSPECTIVE

Although arithmetic and geometry arose as instruments of commerce in ancient times, numeracy as a common demand of everyday life is a distinctive product of the scientific age. Just five hundred years ago the merchants of Venice began for the first time to teach addition, subtraction, multiplication, and division as a means of expanding their commercial influence.[4] Three hundred years later, great universities began to require this "vulgar arithmetic" as a requirement for entrance, alongside Homer and Cicero. Today universities expect students to be ready to learn calculus—which itself was just discovered three hundred years ago—and newspapers expect readers well versed in compound interest, weighted averages, and statistical margins of error.

In our age, the rapid emergence of computers has spawned an unprecedented explosion of data. Thus, what sufficed for numeracy just four decades ago is no longer sufficient today. Today's ordinary business vocabulary includes terms such as *bit* and *spreadsheet*; librarians talk about "Boolean searches" of catalogue data; and graphic artists use "spline curves" for smooth models. Ordinary calculators have keys for functions that only a decade ago were unheard of outside scientific and engineering circles. The extensive efforts by business to reeducate workers to use computers effectively and willingly show just how rapidly standards of numeracy have changed in our lifetime. Numeracy is not a fixed entity to be earned and possessed once and for all.

Although the definition of numeracy—whatever suffices for the practical necessities of life—continually changes, it does not simply expand. Few people any longer need to take square roots by hand, even though such methods were emphasized in school arithmetic for nearly four centuries. Long division, which began its rise in fourteenth-century Venice, has likely passed its prime as hand calculators become as ubiquitous as pencils. By the turn of the century even algebra may be performed more often by machine than by human hand.

This continually changing backdrop makes it difficult to establish reliable standards for numeracy. Indeed, the increasing gap that many observers have noted between the average performance of contemporary U. S. citizens and the implicit expectations of society may be due as much to increased expectations as to decreased performance. It is very difficult to separate these two variables, since today's students are products of today's society, whereas yesterday's students were products of their society. In such a context, talk about decline in numeracy remains more speculation than fact.

CONTEMPORARY EVIDENCE

Today's numeracy should be compared with requirements of today's society. The "nation's report card," which samples the 80 percent of seventeen-year-olds who are still in school, provides a fair measure of what passes for numeracy.⁵ Most students in this sample can perform simple one-step arithmetic problems such as comparing six dimes and eleven nickels, or reading a bar graph. However, only half of these students—that is, about 40 percent of the nation's seventeen-year-olds—can solve moderately more sophisticated problems such as finding 87 percent of 10, or computing the area of a rectangle. And only 6.4 percent of these students—representing only one in twenty of young U.S. adults—can perform simple multistep problems such as calculating total repayment (principal plus interest) on a loan, or locating the square root of 17 between two consecutive integers.

These recent results in the United States confirm evidence gathered a decade earlier by the Cockcroft commission in England.⁶ Instead of relying only on written tests (as is typical in the United States), the British commission interviewed hundreds of adults to determine just how they used mathematics on the job and in everyday life. Interviewers in this study discovered a common perception of mathematics as such a "daunting subject" that more than half of those approached simply refused to take part in the study.

The Cockcroft study revealed intense apprehension in the face of simple mathematical problems: the extent of anxiety, helplessness, fear, and guilt was the "most striking feature" of this study. It documented widespread inability to understand percentages, even those as simple as tips or sales tax. Many thought, for example, that a fall in the rate of inflation should cause a fall in prices.

Two other features of this study are worth noting, for they are undoubtedly as true today in the United States as they were twelve years ago in England. Many people manage to organize their lives so that they make virtually no use of mathematics. By relying on others for what needs to be done or by resorting to coping strategies (for example, writing checks rather than estimating change), they successfully evade the mathematics that confronts them. In the real world, many people survive without ever using any quantitative skills.

On the job, the Cockcroft study discovered a surprising pattern. Most workers who needed to use specific job-related mathematics did so by methods and tricks passed on by fellow workers that had little connection (certainly none that they understood) with methods taught in school. Tradesmen frequently dealt in fractions with limited sets of denominators (e.g., halves, quarters, and eighths), so calculation within this domain could be done by special methods rather than by the general-purpose "common denominator" strategies taught in school. In another example, a worker who had frequent reason to multiply numbers by 7 did so by multiplying by 3, adding the result to itself, and then adding the original number.

The paradox of workers learning (oftentimes inventing) new mathematics instead of using what they have been taught in school is the result of insecurity brought on by their school experience with mathematics. Many otherwise well-educated persons are virtually innumerate; others become "mathophobic," avoiding tasks or careers that require any use of mathematics.[7] Unless the mathematics studied in school is understood with confidence—and all data show that only a minority of students achieves this type of understanding—it will not be used in any situation where the results really matter.

The most important result of school mathematics is the confidence to make effective use of whatever mathematics was learned, whether it be arithmetic or geometry, statistics or calculus. When apprehension, uncertainty, and fear become associated with fractions, percentages, and averages, avoidance is sure to follow. The consequences of innumeracy—an inability to cope with common quantitative tasks—are magnified by the very insecurity that it creates.

AN INVISIBLE CULTURE

Mathematics is often called the "invisible culture" of our age. Although surface features such as numbers and graphs can be seen in every newspaper, deeper insights are frequently hidden from public view. Mathematical and statistical ideas are embedded deeply and subtly in the world around us. The ideas of mathematics—of numbers and shapes, of change and chance—influence both the way we live and the way we work.[8]

Consideration of numeracy is often submerged in discussions of literacy, exposing only the traditional tip of basic skills (" 'rithmetic") for public scrutiny and comparative assessment. Strategies to improve numeracy will never be effective if they fail to recognize that arithmetical skills comprise only a small part of the mathematical power appropriate to today's world. Approaches to numeracy must reflect the different dimensions in which mathematical and statistical ideas operate.

Practical Numeracy

Many mathematical and statistical skills can be put to immediate use in the routine tasks of daily life. The ability to compare loans, to calculate risks, to estimate unit prices, to understand scale drawings, and to appreciate the effects of various rates of inflation bring immediate real benefit. Regardless of one's work or standard of living, confident application of practical numeracy provides an edge in many decisions of daily life.

Those who lack either confidence or skills to employ basic arithmetic, statistics, and geometry lead their economic lives at the mercy of others. Advertisers prey on those who shirk from thinking through the implications of exaggerated quantitative claims. Lotteries take in disproportionate revenue from less well-educated citizens in part because few people with minimal education understand chance.[9] Without practical numeracy, a person is left defenseless against those who would take advantage of his goodwill and resources.

Civic Numeracy

Whereas practical numeracy primarily benefits the individual, the focus of civic numeracy is on benefits to society. Discussions of important health and environment issues (for example, acid rain, the greenhouse effect, and waste management) are often vapid or deceitful if conducted without appropriate use of mathematical or statistical language. Inferences drawn from data about crime or AIDS, economic and geographic planning based on population projections, and arguments about the federal budget depend in essential ways on subtle aspects of statistical or econometric analyses. Civic numeracy seeks to ensure that citizens are capable of understanding mathematically based concepts that arise in major public policy issues.

Civic issues requiring a numerate citizenry arise on many different occasions. Much of the confusion—and near panic—surrounding the 1979 nuclear emergency at the Three Mile Island power plant was due, according to the investigative commission, to reporting by both public officials and journalists that omitted or mixed up important units of measurement. As the commission said, it was like reporting the score of a baseball game as 5 to 3 without saying who had won.

The continuing debate over mandatory AIDS testing provides a good example of quantitative issues hidden just beneath the surface of many public debates. Since no test for the AIDS antibody is perfect, there will always be a small number (perhaps 2 percent) of errors that may produce either false positive or false negative results. The innumerate public infers from this that testing is 98 percent accurate. But since the actual incidence of AIDS in the general population is less than the error in the test, any widespread test administered to a random sample of citizens will produce more results indicative of AIDS because of errors in the test than because of actual AIDS in the population. The personal consequences of these erroneous messages in psychological, economic, and emotional grief are rarely recognized by a public which naively assumes that any accurate test will produce accurate results when put into widespread use.

A public unable to reason with figures is an electorate unable to discriminate between rational and reckless claims in public policy. Debates about acceptable levels of suspected carcinogens, about the efficacy of high-risk medical procedures, and about regulation of hazardous waste all hinge on sophisticated understanding of quantitative issues involving data, chance, and statistical inference. Just as Thomas Jefferson viewed "an enlightened citizenry" as the only proper foundation for democracy, so in today's society we depend on "a numerate citizenry" for informed and productive debate of public issues.

Professional Numeracy

Many jobs require mathematical skills. Today's jobs, on average, require more mathematical skills than yesterday's jobs.[10] Leaders of business and industry repeatedly emphasize the role of mathematics education in providing the analytical skills necessary for employment. One measure of the seriousness that business attaches to mathematics is that American industry spends nearly as much each year on the mathematical education of its employees as is spent on mathematics education in public schools.[11]

Everyone knows that science depends on mathematics. Fewer recognize that mathematical or statistical methods are now indispensable in most professional areas of study. Computer packages, themselves based on mathematical models of scientific or economic phenomena, are widely used to simulate hypothetical situations in areas ranging from medicine to investment banking, from social planning to aircraft design. From medical technology (CAT scanners) to economic planning (projecting tax revenues), from genetics (decoding DNA) to geology (locating oil reserves), mathematical methods have made an indelible imprint on every part of science and industry.

On assembly lines statistical process control is regularly used to ensure quality: workers, most often high school graduates, must learn to use control charts and other statistical tools in the routine operation of manufacturing processes. Bank clerks must be able to interpret to customers the complexities of mortgage rates and investment risks. Doctors need to interpret to patients the uncertainties of diagnoses and the comparative risks of different treatments.

Professional numeracy provides important yet very different benefits to individuals, to businesses, and to nations. For students, mathematics opens doors to careers. For companies, a mathematically competent work force paves the way for new products and competitive production. For nations, mathematics provides the power of innovation to compete in a global technological economy. All benefit when professional numeracy is high; all are hurt when it is low.

Numeracy for Leisure

No observer of American culture can fail to notice the immense amount of time, energy, and money devoted to various types of leisure activity. Paradoxically, a very large number of adults seem to enjoy mathematical and logical challenges as part of their leisure activities. The popularity of puzzles, games of strategy, lotteries, and sport wagers reveals a deep vein of amateur mathematics lying just beneath the public's surface indifference.

Chance and strategy underlie all games of chance, from illegal numbers games to state lotteries, from casino gambling to horse racing. Millions of individuals who are innumerate by school standards thrive in the environment of gambling by relying on specialized homegrown methods, just as the workers in the Cockcroft study relied on special tricks to carry out the mathematical requirements of their trade.

Games and puzzles, ranging from solitaire to chess and from board games to bridge, reveal a different vein of public empathy with mathematical thinking. Many people in widely different professions harbor nostalgic dreams, often well-hidden, of the "Aha" experience they once enjoyed in school mathematics. The feeling of success that comes with the solution of a challenging problem is part of mathematical experience, a part that many persons miss in their regular lives. The popularity of magazine columns on mathematical and computer recreations attests to the broad appeal of recreational mathematics.

So strong is this drive that thousands of amateur mathematicians have devoted millions of hours trying to trisect the angle because they have heard in some remote geometry course that this problem, so simple to state, has defied solution since the time of ancient Greece. What they have failed to hear, or failed to grasp, is that nineteenth-century mathematicians proved that this problem and others like it are impossible to solve. The evidence of the Don Quixotes of mathematics shows that the capacity and drive for mathematics cannot be totally eradicated by unpleasant school experiences.

Many adults romanticize the aura of certainty afforded by the school caricature of arithmetic and geometry: they seek security against a threatening, changing culture by invoking the power of a mathematics they have never learned. Down this road lie numerology, astrology, and pseudoscience. It is truly alarming to discover how many adults trust astrology more than astronomy, numerology more than mathematics, and creationism more than molecular biology.

Both John Allen Paulos[12] and Martin Gardner[13] have documented with convincing examples the deep links between innumeracy and numerology, between scientific illiteracy and pseudoscience. The human need for explanation fills the vacuum of quantitative and scientific illiteracy with beguiling nonsense. Too often, the price of innumeracy is not ignorance, but delusion.

Cultural Numeracy

Like language, religion, and music, mathematics is a universal part of human culture. For many, albeit not for the majority, it is a subject appreciated as much for its beauty as for its power. The enduring qualities of abstract ideas such as symmetry and proof can be understood best as part of the legacy of human culture which is passed on from generation to generation.

Jacob Bronowski documented with superb insight the historical convolutions that blended mathematics, art, religion, and science into a single strand in the story of human culture.[14] Just as the expression of patterns flowered in Moslem art, so the search for pattern drove Renaissance science. Even today mathematicians and scientists commonly employ elegance as a standard by which to judge competing theories.

Two famous twentieth-century essays capture at opposite poles the abiding counterpoint among mathematics, art, and science. G. H. Hardy, the great British number theorist, wrote in his apologia of pure mathematics that "beauty is the first test: there is no permanent place in the world for ugly mathematics."[15] A quarter of a century later, mathematical physicist Eugene Wigner wrote of the "unreasonable effectiveness" of mathematics in the natural sciences as a "wonderful gift which we neither deserve nor understand."[16] Thus the mystery: beauty determines truth, and truth reflects reality.

Although it may sound to some like an oxymoron, mathematics appreciation has always been an important part of cultural literacy. To understand why so many of the greatest thinkers—from Plato to Pascal, from Archimedes to Einstein—rooted their work in principles of mathematics, to comprehend the *sui generis* nature of mathematical knowledge, to witness the surprising effectiveness of mathematics in the natural sciences, to explore the role of mathematical models in the great new scientific quest to understand the mind, to understand how order begets chaos and chance produces regularity—these and countless other facets of mathematical activity reveal their power and significance only on the level of philosophy, history, and epistemology.

The rationale for cultural numeracy parallels that advanced by E. D. Hirsch[17] for cultural literacy: to provide a common background fabric on which to weave the tapestry of civilization. Mathematics is part of this tapestry. Even young children can learn from mathematics the power of thought as distinct from the power of authority. For those with the ears to hear, echoes of Euclid sound in the words of Jefferson: "We hold these truths to be self-evident . . . . " Numeracy in this sense is an intrinsic part of our cultural heritage.

EDUCATIONAL IMPLICATIONS

Traditional school mathematics curricula do not deal uniformly with all aspects of numeracy. A pragmatic public supports two facets (e.g., practical and professional) virtually to the exclusion of the others, although within the two areas that are emphasized, the classroom treatment is often inappropriate to the objectives. Indeed, school mathematics is simultaneously society's main provider of numeracy and its principle source of innumeracy.

The skills required for practical numeracy can be taught to most students during the years of universal primary education through grades six, seven, and eight. Unfortunately, traditional elementary school curricula have concentrated on arithmetic to the exclusion of most other topics. Contemporary recommendations wisely suggest a broader curriculum, including practical geometry, data analysis, calculator skills, chance behavior, measurement, and estimation.[18] In the broadest sense, mathematics is not just about numbers and shapes, but is also a science of patterns.[19]

Beyond grades nine or ten, school and college study of mathematics has traditionally focused on a few very limited parts of professional numeracy. High school courses prepare students for calculus, which is the traditional mathematical standard for the natural sciences. College courses in elementary statistics—which could just as well be taught in high school—provide similar introductions to the quantitative prerequisites for the social and human sciences. However, computer methods have so significantly altered the role of mathematical and statistical methods on the job that most traditional school courses fail today's challenge of providing appropriate professional numeracy.

Civic, leisure, and cultural features are rarely developed in school mathematics, except perhaps in occasional enrichment topics that are never tested and hence never learned well. These aspects of numeracy are slighted because neither teachers nor administrators embrace a broad vision of numeracy. All too often, schools teach mathematics primarily as a set of skills needed to earn a living, not as a general approach to understanding patterns and solving problems. The disconnection of mathematical study from other school subjects— from history and sports, from language, and even from science—is one of the major impediments to numeracy in today's schools.

Students learn chiefly what they are motivated to learn. The evidence of mathematical methods learned out of school—on the job, in the street—shows that when numerical or geometrical methods are reinforced by use, they are both learned and remembered. In this respect, the language of mathematics is just like natural language: effective learning requires immersion in a culture that is speaking and using the language. Children learn to read and write not solely because of their language arts instruction in school, but equally because of the reinforcement provided by other school subjects, and by their environment at home. Where reading and writing are not reinforced at home, the progress of learning is much slower.

Numeracy is rarely reinforced, either in school or at home. Parents, coaches, and teachers of other subjects seldom make the effort to engage children in activities that would use mathematical or statistical methods—perhaps because the adults themselves tend to avoid such methods. No matter how effective mathematics instruction may be in school—and to be honest one must admit that it often is quite ineffective—it will have little lasting value unless student motivation and expertise is reinforced by extensive contact with mathematical, geometric, and statistical ideas in other environments.

LESS OR MORE?

While scientists, educators, and business leaders press for increased levels of numeracy, several social critics have raised questions about the basic premise that more effort leads to better results. Columnist William Raspberry, echoing social scientist Paul Burke, has argued that the wisest social policy is to focus required school study only on what I have called practical numeracy, leaving all other facets to elective study.[20] Within the range of potential meanings of *numeracy,* they adopt the minimalist position—numeracy for survival, not numeracy for civilization.

The issue is partly philosophical—involving the role of numeracy in cultural literacy—and partly strategic and economic: how best to deploy scarce resources (notably, excellent mathematics teachers) to meet necessary obligations of government. If not everybody needs mathematics beyond percentages and simple logic, why strive to teach more to all? Decades of evidence show that we fail both in the larger goal of developing multifaceted numeracy in all students and in the limited goal of developing practical numeracy. Raspberry and Burke argue, in effect, that by trying to achieve the former, we ensure failure even in the latter.

Their analysis rests not only on limited resources, but also on the evidence of hostility, frustration, and failure that mounts rapidly in required mathematics courses in grades eight through ten. As some argue that the laws against drugs are in part responsible for the high incidence of drug-related crime, so Raspberry and Burke argue that requirements in mathematics beyond the level of practical numeracy are themselves the cause of much of the nation's problem with innumeracy. Contrary to current national trends for increased high school requirements, they would reduce required secondary school mathematics to a one-year ninth-grade capstone course in practical numeracy.

One can hardly dispute this analysis because of evidence of current schooling. The typical mode of instruction in mathematics is almost exclusively catechetical:[21] standard texts are discussed bit by bit; standard questions accompany the text; standard answers are taught; and students are expected to recite standard answers with minimum variation or interpretation. Such teaching, developed centuries ago to provide mass religious education, is ill suited as a medium for teaching analytical thinking, creative problem solving, and the art of reasoning. What it produces, more often than not, is just "inert knowledge." Less of this sterile, rigid mathematics would certainly be a net gain for the nation.

The proper question is not whether to have more or less of an outmoded and ineffective tradition, but whether it is possible to do better with more effective school practice. Most experienced teachers and scholars believe that improvement is possible, and indeed under way. In that case, if school instruction does rise to the challenge of numeracy for all, one must still ask whether requirements or electives are the best strategy for public education in mathematics.

When it comes to civic, leisure, and cultural numeracy, the issue is no different than for cultural literacy. Shakespeare and Euclid share parallel pedestals in the architecture of core curricula. For each, schools must struggle to balance the motivation intrinsic to elective courses against the certain exposure of requirements. There is no simple answer.

However, professional numeracy arises from a different motivation—jobs—and requires a separate analysis. Mathematical knowledge is required in two ways in the arena of careers and employment: to get a job and to perform job duties. As the Cockcroft study documents so well, people cope with routine, on-the-job mathematics whether it is learned in school or not. They do not, however, cope well with nonroutine issues: one analysis of the Challenger disaster revealed that managers might have made different decisions had they had better understanding of basic statistics.

It is in securing jobs that mathematics functions as a "critical filter," being required for licensing examinations, college entrance, and course prerequisites. Because they are often less well prepared in mathematics than white males, minorities and women are filtered out in disproportionate numbers from many desirable jobs. Some argue that the role of numeracy on standard exams and course prerequisites should be reduced to match typical job requirements; others, including the president of the National Academy of Engineering,[22] argue that mathematics should become a pump rather than a filter in the educational pipeline from school to job.

The debate about mathematics as a filter, perhaps unnecessary, is a variation on the long-standing educational idea that subjects like mathematics and Latin train the mind. Many trades and professions keep their numeracy standards high in order to select individuals with a certain quality of mind (or, critics charge, of a certain socioeconomic status). So long as this is the case, prudent educators will require young students to continue their study of mathematics not because they *will* need it but because they *may* need it. The consequences for a student's economic future are too serious, and the temptation to opt out of a difficult course too great, to justify electives as wise mathematics policy for students who are still in the required years of schooling.

DIVERSITY

Many manifestations—practical, civic, professional, leisure, cultural—reveal diversity as the norm for numeracy. Just as static descriptions locked in the past are insufficient for today's needs, so narrow one-dimensional descriptors (e.g., " 'rithmetic") are inadequate for the panorama of mathematics in contemporary society.

Diversity in kind is matched—indeed, probably overwhelmed—by diversity in accomplishment. For example, pre- and post-tests of eighth-grade students show that each of the four major tracks (remedial, regular, enriched, algebra) ends the year less well prepared than the next highest class did as it began the year.[23] Enormous variation exists, even at that level, among students who study mathematics. In the eighth grade alone, the four-year spread in entering skills was increased, as a consequence of one year of educational effort, to nearly seven years.

These data are typical of the way students learn mathematics: they learn at very different speeds. Moreover, the more students know, the more they can learn: learning now enables learning later. This is one of the important intrinsic arguments for improving literacy and numeracy. Because of the sequential nature of mathematical knowledge, innumeracy inherited from early years becomes an insurmountable obstacle to subsequent study of any mathematics-related field.

Mathematical learning progresses in proportion to what one already knows. Hence, the range of student learning grows exponentially. The farther one moves up the educational ladder, the farther apart students become. It is not uncommon for the mathematical performance of students entering large universities to be spread across the entire educational spectrum, from third or fourth grade to junior or senior year in college. In no other discipline is the range of achievement as large as it is in mathematics.

One measure of the spread is provided by the mathematical performance of U. S. students as they enter adulthood. We know that on average they do poorly. The weakest leave school, usually as dropouts, with the numeracy level of an average third grader. Solving problems that would stump most college teachers of mathematics, the strongest compete successfully in an international mathematical Olympiad. The gap between these extremes is immense, and filled with students.

The wide variability in mathematical achievement of students, together with the varied types and purposes of numeracy, suggests the futility of any explicit definition of *numerate*. It is neither efficient nor possible for everyone to know the same thing. Reality dictates a continuum of types and levels of numeracy distinguished by purpose, accomplishment, and style.

Demand for civic and professional numeracy—for mathematical skills of citizen and worker—leads directly to increased mathematical diversity of the population. Because students who know more learn faster, increasing educational effort in school mathematics often increases the gap between the strongest and the weakest students more than it raises the average performance of students. Increase in the variance of quantitative skills, not just relative weakness in average performance, is perhaps the most important debilitating social consequence of society's increased demand for mathematical and statistical power.

EQUITY AND EXCELLENCE

Increased variance leads to inequity. In jobs based on mathematics, inequity translates into severe underrepresentation of women and minorities. Concern about this issue has traditionally been based on issues of equity—that all Americans deserve equal opportunity for access to mathematically based careers. Demographic reality now shows that inadequate mathematical preparation of major parts of our work force will produce an America unprepared to function effectively in the twenty-first century. Equity has joined economic reality as a compelling factor in mathematics education.[24]

National projections make the case in stark terms. At the beginning of the twenty-first century—just one decade from now—only 15 percent of net new workers will be white males; the other 85 percent will be women, minorities, and immigrants.[25] Yet advanced mathematics remains primarily an enclave of white males. Without significant (and unprecedented) increase in the proportion of underrepresented populations who take advanced degrees in science, the flow of new scientific and engineering personnel will be well below national need by the early part of the next century.[26]

Strategies for increasing participation of underrepresented groups must encourage both equity and excellence. Equity requires mathematical expectations of *all* students; its focus is to ensure that all students receive a mathematical background sufficient to compete for decent employment and to function as effective citizens in the information age. Excellence focuses primarily on what are often called "pipeline" issues: the need for vast increase in the number of scientific professionals (including teachers, engineers, and technical workers) from underrepresented groups.

Although the goals of equity and excellence sometimes appear to clash, in mathematics education they converge on a single issue: heightened expectations. Equity for all requires appropriate challenge for all—both for those who learn mathematics slowly as well as for those who show special talent for mathematics. Excellence demands that students achieve all they are capable of accomplishing, since nothing less will be sufficient to sustain our national economic and scientific aspirations.

Public emphasis on literacy and numeracy can too easily lead to specifications for minimum performance, which in turn lead to minimum accomplishment. Sometimes such campaigns feature a "back-to-basics" approach which shortchanges all students. Useful numeracy should entail equity and excellence for all. Hence, school mathematics—in curriculum, in pedagogy, and in assessment—should reflect a commitment to equity that simultaneously fosters excellence. In such programs there would be no ceiling on a child's aspiration.

TWO LITERACIES

C. P. Snow introduced the term *two cultures* to describe the schism he found between the scientific and the humanistic, between the world of nature and the world of people.[27] In interviews of M.I.T. alumni Benson Snyder documented two similar "modes" that represent "distinct yet complementary ways of knowing."[28] Numeracy and literacy—the language of nature and the language of people—are the two literacies of our age. Snow's schism and his label remain a reminder that this duality represents a truly fundamental dichotomy.

Despite the gap between them, literacy and numeracy have much in common. In each there is tension between narrow and broad interpretations—between practical benefits and cultural effects. As each is a language, each must be taught in a context of realistic use both to sustain motivation and to ensure mastery. Moreover, the way we use these two languages determines the way we think.

Nevertheless, numeracy remains the more daunting challenge. For each person who never learned to read, there must be a hundred who boast that they were never any good at math. That imbalance is especially troublesome in an age of data and measurement, of computers and statistics. Changing school mathematics is an important ingredient in any program for reform, but one must also look to society beyond the schools for serious change of lasting benefit. Here are some small but important changes that would make great improvements in numeracy:

- *Don't teach just arithmetic.* Numeracy requires a rich blend of statistics, geometry, and arithmetic, catalyzed by careful reasoning rooted in common sense.

- *Don't rely on worksheets.* Students learn best in active contexts featuring discussion, writing, debate, investigation, and cooperation. Isolated facts on artificial worksheets reinforce the image of school mathematics as totally artificial, unrelated to real life.

- *Don't ignore calculators.* Children must learn many ways to calculate—manually, mentally, electronically—in realistic contexts that reflect the world around them. Calculators are part of that world and should be part of school mathematics.

- *Don't rely only on school.* Children are influenced as much by the entertainment and sports industries as by formal school instruction. There is much that those industries could do to promote both numeracy and literacy.

- *Don't use just short-answer tests.* Assessment instruments strongly influence the shape of instruction and learning. In numeracy as in literacy, formulation and expression are more important than simple answers. Tests should reveal how students think, not just what they know.

- *Don't depend only on mathematics.* Although numeracy may be taught in mathematics classes, to be learned effectively it must be used widely in other contexts, both in school and at home, in entertainment and in sports.

Although we can neither precisely define nor measure numeracy, we can improve it. Especially in an age of computers, we really must take steps to improve the level of numeracy in all segments of society. With numeracy comes increased confidence for individuals to gain control over their lives and their jobs. Numeracy provides the ability to plan, to challenge, and to predict; it reveals the power of reason and unlocks the language of nature.

ENDNOTES

[1] Wilfred H. Cockcroft, *Mathematics Counts* (London: Her Majesty's Stationery Office, 1986).

230 Lynn Arthur Steen

[2]Irwin S. Kirsch and Ann Jungeblut, *Literacy Profiles of America's Young Adults* (Princeton: Educational Testing Service, 1986).

[3]William B. Johnston and Arnold E. Packer, eds., *Workforce 2000: Work and Workers for the Twenty-first Century* (Indianapolis: Hudson Institute, 1987).

[4]Frank J. Swetz, *Capitalism and Arithmetic* (Peru, Ill.: Open Court, 1987).

[5]John A. Dossey, Ina V. S. Mullis, Mary M. Lindquist, and Donald L. Chambers, *The Mathematics Report Card: Are We Measuring Up?* (Princeton: Educational Testing Service, 1988).

[6]Cockcroft.

[7]Sheila Tobias, *Overcoming Math Anxiety* (Boston: Houghton Mifflin, 1978), and *Succeed with Math: Every Student's Guide to Conquering Math Anxiety* (New York: The College Board, 1987).

[8]National Research Council, *Everybody Counts: A Report to the Nation on the Future of Mathematics Education* (Washington, D.C.: National Academy Press, 1989).

[9]John Allen Paulos, *Innumeracy: Mathematical Illiteracy and Its Consequences* (New York: Hill and Wang, 1988).

[10]Johnston and Packer.

[11]National Research Council.

[12]Paulos.

[13]Martin Gardner, *Fads and Fallacies in the Name of Science* (New York: Dover, 1957), and *Science: Good, Bad, and Bogus* (New York: Prometheus, 1981).

[14]Jacob Bronowski, *The Ascent of Man* (Boston: Little, Brown, 1973).

[15]Godfrey H. Hardy, *A Mathematician's Apology* (Cambridge: Cambridge University Press, 1940).

[16]Eugene P. Wigner, "The Unreasonable Effectiveness of Mathematics in the Natural Sciences," *Communications on Pure and Applied Mathematics* 13 (1) (February 1960): 1–14.

[17]E. D. Hirsch, *Cultural Literacy: What Every American Needs to Know* (New York: Vintage Press, 1988).

[18]National Council of Teachers of Mathematics, *Curriculum and Evaluation Standards for School Mathematics* (Reston, Va.: National Council of Teachers of Mathematics, 1989).

[19]Lynn Arthur Steen, "The Science of Patterns," *Science* (29 April 1988): 611–16.

[20]William Raspberry, "Math Isn't for Everyone," *Washington Post,* 15 March 1989.

[21]Daniel P. Resnick, "Historical Perspectives on Literacy and Schooling," *Dædalus* 119 (2) (Spring 1990): 15–32.

[22]Robert M. White, "Calculus of Reality," in Lynn Arthur Steen, *Calculus for a New Century: A Pump, Not a Filter* (Washington, D.C.: Mathematical Association of America, 1989), 69.

23Curtis C. McKnight et al., *The Underachieving Curriculum: Assessing U.S. School Mathematics from an International Perspective* (Champaign, Ill.: Stipes Publishing Company, 1987).

24Harold L. Hodgkinson, *All One System: Demographics of Education—Kindergarten Through Graduate School* (Washington, D.C.: Institute for Educational Leadership, 1985).

25"Human Capital: The Decline of America's Work Force," *Business Week* (19 September 1988): 100–41.

26National Science Foundation, *Women and Minorities in Science and Engineering* (Washington, D.C.: National Science Foundation, 1988); and Jaime Oaxaca and Ann W. Reynolds, *Changing America: The New Face of Science and Engineering*, interim report (Washington, D.C.: Task Force on Women, Minorities, and the Handicapped in Science and Technology, September 1988).

27C. P. Snow, *The Two Cultures and the Scientific Revolution* (London: Cambridge University Press, 1959).

28Benson Snyder, "Literacy and Numeracy: Two Ways of Knowing," *Dædalus* 119 (2) (Spring 1990): 233–56.

In the competitive global economy, Japan and Germany are pressing the United States. Our public officials and business-people in the United States explain this competitive decline by pointing to defense expenditures, much larger in America than in Germany or Japan; to an emphasis on short-term company profits rather than long-range strategies; to a low level of consumer savings; to undernourished research budgets; to high interest rates; to huge government deficits. These points are valid. But so is another American handicap.

Our work force is poorly trained. On-the-job training in most U.S. companies does not match the cross-training in various large Japanese firms, in which employees learn several jobs, or of the extensive apprenticeship pattern in German firms. Ill-trained workers with faulty skills severely curtail productivity.

Yet even thoughtful job-training efforts suffer from our severe national educational limitations. New technologies of manufacturing, finance, and service require the ability to read and write and use numbers well. Literacy is a prerequisite for effective job training, and schools are still the main paths to literacy in our country. Tom Sawyer and Huckleberry Finn could scorn schooling over a century ago, but to do so today courts disaster.

High school dropout rates are 50 percent in some inner cities and 20 percent in the nation. By the end of this decade, well over a fifth of the new members of the work force will be immigrants from Latin America, Africa, and Asia, many of whom will have poor command of the English language, the principal language of the international economy. Heroic efforts are required by schools and others to create a functionally literate work force and general population. Neglecting the pursuit of such efforts, which are the foundations of successful job training, will lead to a reduced standard of living as well as to cultural and civic mediocrity.

Martin Meyerson
President Emeritus and University Professor
University of Pennsylvania

Robert M. Zemsky
Director
Institute for Research on Higher Education
University of Pennsylvania

Literacy and Numeracy: Two Ways of Knowing

Benson R. Snyder, M.D.

Than

The longitudinal study of M.I.T. students begun three decades ago included yearly interviews with a random sample of 51 undergraduates during their time at M.I.T. and then eighteen to twenty-two years later. Following their patterns of adaptation and the development of their ways of thinking (about science, about the wider world) through M.I.T. into their careers and personal lives revealed the importance of two complementary but different modes of thought, evident in their language and manifest in their actions. The balance between these modes of thought has compelling implications for students' adaptation to a changing, complex world.

Based on separate yet complementary cognitive skills, literacy and numeracy are subject to various definitions, to which this volume of *Dædalus* attests. Literacy and numeracy are, however, linked to two ways of thinking and are most often learned in specific educational contexts that may sustain one or the other of these modes of thought, seldom both. At the Massachusetts Institute of Technology, the prevailing way of thinking involves the ability to understand and use mathematical notational systems and symbolic language to determine whether a given proposition, when cast in a form which allows for a mathematical solution, is true or false. This way of thinking and its associated language are essential for understanding and commu-

Benson Snyder is Professor of Psychiatry at the Massachusetts Institute of Technology.

nicating in the sciences and engineering. Mastery of this mode of thought is a precondition for serious exploration in these domains, for successful passage through M.I.T.'s curriculum, and for the careers of most of its graduates.

This article draws on my experience in the educational setting of M.I.T., where the mode of thought essential for understanding and communicating the sciences and engineering has been the central discourse for a century, while overall faculty concern with the mode of thought for engaging the humanities has fluctuated from minimal to moderate.

I will review some of the findings from a twenty-five-year longitudinal study of 51 former M.I.T. students in order to address a series of related questions associated with literacy and numeracy. The definitions of the two modes of thought developed during this longitudinal study are discussed in more detail later in this article. For the present discussion, mode one relates to the ways of knowing associated with numeracy and mode two to the ways of knowing central to literacy. How often does mastery of one of these two modes of thought actually preclude the other? What are the educational, psychological, or cultural factors that may contribute to this outcome? What is the role of formal schooling in tipping the balance for or against one or the other mode of thought? What is the long-term outcome when students leave and move on to their careers in the wider world of work and family?

Twenty-five years ago Alfred, an M.I.T. physics major then in his sophomore year, spoke about his undergraduate experience:

> What we're taught here is somewhat intensive and at the same time rather narrow. And it gives a rather narrow perspective on life in general. . . . the only thing of any importance is the development of the mind. . . .

M.I.T.'s core humanities requirement twenty-five years ago when Alfred was speaking about the narrowing of his perspective meant some exposure to the literature, history, and philosophy of Western civilization from Homer to the present in a two-year humanities sequence. The consensus about what constituted "literacy" gave way in the late 1960s to a kaleidoscope of courses from literature to linguistics. This humanities requirement was largely "deconstructed," mirroring events in the outside culture, and was replaced with options to be selected from some 160 subjects in the humanities and related fields. Constraints on these options have recently been introduced, and the writing requirement now tests for competence with the written word, but there is (as yet) little agreement that the mode associated with literacy (two) needs to be a central part of the students' involvement in the subjects that meet the humanities requirement. Literacy, or humanistic understanding, though acknowledged as worthy, has consistently been seen by many students and faculty as simply far less "useful" than the mastery of the mathematical competencies essential for solving problems in engineering or science subjects. Numeracy in this setting is, in effect, largely independent of and of far more consequence than literacy. Still today, entering M.I.T. students can already see this emphasis on one way of thinking. A recent freshman spoke about what it takes to "make it" at M.I.T.:

> You already have to have a certain way of thinking in mind . . . when you come. They want to develop that way of thinking. And if you don't come in thinking that way, it can be pretty hard trying to get it. The way that I think is more humanities oriented, rather than technically oriented . . . though I took a lot of technical classes in high school that I enjoyed. Here there are so many people that have such great technical backgrounds that what I learned seemed trivial to what they already knew. So adjusting . . . took me a while. Most people here just think mathematically. I mean, even when they joke around they always have some mathematical underlying meaning.
>
> I know a lot of people here just don't like humanities. They say they are useless. "What do you need to learn that for?" . . . . They don't see when they read a book; they see words. . . . They don't dig deeper for the purpose.

I had come to M.I.T. thirty years ago from an Ivy League women's liberal arts college where achieving literacy was a far more highly valued educational goal than mastering mathematics or understanding the laws of physics. At the college, students who sought out consultation often spoke of being "bad seeds" or "weeds," evoking agricultural images, whereas at M.I.T., students in distress would often use mechanical metaphors. They would ask to have their "carburetors adjusted" or say simply that they wanted a "tune-up." These students' ways of knowing were reflected in their explanations of their distress as their images of themselves became increasingly defined by their competence in using one or the other mode of thought.

The M.I.T. students' adaptation to this culture with its emphasis on the cognitive mode of science and engineering has been a central concern of my research, though at the time I began to formulate this study thirty years ago, it was not in these terms. I wanted to understand how these students made sense of their world as they moved through four years of a demanding technological education so that I could appreciate the stresses they faced and how they coped with them during their late adolescence and beyond.

In 1961 I began a longitudinal study of the 893 freshmen in the class of 1965 which traced the paths these students followed during their undergraduate years.[1] Identifying and inquiring into those significant interactions that characterized their separate passages allowed us to explore the impact of their undergraduate education on their patterns of adaptation and to investigate their emotional and cognitive development. Briefly, data on their academic performance, their family and prior educational experience, and their scores and item responses on a psychological and personality inventory were correlated with their movement through the maze of the formal curriculum. A central part of the study involved interviewing a 5 percent random, stratified sample of this class (54 individuals) four times during the course of their undergraduate years. There were also interviews with 10 faculty members. Selective classroom observations were undertaken. The major findings from this phase of the study were published in 1971.[2]

Twenty years after these former students had entered M.I.T., I again began to interview the original 54 participants. By 1987 I had spoken at length with 51 of them in their offices or homes.[3] These follow-up interviews focused on their subsequent adult and career development: on how these individuals dealt with, responded to, and thought about their educational experience and their careers, their relationships, and their other concerns. The recorded interviews were transcribed and then coded in a number of categories by research assistants. During the analysis of these narratives, we paid particular attention to their language as these people articulated their thoughts and feelings and described their actions and decisions from age eighteen through their late thirties.

TWO MODES OF THOUGHT

Though the students' ways of knowing were apparent at the outset of the research, the significance of this observation increased as the follow-up interviews were analyzed. The study of the language these individuals used in the narratives of their life experiences through M.I.T. and on into their positions at midcareer revealed the importance of two complementary but different ways of thinking in their careers and in their continuing relationships. The following brief definitions of the two modes are based on analysis of the interviews with 51 participants.[4]

Mode One

This mode of thinking has a close connection with mathematical concepts and draws on those formulations which are fundamental in the natural sciences, where forces are acting on objects that do not have intentions. Subjects employing this mode of thought are concerned with determining the falsity or truth of propositions with certainty, with "hard" data that can be replicated over time. Predictions of outcomes are precise and unambiguous. The goal is to find causes that are regularly connected with effects, where predictions are least likely to be disturbed by historical or contextual patterns. The most frequently used formulations in those rated high on this mode were Newton's laws of motion, the laws of electricity and magnetism, and the relatively new, highly complex mathematical formulas for processing information in order to separate signal from noise.

Mode Two

This mode of thinking refers to efforts to understand animate beings, where the objects of inquiry have intentions, especially in the social and psychological world of human beings. False or true propositions are relative and subject to constant revision. Uncertainty is expected. The "truthfulness" of a statement about human intentions is necessarily linked to both a specific time in history and an appreciation of the present context. Thoughts, feelings, and actions are attended to in an effort to understand human intentions. Predictions about possible actions are conditional. Not least, knowledge of other actors' intentions must account for the particular time and situation. Empathy and intuition often play a role in "knowing." Those rated high on this mode of thought frequently referred to literature and history.

Over the course of the study, the tension between these two modes was conveyed by most of the participants. Alfred, the physics major who had described the "narrow perspective on life in general" at M.I.T., spoke again to this issue during his junior-year interview in 1964 when he recalled his response to two distressing events. At the time of Kennedy's assassination the year before, he had been surprised to see people on TV crying in the streets. He found this response contrasted dramatically with the constrained, controlled reactions of his classmates and professors. Later that year he had been confused by his unexpected, though temporary, inability to work following the break-up with his girlfriend:

> I found that my whole way of thinking . . . seems to prevent me from . . . well, reacting in any sort of a natural manner to such a situation . . . because I'm constantly analyzing myself. . . . This whole way of thinking has made it impossible for me to react.

Twenty years later we met again. Alfred had a Ph.D. in physics and had spent ten years in an outstanding R&D lab. Then, in part out of "restlessness" with his research, he had made a major career change. Two years before our interview, he had moved to a senior management position in a high-tech, start-up enterprise. Early in the interview, he brought up and reflected on his way of thinking since M.I.T.:

> What I mean by analytical thinking, I guess the natural model for me, is that of the physical sciences, where things are put out very sharply in terms of cause and effect, in terms of variables that can be quantified, in terms of functional relationships that can be described almost in a mathematical sense. I think there's definitely a weakness to the analytical style that relates to a fundamental distrust of intuition.
>
> So many times in dealing with people, you're never really sure what the answer is, at least in any absolute sense. People just don't correspond to actual exact answers. . . . You just sort of have to wing it and see what happens. . . . That sort of runs directly counter to what I've termed the analytical approach, where you can calculate and evaluate and you're very precise about everything.

What I've found out in my own career as well as in my personal life is . . . the tendency to rely almost entirely on analytical thinking really slows me down. If I can analyze a problem, I trust the answer. If I can't analyze a problem, if I have to resort to intuition or a gut feel, I don't trust the answer, and as a consequence I'm hesitant to act. It's a confidence issue. . . . How do you bring yourself to the point where you're willing to deal with situations where your analysis is inapplicable, or there aren't enough data to analyze without perhaps making a fatal mistake of hesitating so long and trying to work on things on an analytic basis that the situation disintegrates before your eyes?

In contrast to Alfred, another physics major, John, had from freshman year on expressed his delight in the complexity of both physics and humanities subjects. Paradox had not put him off; rather, it had intrigued him. In his senior year he had deliberately neglected the assigned problem sets in an advanced-level course on Newtonian mechanics and spent his time instead reading Newton's *Principia* to reach a deeper understanding of the underlying principles. He had said at the time he was "protesting" against the pressures to "selectively neglect" and wanted to know "what was really going on" instead of focusing on formulas for problem sets or on the quizzes. He was both surprised and disappointed when his "protest" ended with his receiving an A on the final exam and in the course as well. After receiving his Ph.D. in physics from a leading university, he sought a postdoctoral fellowship in another field and eventually, after several years, went on to develop an innovative and outstanding group in bioengineering. His reflection on his now highly successful career conveys a rich mix of both modes of thought:

You need a tolerance for error so you can make it and learn from it. When it gets to where everything has to have a high probability of short-term success [referring to problem sets at M.I.T. and current career concerns]—or there isn't enough looseness in the system any-more—it's very sad.

The comments of these two participants convey the essential difference between mode one and mode two.

IMPACT OF HIDDEN CURRICULUM ON WAYS OF KNOWING

The Hidden Curriculum reports much of what was learned from the longitudinal study of the class of 1965. One of the central, though tacit, tasks that students had to master was coping with the massive overload. Most managed this by "selective neglect" of some of the demands and by limiting their other interests so that they could narrowly concentrate instead on preparing for quizzes by solving problems. This concentration put a premium on their facility with the ways of knowing associated with science and engineering. The students whose self-esteem was most tightly linked to their grades expended even greater effort honing their skills with the scientific mode of thinking. Their attention to humanities subjects in the face of the overload meant that such subjects and the mode of thought relevant to human intentions were often casualties of selective neglect. These more "instrumental" students often expressed relief about being able to spend their time and effort primarily on passing quizzes. Other more "expressive" students had to constrain their curiosity about the underlying concepts in both technical and humanities subjects and frequently expressed their resentment at having to limit their attention to only manipulating formulas needed for quizzes.

These students had come into M.I.T. in 1961, four years after the Soviet Union had sent Sputnik into orbit around the earth. This event had intensified an emerging national effort to upgrade science education in American high schools. Space had become the new frontier. A sense of mission, "a calling" 1 student said, for service to the country informed these students' decisions to pursue engineering and science both for the country and for themselves. There was the Peace Corps as well; 2 in the study joined after graduation. The students thus had options ranging from helping to put a man on the moon to teaching math in Southeast Asia. A mix of practicality and idealism was evident in most of their early interviews.

Demonstrated competence in mathematics and science had helped put these students on the path that led them to M.I.T. The National Science Foundation science projects and enriched math and science courses in high school figured prominently in the students finding that, when challenged, they could do well in these disciplines.

The majority of the students came from middle-class homes. Their standing among their peers was based far more on being able to use their minds or hands in solving puzzles or problems than on having the tasteful appurtenances of middle-class life. Two metaphors frequently used by faculty and students to describe an M.I.T.

education, still heard today, are "tempering steel" and "learning to drink from a fire hose." This was not a setting that encouraged quiet reflection on aesthetic issues or the nuances of human interaction. They had come into an institution, almost regardless of department, where the mastery of mathematics and quantitative skills, applied to problems, was the central assignment. Literacy was, at most, a second priority for the vast majority.

One finding from the original study illustrates the hidden curriculum's impact on certain students that M.I.T. had especially sought out for admission. Their early withdrawal from the school relates at least indirectly to the institution's pressure on freshmen to master the narrow scientific mode of thinking. A psychological test had been administered to almost all entering freshmen.[5] Two groups of students were compared on the basis of their responses: one group (56 students) consistently expressed a desire to seek out new, complex social and cognitive experiences; the other group (59 students) responded to the same items very differently, saying that they were careful and orderly, that they would avoid ambiguity where they could and would prefer to take minimal intellectual risks. Through withdrawal or disqualification, the group seeking new experiences who scored high on complexity lost three times more the number of students in the first year than the second group did. There was no significant difference in attrition between these groups in subsequent years. The grade average was slightly but consistently higher in the second group, despite the fact that there was no significant difference on the admissions scores of the two groups. The "surviving" students from the first group had followed different and more varied academic paths than their low-risk-taking classmates throughout their remaining three years at the institution. One of the interviewed students who was in this high-score group was proficient in both ways of knowing. He lost his scholarship in sophomore year because of a C in a midterm physics exam and had to withdraw from M.I.T. He went to an agricultural college and then to a prestigious university for a Ph.D., however. He became a professor in one of the sciences and the author of both a textbook and a novel. The intellectual curiosity that characterized these intellectual risk takers was a quality that many faculty members sought in students. The institution wanted these students, admitted them, and then saw a disproportionate number of them leave.

Two-thirds of those interviewed when they were undergraduates had largely avoided grappling with the uncertain nature of knowledge about human intentions, which are obviously not driven by the laws of physics or the logic of mathematics, as Alfred's comment on "hesitating so long" illustrates. Many subjects had sought to understand, to predict, and often to "manage" the uncertainty of human affairs by sorting out the net impact of one variable among many. This search for order was reflected in the mode-one students' narratives, which were more literal and concrete than the mode-two narratives. The mode-one students made fewer references to psychological or contextual factors influencing their own or others' actions than the mode-two students.

In 1963 a sophomore math major had spoken about his required humanities subject:

> To me [the books] are very boring . . . so I just don't read them. And I've gotten a C so far. As far as I'm concerned, this is really a joke.

Twenty years later, as a successful thirty-eight-year-old computer scientist, he commented on the persistence of his way of thinking over the years since I had talked with him as a student:

> I never really thought much about love during my first marriage. . . . In retrospect I think I felt it, at least at first. . . . I think I handle problems in my relationships much the same way I handle problems on the computer. I don't know if I've changed my mode of thought so much as I've expanded the collection of things that I apply my mode of thought to.

These individuals' emphasis on mode one is reflected in their early disdain for their humanities subjects and in their relative isolation in personal relationships.[6] To appreciate what their education may have contributed to students in speaking and thinking this way, it is relevant to consider the pressures on their time, their constant need to judge what would be most useful for their academic survival. There were certainly other outcomes: the 14 students who entered with both modes survived the pressure and maintained both ways of knowing through graduation.

One student majoring in chemical engineering in 1964, who was deeply immersed in subjects requiring mode one, spoke as a sophomore about the multiple pressures and how he was coping with them.

These pressures were accentuated by his decision to graduate in three years, a decision he came to after losing his scholarship when he received a B in a core freshman subject. He gave some indication of using mode two, but he didn't have time to "indulge" in more than a few subjects where mode two was central. He described, with enthusiasm, a current music subject:

> One of the first things we learned from thermodynamics ... is the entropy of the system is lower if there's more order ... and things that are more ordered generally seem to be more pleasing. When Bach wrote his fugues ... he just knew what it [the music] sounded like and he put it down ... and all this analysis came later ... trying to pose an order to it is ... empirical idiocy.
>
> Listening to music is like reading a classical novel. The more you read it, the more you get out of it. My mother one time asked me why do I read books over and over again.... The first time it's like listening to a melodic line—you just get the plot. When you concentrate on the details, you find that they're really not so much in the background as you thought they were.

After a decade as an engineer in a major corporation, he weathered crises in his marriage and career to become an innovative manager in another firm. There he employed his considerable competence with both modes of thought and gained material success and personal satisfaction.

THE NETWORK OF ENTERPRISES

An important development during the students' undergraduate years was the close relationship between their increasing mastery of one or both modes of thinking and their ability to then explore a network of related questions: finding the answer, solving the problem that would expand the set, or suggesting further questions that would engage them. These questions, these concerns really, that engaged their minds as undergraduates typically went back to simpler forms in early adolescence and were often evident in elaborated and more sophisticated forms in the follow-up interviews. Howard Gruber's insightful term for this phenomenon in which individuals' intentions can be organized is a "network of enterprises," the projects, problems, and tasks to which individuals are committed and which recur as similar or related concerns over extended periods of time.[7]

One student's rapt involvement with ham radios at age twelve, for example, in which his attention was focused on separating the signal from the noise, became, at thirty-eight, transformed and elaborated in his using ultrasound to obtain "signals" from the ambient noise of the human body in order to measure characteristics of blood flow. When interviewed in the mid-1980s, he was working on discrete circuit design in several contexts:

> I rely very heavily on the theoretical background that I picked up at M.I.T. I wound up using a bunch of statistical communication theory in my thesis. . . . I wanted to show that this signal-processing technique would measure what it was intended to measure . . . a new way of doing the signal processing. It was a fairly unique idea.

Most of these individuals continually sharpened the skills and competencies that enabled them to pursue new, more complex clusters of problems. There were others, however, who applied mode one to domains which were not subject to solutions based on this way of knowing (dealing with a roommate's rage, for example). This was in contrast to still others who limited themselves to those concerns and problems where mode one was appropriate. The most innovative group, the ham radio adolescent for one, used a mix of modes to both frame problems and solve them. A central finding was the close connection between the use of both modes and the expansion of the network of enterprises. Those with only mode one were found to have more often narrowed their set of concerns and limited their network of enterprises.

George, a modern-day "bricoleur," illustrates the connection between his competence with both ways of knowing and his engagement as he has expanded his network of enterprises. George's interest in fixing things "to see how they worked" began in childhood and brought him to M.I.T. "I've been playing around with my hands as long as I can remember . . . tinkering around," he said. He had changed his major three times because he missed having his "hands on things" and because he was dissatisfied "with just sitting down with a page of numbers . . . until you figure out you have the answer." As an engineer, he found settings where he could "fix things" with a creative flair. In several firms he had been confronted with evidence that they wanted only short-term "fixes," not his suggestions about how underlying flaws in the design of the machines he repaired could be addressed. He seemed motivated by the satisfaction he obtained from "making something work that had failed to function." Over almost twenty years he had become an astute observer of not only the machines he worked on, but also the firms he worked for. With excitement and some misgivings, he spoke about his plans to form his own consulting company where he could employ all of his interests and competencies to deepen the managers' understanding of their machines as a means of improving their management.

In contrast to George, Martin limited his concerns to those where only mode one applied. A programmer for military guidance systems, he described increasing constriction in the range of his questions and concerns from his sophomore year on. His interest in electronics went back to age ten when he had begun taking apart radios and television sets. His parents had discouraged this activity because of "the mess" he had usually made. By junior high school, he was winning awards in math. His motivation for studying math had begun to ebb during his second year at M.I.T., though his aspirations for graduate school remained. In his junior year he had said:

> I have a few tightly defined skills [algebraic manipulation] that I'm really good at. There are whole areas of knowledge or ability that I just don't seem to possess at all. . . . maybe I'm not very good at probability. I gave up on humanities after my first term.

By his senior year, he longed for a nonstressful job for a few years, after which he would perhaps return to M.I.T. for a Ph.D. in math. Seventeen years later we met again in his home close by the facility where he had been employed since graduation:

> When I got out of college I was completely uninterested in anything that required . . . any further studying or learning or deep thought. . . . I was just looking for a job like applied computers. . . . I found it at this place out in the woods. I moved into a dormitory, and the little room that I had was exactly the same kind and size as my room at M.I.T., thirteen by eighteen tiles, and my life was measured by this constant.

The work itself, he said:

> is all very simple mathematics. I've steered away from the complicated stuff. . . . I get a lot of personal satisfaction from writing computer programs. It really surprises me how much I like it.

Following his divorce after several years of marriage, he participated in a human relations course:

> I think it opened a door. . . . I realized that there was this huge gap, a
> kind of dead zone in me. I've been trying to work on getting it
> developed now, but it's a very slow process.

These brief accounts of two individuals, one expanding his network of enterprises with both modes and the other narrowing his
network of enterprises with mode one, introduce discussion of the
ways of knowing observed in the 51 participants in the follow-up
interviews.

CHANGES IN WAYS OF KNOWING

It was not surprising that in their senior year, 42 of the 51 subjects felt
that mastery of mode-one thinking and their skill in exercising this
mode had become an integral part of their sense of self. Their
self-esteem was sustained by successfully using this mode. They often
spoke of their dismay when mode one didn't apply.

Close study of the language of 30 participants shows that they had
primarily used the mode-one way of thinking throughout their
undergraduate interviews. All had majored in engineering or science.
At graduation, 15 individuals showed a rich mix of both mode one
and mode two. As undergraduates, they had majored in engineering,
science, management, social science, and humanities. The 5 students
who had used primarily mode two in their M.I.T. interviews had
joint majors in science or engineering with humanities or social
science.

Four groups stand out in terms of their ways of knowing at M.I.T.
and at follow-up. Clearly, these findings on their predominant modes
of thought indicate that their definitions are more complex than
simply saying that numeracy equals the first mode of thought and
literacy equals the second.

"The Expanders": From Mode One to Both Modes

The most striking shift in the relative emphasis on modes of thought
over almost two decades occurred in the group of 30 who had shown
primarily the first mode of thought as undergraduates. In their
follow-up interviews, two-thirds (20 of the 30) showed evidence of

having made significant use of both modes. Most described a deepening level of intimacy with family and friends over the past two decades, sometimes gained through dealing with conflict or loss. Being called an "unfeeling automaton" by his adolescent daughter had been the beginning of his process of "constructive change," an engineer recalled with humor. Three-quarters of the expanders were married at the time of their interviews. Their occupations included engineering in both high technology (solar energy, computer design, etc.) and consumer and service industries (design of absorbent fibers, diesel engines, etc.), middle and senior management (of from small to multinational corporations), and research in computer science and biomedical applications of engineering. Several were in medicine and law. Most of this group described high intrinsic satisfactions from their work.

"The Nonexpanders": Mode One Throughout

One-third (10 of 30) of those in the group high on mode one and low on the second mode had only minimal or no discernible change from the first way of knowing in the follow-up interviews. For most of the nonexpanders, their work was the center of their lives, even though extrinsic rewards tended to be higher than intrinsic satisfactions. Their circle of friends was more limited than that of the expanders. Less than half (4 of 10) were married at follow-up. Solving work-related problems seemed to take precedence over sustaining relationships. Their occupations included software and systems engineering (in defense industries primarily), middle-level management (being project directors for missile-guidance hardware, etc.). Four were directly engaged in some aspect of nuclear weapons systems, while only 2 others of the 51 were in similar situations.

Users of Both Modes Throughout

Thirteen of the 14 individuals employing both modes as seniors were still employing both ways of knowing in their follow-up interviews. All of this group had sustained ongoing close relationships; 12 had marriages that seemed to work. One was single. They had an expressive rather than an instrumental involvement in their occupations, where intrinsic rewards were prominent as they described the issues that engaged them. The group included professors of physics, biology, and medicine, administrators of interdisciplinary groups, senior corporate executives, bioengineers, an entrepreneur, and a senior computer engineer.

One member of the group who had been high on both modes at M.I.T. was using primarily mode one at follow-up. A computer programmer, single, in a low-level administrative role, expressed his conviction that the computer itself would render him obsolete within a decade if he did not stay alert to its encroachment on his special competence.

"High Mode-Two" Participants: Modest Increase in Mode One

The 5 individuals rated high on mode two and low on mode one at M.I.T. at follow-up showed a modest increase in their use of mode one, while they remained high on mode two. All were married, and their relationships were clearly important to them. No one in this group was in a science or an engineering career. They were pursuing occupations different from those of most of their classmates. Four found strong, intrinsic rewards in their work—as a farmer, a manager of a TV station, an architect, and a minister—while the 1 remaining member of this group said his work was simply a way to make a living.

There were 2 individuals who had experienced serious psychological restrictions on their ability to employ either mode of thought; hence, they were not rated. One was unemployed, the other a low-level computer programmer. Both were single when interviewed.

In summary, 76 percent of the original cohort were using both ways of knowing almost two decades after leaving M.I.T., while 20 percent were persisting in their reliance on mode one.

Three further observations extend our understanding of what we have seen so far about the ways of knowing: one concerns the response of these individuals as undergraduates to their humanities subjects, another reports on their use of psychiatric and other counseling over the entire period of the study, and the last is a comment on the most "creative" individuals in the study.

RESPONSE TO UNDERGRADUATE HUMANITIES

All M.I.T. students in 1961–1963 had taken the same two-year required humanities sequence, which presented a unique opportunity to obtain data on the possible relationship between the individuals' ways of knowing (then and now) and their responses as undergraduates to this shared humanities experience. When the analysis of the follow-up interviews had been completed, a research assistant (new to the project) reviewed all comments on these humanities subjects in the undergraduate interviews and rated them on a five-point scale: from strongly negative (1) to strongly positive (5). The distribution of the response ratings to humanities in each of the four "outcome" groups at follow-up were then compared.

All 20 of "the expanders" (formerly mode one and now mode one and two) had ratings of 4 or 5, positive or strongly positive. Typical of their comments was: "You enjoy reading the [humanities] books ... not quite so hard and fast [as technical subjects] .... It's more a part of you."

All 10 of the nonexpanders (mode one) had ratings of 1 or 2, strongly negative or negative. Examples of their comments bear this out: "Books are boring. I don't read them."

The 13 users of both modes and the 5 high-mode-two users had similar responses, which differed from those of the preceding groups. Their ratings ranged from 2 to 5, moderately negative to strongly positive, varying with the professor and the content of the subject. They were specific and discriminating in their comments, which ranged from "very well taught," for example, to "the professor keeps apologizing for the course—why?"

The results from this modest exercise are far more robust than anticipated. The expanders had all been positive about these humanities subjects. Many seemed to welcome this respite from mode-one thinking. In marked contrast, the humanities course had a low priority for the nonexpanders, who described the subjects as "extraneous," "too soft," and "too ambiguous," and often expressed impatience with "the fuzzy thinking." On the other hand, the users of both modes and the high-mode-two group had responded critically to poor teaching and positively to some excellent professors and were far more tolerant of the use of both modes than the nonexpanders group.

In brief, the content of the humanities core subjects and the mode-two way of thinking required for its mastery had actively engaged the expanders, who did not disparage the usefulness of mode two in understanding literature and history. The mode-one nonexpanders gave little or no indication of such engagement in their first two years at M.I.T.; mastery of mode two had not been important to them.

The preceding observation and the two that follow are like a collage. One needs to hold each piece in mind as the whole is put together.

USE OF PSYCHIATRIC OR OTHER CONSULTATION

Between freshman year and the follow-up interview, 19 individuals had some consultation. Of the 14 consulting the psychiatry service while at M.I.T., 6 were users of both modes and 2 were high-mode-two users. Both groups had come because they were troubled by their mismatch with M.I.T. All 8 had been reasonably aware of their feelings and had spoken about them directly.

The other 6 consulting the psychiatry service as undergraduates were high-mode-one and low-mode-two. Most had presented their problems in terms of their difficulties in action less than in terms of their feelings. They complained of "procrastination" or said they were "not organized," and 1 wanted a "tune-up." At follow-up, 2 were expanders and 4, nonexpanders.

Those high in their facility with the second way of knowing had had more extended discussions with their psychiatrist than those showing minimal evidence of having used mode two. Instead, mode-one undergraduates reported receiving brief reassurance from the psychiatrist and then being sent on their way. From the follow-up it was evident that this group's emotional problems had not been trivial at the time. (One from this group called me at home on a Sunday because of our earlier research interview. Since he said he was desperate, I saw him that afternoon. He had been to the psychiatry service a month before because he couldn't study. Told he had sophomore slump and that he should pace himself, he had just failed three finals. He feared losing his scholarship and felt suicidal.)

In retrospect, their mode-one language may not have been sufficiently attended to by some of the staff. Some psychiatrists seem to have been put off by their mode-one students' need for precision and may not have listened attentively enough to hear the students' underlying, sometimes painful, confusion. Professionals, whether therapists or professors, should know enough of the mode-one individuals' language and concerns to be able to translate the "latent" message and respond in terms that lead to further communication. A psychiatrist had interpreted the request for a tune-up as an insensitive joke; a humanities professor had been annoyed when one student dismissed even Descartes as "soft."

Subsequent to graduation, 9 individuals had had some psychological consultation: 4 of them had been to the psychiatry service at M.I.T.—2 expanders and 2 nonexpanders. Of the 5 who had not been seen in the psychiatry service, 4 were expanders and 1 was a nonexpander.

In sum, 6 of the 9 individuals seeking subsequent consultation were expanders, while 3 were not; 5 of these expanders had sought consultation because of difficulty with close relationships. In a context of attending to a personal crisis that mattered deeply to them, 4 of these had explicitly described coming to appreciate another way of knowing (mode two).

CREATIVITY AND WAYS OF KNOWING

As noted earlier, the first-year attrition of the intellectual risk takers had been far higher (3 to 1) than the cohorts seeking certainty. The subsequent attrition from these cohorts had been the same.

For the follow-up study, a set of criteria for creativity had been developed. They included significantly reformulating a concept or design, initiating successful innovations, or making major original contributions in any field. Of the 10 individuals who fit this operational definition, 5 came from the 13 in the both-mode-users group. The other 5 came from the 20 in the expanders group. There were no nonexpanders (mode one only) in the creative group.

Reviewing the early interviews of those expanders in this group, we could discern brief flashes of curiosity and originality behind their constant contending with assignments. John's "rebellion," for instance, was not unique among the more creative students; many had felt constrained by the hidden curriculum. All 10 who met the criteria for creativity had been articulate about their intentions and were increasingly successful in following them over the period of this study. They, more than most others, actively sought out settings where they could pursue their central intellectual concerns.

In this small sample, creativity after graduation was dramatically associated with the use of both modes of thought and a high degree of intentionality in undergraduate and career choices. These people were active, not passive, in structuring opportunities to pursue their major interests.

CONCLUDING OBSERVATIONS

Comparing the 39 individuals with evidence of both modes at the time of the follow-up with those 11 still using primarily mode one reveals even further and more subtle differences between these two groups, which are consistent with those differences I have examined here. All the interviews were reviewed to determine the kind of relationships the participants described having with those who mattered most to them, the range of interests that engaged them, and their reflections on the meaning and value of their work to themselves and to others. What the participants said about these areas—and particularly what gave them pleasure, delight, and a sense of wonder—suggests that these two groups experienced their lives in significantly different ways. The categories they constructed to give meaning to their lives were significantly related to their ways of knowing.

What should give us pause, as well as some hope, since it goes against some current assumptions about adult development, is those 20 individuals (40 percent of the 51 and 66 percent of the group of 30 primarily using mode one at M.I.T.) who came to use both ways of knowing during their late twenties and early thirties. Achieving a balance between these distinct modes of thought is demonstrated vividly in their search for intimacy, the quality of satisfaction in their work, and the diversity of projects that also engaged them (making and playing baroque musical instruments, painting, raising thoroughbreds, serious mountain climbing, writing novels).

Almost all of the participants highly valued their ability in mathematics and the mode-one way of thinking. However, a majority delayed serious sustained engagement with both ways of knowing until their midtwenties or later. This pattern was most apparent in those highly intentional individuals who feared that the risk of academic failure would increase if they took time from the constant assignments to wonder or to pursue a paradox, since many felt the pragmatic mode-one culture defined such thinking as "soft," as a potential "waste of time." Listening to their narratives, one hears how they used their considerable skills with both modes of thought to free themselves in diverse ways—on a number of levels—to explore a wide range of important technical and human problems (such as the design and development of new instruments with significant medical applications, the design of highly energy-efficient automobile engines, the implementation of effective Affirmative Action programs in major corporations).

The 20 percent in this cohort who did not develop facility with the second way of knowing (10 of the 51) present us with a challenge to understand how they remained so firmly rooted in the first mode, consistently using this mode to make sense of both the physical and the human worlds. For some, this persistence of mode one was associated with specific psychological conflicts in developing their potential facility with mode two. On yet another level, their continuing reliance on mode one seems to have been undisturbed by their education. We know that their humanities subjects had not challenged them in this regard. For some, this persistence of mode one may, according to the evidence at hand, have been associated with specific psychological conflicts in developing their facility with mode two.

There are, however, other clues in their narratives, from their late adolescence and again when they were nearly forty: they spoke about their sometimes painful loneliness, their isolation, and their relentless search for certainty or perfection. They needed to have the right word, the right equation and its solution, in order to feel good about themselves. Thinking in the first mode became itself invested with so much significance for the nonexpanders that when faced with evidence that their thinking was not "working," they were puzzled and often felt at a loss. One computer programmer, after his divorce, put it starkly: "I've largely dropped out of thinking as a mode of existence." An engineer slowly came to a decision "to think about relations that matter to me, but I didn't know how to." Another engineer in high technology spoke of his isolation "from others" as he dedicated himself to his pursuit of "neat" solutions to the intricate problems in his classified job designing weapons systems. He described his "pleasure" in his work as similar to doing crossword puzzles. He had acquaintances but no close friendships, and so human puzzles had been at a minimum throughout his M.I.T. years and beyond. By his colleagues at work, he was considered most successful, a "doer" with high skills, though he had been told that his arrogance seemed to put his colleagues off. Their response to his certainty about the correctness of his positions sometimes puzzled him, though more often made him angry at their "ignorance."

The group operating primarily with the first way of knowing often attempted to understand the nature of their social world and to manage its complexities by employing analogies derived from familiar techniques and instrumentation which gave them data several levels removed from actual events. Direct experience was therefore often replaced by modeling and simulation. The "utility" of mode two remained suspect for those in this group. However, this emphasis on mode one is not limited to these individuals in science and engineering. It is seen as well in people in other fields who increasingly rely on a way of knowing that minimizes the complexity of human experience by constructing quasi-mathematical models of situations as preconditions for action.

There is a real risk that as psychiatry emphasizes psychopharmacology, attending more to symptoms and diagnostic categories than to the dynamic interplay of unique psychological states, the reliance on mode one may increasingly replace mode two as the primary way of knowing. Both ways of knowing are necessary for understanding the successes or failures of an individual's intentions. Mode one alone is not sufficient for dealing with the ambiguity and complexity of the human condition.

The pressures to depend primarily on mode one that these students faced in the early 1960s are more acute for students today. Over the past two decades the scientific and technological fields have increased in breadth and depth, with ever more sophisticated models often employing complex computer systems which lead to simulations that range from the structure of molecules to the political behavior of institutions and nations and even to the hardware of computers.

The amount of information to be processed and accounted for has increased exponentially. These and similar developments tend to distance both students and faculty members from direct hands-on experience of raw data. For those using mode one, this distancing, especially when their near-term predictions derived from the model are successful, increases their emphasis on mode one and further diminishes their concern for the possible relevance of mode two to the task at hand. Those using both modes of thought consistently attend to a far wider range of possible consequences of the model's predictions. John, for example, welcomed "error so you can make it and learn from it" as he modeled the potential patterns of accidents "waiting to happen" in a hospital operating room.

In summary, more than two-thirds of the participants in this study relied primarily on mode one during their undergraduate years. Certain characteristics of the setting at M.I.T. contributed to this outcome. This institution's necessary emphasis on science and engineering subjects and the rapid pace and high pressure to master assigned tasks had the consequence of limiting the time available to develop and practice mode two. In effect, both the formal and the hidden curriculum in the early 1960s tipped the balance in favor of mode one.

Over the long term, slightly more than three-fourths of these individuals were using both modes at follow-up. The former emphasis on mode-one skills did not preclude the emergence over time of mode-two thinking for this group. Half of the most creative and two-thirds of the "able average" individuals spent a decade or more developing their facility with mode two and came to value this way of knowing far more later than during their undergraduate experience. By the follow-up interviews, they had either sustained or gradually incorporated mode two and were using both modes in their personal and professional lives. Mastery of mode one, combined with mode two, became essential to their efforts to understand and deal with a variety of technical and human concerns.

Our educational institutions have yet to grasp this dilemma seriously and resolve its inherent contradictions in order that more of today's students graduate with appreciation for and real understanding of both modes of thought.

ENDNOTES

[1] The Student Adaptation Study was funded by the Bing and Grant Foundation (1961–1963) and the National Institute of Mental Health (1964–1969). A number of individuals participated in this study. Among the principal collaborators were Merton Kahne, Malcolm Parlett, John Rule, John Seeley, and Martin Trow.

[2] Benson Snyder, *The Hidden Curriculum* (New York: Knopf, 1971).

³The follow-up study was funded by the Ford Foundation (1982–1985). In a companion study, my collaborators Lora Tessman and Kenneth Manning conducted interviews with 25 women and 2 minority men from the class of 1965. The findings from these retrospective accounts are not included in this discussion of the prospective data from the longitudinal study. Lynn Goldschmit coded the 51 interviews of the original group reported here.

⁴Geoffrey Vickers, *Human Systems Are Different* (London: Harper & Row, 1983), and *Value Systems and Social Process* (London: Tavistock Publications, 1968). Discussions with Vickers about the early follow-up interviews were important in formulating these two ways of knowing, particularly in relation to his concept of appreciative systems; Jerome Bruner, *Actual Minds, Possible Worlds* (Cambridge: Harvard University Press, 1986). Bruner contributed much to my appreciation of the relationship between these two ways of knowing.

⁵Paul Heist et al., *Omnibus Personality Inventory Research Manual* (Berkeley: Center for the Study of Higher Education, University of California, 1962).

⁶There were no data on these individuals' ways of thinking in early childhood. However, this is an interesting issue raised by the contributions of Howard Gardner and Jerome Bruner to our understanding of cognitive development, which locate the origins of these and other modes of thought in infancy.

⁷Howard E. Gruber, *Darwin on Man: A Psychological Study of Scientific Creativity* (New York: E. P. Dutton, 1974). Gruber introduced the important notion of the "network of enterprises" as he carefully traced Darwin's development of the various enterprises that had engaged him while he formulated his theory of evolution. For specific reference to this point, see Howard E. Gruber, "Networks of Enterprise in Creative Scientific Work," chap. 9, *Psychology of Science: Contributions to Metascience,* ed. B. Gholson et al. (New York: Cambridge University Press, 1989).

Doing Badly and Feeling Confused
Stephen R. Graubard

Illiteracy was endemic in the United States at the time the Constitution was ratified and remains so today—tragically. While schooling through the secondary level became accessible to many social classes and ethnic groups in the early twentieth century, the wholly excluded, the undereducated, and the poorly educated remained prominent. Now, with discussion of the nation's educational problems widespread, and a wish by some to believe that conditions were once better, the confusion about what to do is massive. The remedies proposed omit such intangibles as dignity, responsibility, and equality, terms that have little meaning in a society that is crass and shortsighted, insufficiently intellectual or commercial.

As the nation moves into the final decade of the twentieth century, there are compelling reasons for stocktaking; education, in the broadest sense, needs to figure centrally and prominently. There is no domestic issue of greater urgency, none on which the nation is more prone to romanticize the past, to misconstrue the present. Until there is some understanding of what is today being attempted in the educational arena—however unsuccessfully—placebos will continue to be offered for social and cultural conditions that cannot respond to such mild and innocuous medication.

The historian, allowed to ignore conventional calendar chronologies, permitted to invent his own (particularly when it serves a major

Stephen Graubard is Editor of Dædalus and Professor of History at Brown University.

intellectual purpose), understands that not every century must begin with a year ending in two zeros. Just as the eighteenth century may have ended some time before 1800 (in 1789, for example, or possibly later, in 1815, depending on what one is seeking to demonstrate), a good argument can be made that America's twentieth century began not in 1900 but in 1917, the year when Congress accepted Woodrow Wilson's call for a declaration of war against Germany, the year also of the Russian Revolution.

By using this wholly legitimate historian's device, William McKinley, Theodore Roosevelt, and William Howard Taft are joined to a company that includes such late-nineteenth-century presidents as Grover Cleveland and Benjamin Harrison. It does nothing to diminish the uniquely twentieth-century features of certain of his later policies to suggest that Teddy Roosevelt, leading his Rough Riders up San Juan Hill, was as remote in understanding what the new century would bring as Benjamin Harrison was in a much more inconsequential ceremonial, which led him to invite gentlemen with American prerevolutionary antecedents to the official celebrations of the centennial of the federal republic. Anyone in 1889 suggesting that descendents of other early North American inhabitants might also be asked, including representatives of the Indian nations, and a number of recently emancipated slaves to serve as symbolic surrogates for blacks brought over to the New World in the seventeenth and eighteenth centuries, would have been thought mildly eccentric. Such individuals did not figure as early Americans. The fact that blacks constituted more than 19 percent of the American population in 1790, according to the first census, had no significance.[1]

An educational census of twentieth-century America that made 1917 its starting point would necessarily rely on the 1910 census figures. This census established the population of the country as 91,972,266.[2] Of this number, 88.7 percent were white and 10.7 percent, black. All the others, including Native Americans (then denominated as American Indians), Chinese, Japanese, and Filipinos, formed a very small part of the total. By 1920, when the population had risen to 105,710,620, in great part because of massive annual European immigrations in the immediate prewar years, substantially reduced after August 1914 by the hazards of travel in U-boat-infested Atlantic waters, the white population had grown significantly; there was no equivalent growth in the black population. Indeed, in 1930, a decade later, the American black population stood at an all-time census low; 9.7 percent of the United States population was black.[3]

Why is any of this significant? Because it tells a great deal about how the country was changing demographically in the twentieth century, why given the size of the total population, the large cohort of European immigrants, adults and children, merited attention of a kind that would not have been awarded much smaller groups of preponderantly English-speaking immigrants in the nineteenth century. Together, the new arrivals constituted a major element in the American population; their schooling, which mandated literacy but also assumed a certain responsibility for the more difficult task of acculturation, ought to have been a matter of great consequence. It is interesting that though educational issues figured prominently during the period, other questions, seemingly more compelling, held center stage. It may have been that Americans, like so many others at the time, assumed that literacy was a competence easily achieved, that the national will to support elementary school education was all that was needed.

If this was believed, the experiences of 1917 and 1918 ought to have produced serious second thoughts. Many among the several million young men eligible for the draft, both white and black, summoned to serve in what were then racially segregated military units, when submitting themselves for physical and mental examination, showed disconcerting intellectual and physical weaknesses. The educational deficiencies of the nation's youth were nothing less than startling.[4] The nation learned of these deficiencies, but chose not to become too preoccupied with conditions that suggested gross inadequacies in primary schooling. Generous access to elementary school had not produced the anticipated results. More important, some of the young were being left out entirely. This knowledge, like so much else learned during the war, did not lead to resounding calls for school reform.

Indeed, in the general euphoria that accompanied America's entry into the war, which took on even greater and more irrational dimensions following the swift victory achieved in November 1918, many in the country tended to be confirmed in their high opinion of themselves. There was no democracy quite like the American, no system of government more rational, more benign, more just. The country, having absorbed tens of millions of immigrants who showed their patriotism and ardor unmistakably, might have reveled in this spectacular success. Instead, a deep antipathy to massive new immigration showed itself. Policies that would have allowed the free and easy entry of the prewar years became exceedingly unpopular. Some of the opposition to liberal immigration programs came from working men, fearful at a time of economic recession that their jobs would be threatened by a new influx of cheap labor. An even more unsavory and bellicose opposition came from latter-day "nativists," who had periodically enjoyed a certain prominence. They now came forward again to claim that the national "stock" was being compromised, diluted by a too-free admission of inferior men, women, and children who did not resemble in race or religion the early and virtuous English, Scottish, Dutch, and German settlers, who had done so much to build the nation.[5]

Those who came to the United States in the first and second decades of the twentieth century, and it is important to emphasize the substantial numbers that arrived in the first decade, were overwhelmingly emigrants from southern and eastern Europe; many were illiterate. While we lack precise information about that number, particularly how many lacked the skill to read and write in any language, they may have been numerous. There is much to suggest, however, that many were literate in their mother tongues and that this literacy helped create the market for the large new ethnic newspaper enterprises that flourished. This foreign-language press, among its many accomplishments, kept alive certain European linguistic, cultural, social, and religious traditions; it served also to instruct the new arrivals (and many who had come previously) in the mysterious ways of a political and economic environment that was alien.[6]

The civil unrest in eastern Europe, the tensions within the Austro-Hungarian Empire, the circumstances peculiar to czarist Russia, not to speak of those within the kingdom of Italy, all contributed to these vast popular emigrations. So, also, did the undeniable attractiveness of the American economy, which despite its perpetual tendencies to "boom and bust," seemed remarkably robust and resilient, particularly when seen from across the Atlantic. However important the economic imperatives for emigration may have been, particularly for certain ethnic groups, religious factors were no less significant for others. Together, they created an American population mix that was ethnically and religiously totally different in its configuration from any that had existed in the nineteenth century. Even after the hunger of the 1840s had led to massive Irish Catholic immigration and continental revolutions and civil disturbance had served further to populate the New World with new peoples, many in the United States persisted in seeing the country as essentially a Protestant Anglo-Saxon enclave.

By 1930, the sustaining of that illusion was becoming increasingly difficult. Even after eastern and southern European emigration was virtually halted by 1924 federal legislation, with its all-too-obvious preference for specific ethnic "stocks," excluding some almost entirely, the foreign-born white population of the country numbered 38,727,593.[7] Concentrated principally in the mid-Atlantic states, but prominent also in the central states, with significant numbers in New England and the Pacific states, relatively few chose to settle in the South or the mountain states. The ethnic and religious distributions tell a familiar tale. Most immigrants settled where others of the same region, religion, or ethnicity had preceded them. Family, friends, and neighbors were therefore immensely influential in shaping behavior, in bringing new arrivals to understand the complexities of American life and helping them learn to cope with its intricacies.

The story of the black migration from the South needs also to be recalled. The First World War accelerated a process that had begun earlier; it led some 454,000 blacks to move north, principally into the Midwest and the mid-Atlantic states. In the 1920s, this migration took on major new dimensions: 749,000 blacks resettled in the North. The Depression caused these numbers to decline appreciably; in the 1930s, only 172,475 Southern blacks migrated.[8] The march northward and westward began again, however, more significantly and more dramatically, with the coming of World War II. Fueled by vast new employment opportunities created in an overheated economy suddenly working to sustain a greatly expanded civilian and military sector of quite unprecedented proportion, labor shortages were acute.

It is in the context of these massive and continuing population movements, taking on so many new and unanticipated dimensions, that any study of twentieth-century American literacy, however defined, must be considered. If one consults the Bureau of the Census statistics, all illiteracy in the United States fell from 7.7 percent in

1910 and 6.0 percent in 1920 to 4.3 percent in 1930. Among the foreign born, it stood at 12.7 percent in 1910, 13.1 percent in 1920, and 9.9 percent in 1930. Among blacks, the illiteracy rate was 30.4 percent in 1910, 22.9 percent in 1920, and 16.3 percent in 1930.[9]

Someone consulting these statistics without knowing what they reflect, particularly in the later years, would take them to mean that the country—the white population at least—was well on its way to becoming a literate society. A closer examination of the statistics would reveal that the Mexican rate of illiteracy stood at an alarming 27.5 percent, the Indian (Native American) rate at 25.7 percent, and the Chinese rate at 20.4 percent.[10] Given that the criteria used by the census for establishing literacy rates were immensely flexible, that they allowed literacy at various times to be equated simply with the ability to read or write in any language in the most elementary sense,[11] they cannot be taken too seriously. In any case, such statistics told nothing of what children were being taught in American schools, what they were learning, how long they were staying.

After World War II, in 1945, Vannevar Bush submitted a brief report, *Science: The Endless Frontier*, to the American president, Harry S. Truman. Originally commissioned by Franklin Roosevelt to write the report, Bush discussed school attendance in ways that suggested how limited the access to elementary and secondary education had been. Without dwelling on questions of literacy, Bush emphasized the number of adolescents lost to education before they completed elementary or high school. The man who enjoyed a certain renown for assisting in the development of the atom bomb expressed succinctly but powerfully certain of his educational concerns. He wrote:

> The country may be proud of the fact that 95 percent of boys and girls of fifth grade age are enrolled in school, but the drop in enrollment after the fifth grade is less satisfying. For every 1,000 students in the fifth grade, 600 are lost to education before the end of high school, and all but 72 have ceased formal education before completion of college. While we are concerned primarily with methods of selecting and educating high school graduates at the college and higher levels, we cannot be complacent about the loss of potential talent which is inherent in the present situation.[12]

As late as the end of the Second World War, most American children did not graduate from high school. In the time of Woodrow

Wilson, and in the decades following, when blacks lived predominantly in the South, those who attended school at all were required by state laws to study in race-segregated facilities, in theory separate but equal, in fact notoriously unequal. High schools for blacks were virtually unknown. Instructed in archaic ways, in inadequate facilities, in subjects intended to prepare the greatest number for menial labor, many (and not only those who came from impoverished families living on the land as sharecroppers or tenant farmers) habitually ended their schooling long before they reached adolescence. In the burgeoning cities of the country, particularly in the North, while there was no equivalent legally enforced racial segregation, residential requirements, in effect, though by no means completely, separated the races. No one, not even in the most flourishing years of the New Deal, believed that blacks enjoyed equal access to schooling, that the same vocational and professional opportunities were available to them.

In the high schools of pre–World War II America, relatively small numbers, preponderantly white and middle class, opted for the academic course whose diploma allowed them to seek admission to colleges or universities. While their number, by comparison with most European societies, was high, they remained in the United States, as elsewhere, a distinct minority. Vannevar Bush, basing his judgment on his World War II experience, insisted that too much talent was being wasted. For him, equity and the national interest recommended a more substantial commitment to keeping young people in school.

With the earlier introduction of mandatory school attendance and obligatory minimum school-leaving ages, linked to a growing concern with protecting children against premature labor-force entry and work exploitation, federal and state health, labor, and education legislation ought to have resulted in most children being legally required to stay on beyond elementary school. There were sufficient loopholes, however, by law or custom, to allow systematic evasion of these rules. More important, though less observed and less commented on perhaps, were the subtle and pervasive social and racial distinctions that made certain kinds of schooling appropriate for some but virtually impossible for others. Even if one looks only at the high school population of pre–World War II America, one cannot fail to note the high proportion who opted for programs that were commercial or vocational. While no stigma attached to either of these, particularly among children of certain social or ethnic origins, the commercial programs, predominantly clerical and secretarial, had a particular appeal for girls, most often children of working-class parents. The boys, again with differences relating principally to family income and ethnic origins, were as likely to choose vocational programs, often of the simplest mechanical or manual kind—the only ones generally available—as they were to select courses of study that would enable them to go on to college. The schools of America were confirming children in their social origins, and while mobility allowed some always to escape, there was no easy exit for millions of others.

Where state universities existed—particularly in the Middle West, and where racial differences were insignificant or muted, at least until the beginning of the Second World War—high school graduation was a virtual guarantee of an almost tuition-free higher educational opportunity. Many second-generation white American boys and a significantly smaller number of girls opted for State U., where they discovered in varsity sports, fraternities, and sororities, and all manner of extracurricular activities, the essential components of a life-style rapidly establishing itself as part of a new national culture and folklore. Where requirements for admission were low, but where individual state universities resolved to maintain reasonable academic standards, a revolving-door policy of entry and withdrawal took hold. Of the large number admitted, many failed to graduate; a good number left during or at the end of their freshman year.

Even where such high standards prevailed, with its obvious appeal to children of middle-class parents, education in the liberal arts remained fairly uncommon.* Many who went on beyond high school—particularly girls—opted for a local normal school. Joining the ranks of elementary school teachers, generally for a brief time

---

*"The report of the Douglas Commission on Industrial and Technical Education in Massachusetts of 1906 reinforced this trend. Not only was there now a demand for public vocational education in the country, there was a concomitant denigration of 'literary education.' The latter was pinpointed as the weakness of the American school system by Theodore Roosevelt in his annual presidential message to Congress in 1907. Although he spoke only in terms of males, girls' education was also affected. Cooking and sewing courses, labeled in turn housewifery, domestic science, home economics, were considered vocational, and qualified for federal subsidies. Commercial training for girls received no such grants.

"Thus in its first effective role in girls' education, the federal government opted to prepare them for unpaid housekeeping rather than paid jobs." (From Phyllis Stock, *Better Than Rubies: A History of Women's Education* [New York: G. P. Putnam's Sons, 1978], 189–90.)

only, many "retired" at an early age into marriage. Others chose nursing, thought to be a calling particularly suited to a sex held to have unique nurturing and caring capabilities. Still others, terminating their formal education before high school graduation, and using their typing skills acquired in the classroom to join a rapidly growing clerical force increasingly dominated by women, saw work as a temporary financial necessity. Only those who remained unmarried, unable to find suitable or acceptable life partners, sometimes openly disdaining the domesticity that seemed the inevitable concomitant of marriage, entered what would today be called, rather loosely, the professions. For women, this often meant teaching in school or college (the great majority in the former; a less significant number in the latter, sometimes in single-sex institutions, more frequently in second- or third-rate colleges, rarely in research universities.[†])[13]

Librarianship, like nursing and health care, social and philanthropic work, became the professions, paid or unpaid, of women. Occasionally women made their way also into law or medicine, professions chosen overwhelmingly by men in a financial position to pursue years of postgraduate study. By the 1930s, the expense of such professional education generally required students to be sustained by their parents, even where tuition remained moderate or low. The prospect of lost income over many years, followed by minimal income during a long professional training period, did not make such professions very accessible or indeed desirable to many whose parents lacked financial resources.

It is not entirely an accident that Theodore Roosevelt, William Howard Taft, and Woodrow Wilson—the first three presidents of what is chronologically the American twentieth century—should have been the "sons" of Harvard, Yale, and Princeton respectively, that all were the children of genteel Protestant birth who gained immeasurably from their loving, demanding, and concerned parents. Secure in their claim to an ancestry that no American could question,

---

[†]The 1921 study of the Association of University Professors found that in 29 all-male universities, only 2 of approximately 2,000 faculty members were women. In 104 co-ed institutions, there were 1,646 out of a total of 12,869 faculty, or 13 percent. In 14 women's colleges, the faculty was made up of 738 women of a total of 989 faculty members, or nearly 75 percent. However, over all, women faculty members held only 4 percent of the full professorships, 7.9 percent of all professorships, and 23.5 percent of instructorships. This study is cited in Thomas Woody, *A History of Women's Education in the United States*, vol. 2 (New York: The Science Press, 1929), 329.

that gave them substantial psychic and other rewards, they knew that they belonged, incontestably. Each in his own way believed in education and thought the enterprise important, though none could claim himself to have had a significant public school experience. Still, they showed their regard for intelligence and learning in the manner in which they comported themselves, in office and out. No one surveying their lives, knowing their political concerns, could claim that they saw the American school system for what it was, were disconcerted by its failings, or felt an urgent need to argue for making educational opportunity of better quality available for all. While it would be wrong to say that they averted their eyes from the educational experience of large segments of the American population, no one of them, and none of their immediate successors, thought it imperative to argue for radical or even moderate reform that would create new possibilities for blacks, women, children, and adults of various ethnic and racial groups. They, like their fellow-citizens, saw little need to preoccupy themselves with such issues, nor, if the truth be told, did it much engage the great reforming president, who in time succeeded them, Franklin D. Roosevelt.

Indeed, education did not figure prominently as a national political issue at any time in the 1920s or the 1930s, or during World War II. The country, seized with quite other matters believed to be more urgent and consequential, was inclined to leave educational issues to teachers, principals, and school superintendents, to "professionals"—women and men who could be relied on to work closely with impartial school boards and all, in theory, responsible and responsive.

There was enough in American schooling to praise, particularly when contrasted with educational conditions abroad, for those disposed to esteem all things American, to insist on the unique virtues of American education, whatever its minor and inconsequential flaws. Numerous indices—the American passion for statistics guaranteed their elaborate preparation—supported the most sanguine opinions. In the prosperous 1920s, when high school building and public school attendance reached levels previously thought unattainable,[14] when colleges, public and private, admitted men and women in unprecedented numbers and provided them with a broad range of vocational and professional opportunities, there were good reasons to exult in what seemed to be a growing and increasingly prosperous and various educational enterprise. Few at the highest levels of government or industry thought to look beyond the raw statistics, to determine who was being left out and why.

Even in the 1930s, when economic depression created grave problems for many schools, with whole systems becoming virtually bankrupt, the obligation to retrench, reduce salaries, lay off personnel, and pare all unnecessary costs led few to argue for a more rational and equitable system. The economic catastrophe, whatever its causes, did not derive from an insufficiency of willing or able hands. In these circumstances, there was no reason to dwell on the defects of an American school system that enjoyed a well-merited legitimacy; the fact that schools judged children in terms of race, gender, social class, and religion simply reflected the general opinion, indeed the general will.

Given the character and work expectations of so many who lived in these early twentieth-century American immigrant communities, raw, impoverished, and fragile, protected by religious and family networks but defended also by corrupt political party machines (established in the new urban America in some part to safeguard their interests), there were numerous devices for defending men and women who had been effectively ostracized, shunted aside. All manner of hastily created fraternal and neighborhood institutions existed to make their lives more tolerable. Ethnic pride, often an odd amalgam of aggression and self-doubt, which might show itself in rude and hostile expressions of contempt for others, "lesser breeds," not necessarily of other races, but frequently of other religions and languages, created the hazard of perpetual violence and insult, made scarcely more palatable by the ignorance and superstition that they revealed. The American immigrant enclaves were frequently rough and tumble; tolerance, the easy acceptance of others, an explicit dedication to the nation's putative commitment to the equality of all races, religions, and ethnic groups, was fairly uncommon.

Given the social and psychological differences among men and women coming from disparate foreign cultures, the mere fact of their being required to live in close geographic proximity in America's rapidly expanding cities did not make for amity, rarely for close cross-cultural personal or community ties. Indeed, among the many ways in which immigrant groups lived apart, sometimes seeking to perpetuate their isolation, were the markedly different attitudes they showed in confronting the opportunities created by the promise of free public education. Not all immigrant groups grasped with equal ardor the possibilities created by free elementary schooling. Indeed, in time, the same misgivings existed in respect to public secondary education. Many Catholic parents, for example, looked with great favor on what they perceived as the more attractive prospects created by their own church schools, committed to protecting the moral and religious principles of children placed in their care. To secure children against the hazards created by an American value system, too openly Protestant or secular, seemed a very appropriate educational goal.

Increasingly, many of the more affluent Protestant families also sought "protection" of their children by removing them from schools that others of their social class no longer patronized. In doing so, these families created powerful incentives for founding new private boarding and day schools, all aiming in some sense to be "exclusive," best defined as having the power to exclude. Both Catholics and Protestants, for compelling reasons, fearing very different forms of contamination, craved schools where their children would be educated among their own. The austere Protestant schools of the affluent, particularly conspicuous in certain parts of the country, were often unabashedly committed to the values of a specific social class, thought to be a besieged minority seeking to survive in an America becoming less civil, less civilized.

While many of the well-to-do Protestants most active in supporting these new forms of private elementary and secondary education would have been astonished to learn that their motives for separation in any way resembled those of Catholic bishops, priests, and nuns busily building their own schools and staffing them, each, independently, belonging essentially to the same educational universe for all their doctrinal and social differences, were seeking an escape from the American public school system. That the Catholic day schools, with their more socially diverse student populations, showed a certain hostility to the democratic principle of mixing, familiar also to Protestants concerned with avoiding a too-close association with those they conceived to be "alien," was an unpalatable fact not always concealed. In important ways, each was questioning whether the common school, the American public school, was the most appropriate place for their children, whose needs for discipline, attention, moral and spiritual instruction recommended attendance in quite other kinds of institutions.

Such concerns scarcely touched the black world at all, desperately seeking for any kind of instruction. While many felt keenly the injustice of American law and custom that challenged them in their self-esteem, reducing them all to a sort of second-class citizenship, there was little help to be had from federal, state, or local authorities. Apart from the charity and philanthropy of numbers of well-meaning Northern whites, individuals who could be counted on to do something to help, knowing full well that their educational interventions would be resented, regarded by many white Southerners as an unjustified interference by outsiders, the blacks were compelled to rely largely on their own resources. Family, church, and community, segregated and preponderantly poor, were called upon to support black schools in the South, where for eight decades after the abolition of slavery the public support of black education, with few exceptions, was minimal. It is surprising that in these circumstances as much was accomplished as appears to have been the case.

The creation of a handful of superb schools like the Dunbar High School in Washington, D.C., and the Avery Institute in Charleston, South Carolina, suggest that black aspirations for good education, defeated in so many other American communities, were at least occasionally realized. So, also, the accomplishments of the black colleges of the South need to be remarked on. Learning from the much earlier example of such noted midwestern state universities as Michigan and Wisconsin, which had instituted major college preparatory programs allowing for the admission of white students who would otherwise have been barred—having no access to adequate high schools in their region—the black colleges of the South served a population whose secondary schooling was frequently minimal and inferior, only occasionally compensated for by the informal instruction offered by preachers and parents.

To recollect all these things—to dwell on what some may think to be an excessive preoccupation with the defects of American primary and secondary education before 1945—is not to deny the real accomplishments of the American public school system. In certain parts of the country, and for certain groups, free public education worked, creating the opportunities advertised by its more ardent advocates. Nor, for the matter, should the achievements of the several private school systems—Catholic, Lutheran, Jewish, Episcopal, and secular—be denied. Still, a too-generous estimate of what they collectively accomplished ignores many facts: among those who attended these schools, despite the best efforts of teachers, parents, principals, school boards, nurses, and truant officers, all seeking to impose some sort of rational discipline, intellectual as well as personal, the failure to create a deep and abiding commitment to learning was commented on by many. Granted that the strictures of someone like Thorstein Veblen, speaking adversely about America's colleges and universities, may have been too severe,[15] others, including many abroad, thought American primary and secondary schooling to be haphazard, dominated by too great a concern with sports and school spirit to the detriment of scholarship. To say that all too many learned relatively little, that these and other deficiencies showed themselves most glaringly in the intelligence and other testing initiated after the introduction of conscription in World War II, is to make too much of the results of standard aptitude tests. Still, the fact that hundreds of thousands of boys of eighteen, compelled to serve, were found to be both illiterate and innumerate, by even the most rudimentary standards, must be said to indicate some measure of failure.

It takes nothing away from the American schools' real achievement with millions of others to note these deficiencies. Nor, for that matter, does it diminish the role of American elementary and secondary education to say that it failed almost entirely to serve all the races; insufficient funding, combined with inadequate and uninspired teaching, reinforced by distinctive forms of American nativism, provincialism, prejudice, and class feeling combined to keep many out of schools almost entirely, providing them with such superficial instruction as to make it all meaningless, almost useless. Countless others, less badly served, were compelled to accept inferior instruction, thought to be sufficient for the world of work.

This, it must be said, is not the plaint of those who have argued that the pre–World War II traditional schools, with their emphasis on memorization, correct deportment, respect for authority, and perpetual recitation and testing, failed to understand or appreciate the psychic and intellectual needs of children. While the principles of "progressive education" never effectively ousted or replaced the more traditional pedagogical practices of the large urban school systems, they had an influence. Principally serving greatly expanded white middle-class populations, recently removed to the suburbs, who had no great wish to send their children away to boarding schools and saw no reason to enroll them in private schools for which they would have to pay tuition, suburban progressive schools provided alternative education. These parents, like so many others, sought protection; they would find it in public schools of their own, intended for others of their social class. They hoped that these schools, with their innovative curricula and their commitment to certain kinds of freedom, would prepare their children admirably for the colleges and professions for which they were destined. While these schools offered much in the way of pedagogical innovation, they never seriously addressed the political and social issues that made American education class-ridden, religiously, ethnically, and racially separated. The "progressives" were doing precisely what others were also attempting, protecting their own.

Because of a studied indifference to the continuities (and changes) characteristic of American elementary and secondary education in this century, there is a certain unwillingness to confront certain disconcerting facts. The proposition that in educational matters, Woodrow Wilson's America was not so different from that of Harding, Coolidge, Hoover, Roosevelt, and Truman, that more fundamental change began, very tentatively, in Eisenhower's time, proceeded more rapidly under Kennedy and Johnson, and has taken on wholly new dimensions under a covey of Republican presidents who have occupied the White House almost continuously for over twenty years, may seem unnecessarily contentious, particularly if it is suggested also that many of these changes have been unintended.

Educational issues, once concealed, scarcely spoken of in major public political arenas, particularly at the national level, have claimed new attention. This is not to suggest that late-twentieth-century Americans are significantly more preoccupied with the problems of the "invisible" parts of the population, though they may speak of them more frequently, and, given the political changes that have occurred in voting rights in recent decades, somewhat more circumspectly. In the attention given to America's schools and cities by the media, the jubilation of an earlier day is difficult to sustain. Inevitably, less exaggerated and extravagant claims are made for institutions so recently praised for their uniqueness.

While the educational Cassandras of our day, anxious to demonstrate and document the "decline and fall" of once noble educational institutions, recently sapped in their foundations, have gained a certain notoriety for their views, their innocence of history—their insistence on equating their personal autobiographies with the life of the nation—have limited the utility of their nostalgic proposals. Though we may, for the sake of convenience, attach presidential names to the two distinct parts of the century, a good argument can be made that the specific educational policies crafted in Washington, D.C., since the end of World War II have counted for relatively little, that other federal policies, touching on health, family, and welfare, together with any number of judicial decisions, have counted much more heavily. More important than either, however, have been the major economic, social, and cultural changes that have taken place in the country that have had little to do with federal politics as practiced in the nation's capital. They have contributed to the transformation of an American society that has suddenly discovered itself to be immensely rich, imagining itself, quite correctly, to be also very poor, knowing neither how to evaluate its wealth nor how to define its poverty. Unprecedented affluence has made the grinding poverty of the inner cities seem obscene in ways that would have been inconceivable in Wilson's day. It has also made many acutely conscious of how much family and race continue to define an individual's possibilities in life.

Despite incomparably larger federal expenditures for elementary and secondary school education, wholly unprecedented in the pre–World War II national budgets, despite judicial, legislative, and executive actions taken to effect school and work integration, together with the outlawing of various traditional forms of discrimination, including the enforcement of the provisions of the Civil Rights Act of 1964, and the larger appropriations voted by state legislatures, responding to various kinds of public pressure, not to speak of expressions of alarm from business, professional, and other powerful economic constituencies, the bright promises of yesterday have not been realized. Lyndon Johnson's "War on Poverty" has not been won; it has been replaced by a new domestic war, the "War on Drugs." Johnson, who wished to be remembered as the century's "education president," recognized the importance of Head Start and understood what he and Congress had achieved with the passage of

Title I of the Elementary and Secondary Education Act. Yet, neither of these admittedly precedent-breaking federal educational interventions—and not only because of an absence of sufficient funding—have been sufficient to instruct another would-be education president in what needs to be done.

Now that the post–World War II era is definitively ended—1989 did much to make that credible to a society prepared to believe that certain things were preordained and would never change—it may be useful to think objectively and critically of what the Second World War did to change America, how much it may have set the country on a course that needs now to be abandoned. Victory in war, as most informed observers know, is always preferable to defeat; it exacts a price, however, and the time may now be appropriate for the United States to consider what price it may have paid for its relatively easy triumph over dangerous and sinister forces. Such questions are too rarely asked in the United States today.

That World War II made certain forms of traditional American prejudice intolerable, that it made specific conventional American practices with regard to race and religion seem unjust—particularly where they involved the virtual exclusion of individuals from education or employ on no basis other than race or religion—is frequently mentioned. Just as significant, perhaps, is another change, less frequently remarked on. The whole concept of majority and minority as de Tocqueville saw it may today be in need of drastic revision. In a society where women outnumber men, where the aged are numerous and the young are conspicuous, where blacks and others, preponderantly poor, are bearing children in numbers that make white birth rates seem positively regressive, where a state as large and industrially powerful as California is expected to have a demographic profile by the end of the century that mocks the "Anglo" prejudices of yesterday, there is a compelling need to look again at what majorities and minorities are, how they relate to each other, what they may be expected to agitate for in the last decade of the twentieth century and in the first decades of the twenty-first. Will the behavior patterns created after 1945 perpetuate themselves, or will they be displaced? Can they be maintained when the population mix of the society is again changing so dramatically?

To ask such questions is to betray a partiality for a truism that may be considerably more incendiary than others that are more avowedly ideological. It is to suggest that we have yet to understand what has happened to American society since 1945, and since the country so blithely extended its influence over great parts of the world, entering wars as if they were wholly natural events, doing so in a fashion that would have shocked the architects of the American Constitution. Or, to put the matter another way, we may still be thinking too much in terms of United States power, mistaking a temporary superiority achieved at a time when many others had fallen, taking that to be a final judgment of American democratic superiority.

That immediate postwar habit has not been lost. Looking at issues of race and religion, for example, congratulating ourselves on the undeniable progress made in extinguishing all manner of crude and irrational prejudices and injustices, there is a definite disinclination even to consider the possibility that everything in these sensitive areas, particularly as it pertains to race, remains to be done. This, an unsettling idea even to those given to a certain skepticism about the recent accomplishments of the American democracy, must be entertained.

With respect to literacy, candor requires an admission that few societies in history have given so many of their citizens educational experiences of greater and more imaginative variety, at so many different levels.* Not the least of the accomplishments of the country has been to dignify so many subjects, so many skills, and to offer instruction in all. There has been a refreshing unwillingness for Americans to make certain activities appear more important than others, to "privilege" them in one way or other. If we have found it perfectly reasonable for a former movie star to inhabit the White House, and for grasping and not wholly orthodox business tycoons to gain fame and fortune through their manipulative efforts at corporate takeovers, we have not known how to dignify whole races—including those who have been on this continent for centuries—particularly when they are impoverished and at risk. On a more general level, we have also lacked the capacity to show that fine discrimination which knows how to dignify an essential service, and to do so in a way that is neither patronizing nor maudlin.

---

*Since the year 1890, the secondary school population has practically doubled every ten years. The increase in the high school population from 1890 to 1930 was twenty times greater than that of the general population. (See James H. Bedford, *Vocational Interests of Secondary School Students* [Los Angeles: Society for Occupational Research, 1938], 1.)

Where the concept of dignity is so little understood, where the concern with equality, which men as different in their ideological proclivities as Jean-Jacques Rousseau in the eighteenth century and Alexis de Tocqueville in the nineteenth saw to be central, we take pride—or used to—in American social engineering techniques, in the capacity to be pragmatic. If the schooling system has broken down, the national task must be to find the cause of the breakdown, to repair it. Taking it to be some sort of social malady, we search incessantly for cures. The responses are all predictable; many are now shopworn. Some of us choose to find the culprit in teachers, unwilling or unable to teach, lacking the competencies they profess to have; others condemn parsimonious legislatures, unprepared to make appropriations of the size thought to be essential; still others dwell on the toll taken by swollen political and educational bureaucratic establishments, unwilling to cut their numbers, to reduce red tape, their principal commodity of exchange; a few choose to blame parents, not only the children who today bear children, mostly illegitimate—a term now much out of fashion—but the millions of others, maintaining broken homes, who have scant time or interest for their children's welfare, who neglect them very much as strangers do. And, always, there are those who blame the youths themselves, undisciplined, unruly, knowing little, showing scant respect for others, having little regard for themselves. And, when all these explanations fail, one asks what the man in the White House is doing, what it means that senators, representatives, and other federal officials are so impervious to the nation's educational needs. The final scapegoat—the ultimate expression of our post–World War II American mass-media civilization—is that iniquitous force called television, with its violence and its inanity, its failure to instruct in anything that can be said to have civic value.

This, an abbreviated though not wholly distorted litany of the complaints most frequently heard today, implies that remedies exist for our educational distress. They generally involve some major new federal financial commitments and a restructuring of schools and their curricula. While both may indeed be necessary, defining these remedies in more precise terms, making them reasonably palatable to large publics, is a task that goes well beyond the capacities of many who seriously recommend them. That the problems of illiteracy and poor schooling have been endemic in American society, that they are deeply rooted in long-standing social habits, not easily transformed by federal or state legislation, or by school reorganization, is a proposition too disconcerting for many even to consider.

Where so much effort has been made to find relief for social situations recognized to be grave, where money and time has been expended over many years, the idea that all such remedies need now to be supplemented must seem bizarre. Yet, it is precisely this kind of thinking that is lacking today. There is no Japan or Federal Republic to consult that will teach the United States how to become productive again; there is no road back to the teacher-directed and teacher-controlled system of education that worked so effectively for those ready to accept or tolerate such leadership. If the White House is indeed a "bully pulpit," the message cannot be "Tighten your belts; look to your principles; remember that you are an American." Such injunctions carry little weight in our free-spending, wasteful, and skeptical age, in which too many constantly search for "the main chance."

If the United States wishes seriously to provide some sort of meaningful literacy to all, it cannot do this without a major revolution in its social habits: it must give attention to its regrettable tendency to patronize or ignore the poor, particularly those who belong to minorities, while it insists on its good intentions. Nor can the country continue to infantilize and cosset the white majority, not so much because such preference gives an advantage resented by others, but because it contributes to a kind of innocence among the privileged young that makes them incapable of understanding the world they live in. It leads them to exaggerate their own competencies, to mistake money and celebrity for achievement, all the while despising or ignoring those who are permanently down, especially those thought to be responsible for their own misfortunes.

To ignore the poor is serious enough; to be afraid of them, having no real rapport with them, to apply subtle double standards, and to avoid any kind of criticism of their work even when it is patently shoddy is to insult them. When those who are privileged are equally ignored, though in different ways, allowed to slide through, never made to understand the dignity of work, the necessity of choice, the importance of service, the results are as we find them today. Too many bearing college certificates are barely literate. Very few have skills that show a real capacity for numeracy on any meaningful level.

The habit of the society to "privilege" all learning has allowed too many to learn too little, to ignore things that are essential, not only in the making of an educated man or woman, but in discerning what it means to be morally and intellectually responsible.

Again, in this regard, de Tocqueville is an excellent teacher. Dwelling on the role of law and religion in early-nineteenth-century America, he recognized that the respect given each guaranteed a fidelity to principles that transcended the present, that led the nation to show respect for things not wholly contemporary, entirely temporal. Without ever using the term *vocation,* de Tocqueville understood its meaning, with all of its sixteenth-century Protestant connotations. Until teaching is again seen as a vocation, until its unique importance in the contemporary world is recognized, no provision for salary increases or for additional instruction to make teachers more proficient can significantly alter the profession. This is not to argue against improved conditions of work, against any number of other recommendations calculated to attract more able individuals to teaching. It is only to insist that something of a more fundamental nature needs to be attempted. The profession must be given a dignity that it has lacked for far too long.

If medicine and law reformed themselves as professions in the United States late in the nineteenth century—the latter seeking to retrieve an eminence it had lost, the former having never enjoyed very high repute—the time has come for education to attempt a comparable reformation, perhaps in time leading other professions to do the same. It will not be accomplished by simple devices, by schools of education reforming curricula, by teachers' salaries being raised. It can be achieved perhaps by the profession assuming a much more deliberate moral stance, which would establish the unique role of education in the modern world, which would enlist the support and enthusiasm of the American people. The nation is threatened with becoming not only less prosperous, but less relevant to the concerns of the world. The United States is losing its reputation for modernity, efficiency, empathy, and sympathy. In the effort to create school systems that will serve the social and economic needs of the society in ways that it never previously thought to do, the country has a unique opportunity to demonstrate again its democratic potential.

So, also, returning to an older tradition, the concept of vocation needs to be thought of again in respect to parenting. To say this is not to defer to any specific religious creed, let alone to suggest that certain contemporary social phenomena—frequent divorce, sexual promiscuity, drug abuse, and the like, incontestably grave social conditions that affect all behavior—are at the root of the contemporary education crisis. It does suggest, however, that children need to be seen and treated as such, cared for in a way that repudiates the neglect common among adults who are themselves unschooled and poor, but also among many others who are neither, whose ambition to be cool and successful masks another perhaps even more insidious form of poverty. So long as there is a middle-class emphasis on the "sophistication" of certain children—worldly and well traveled—and an implicit or explicit disdain for the "barbarism" of those who choose to subscribe to other values, with an even greater disdain, rarely expressed openly, for those of other races and social classes unfortunate enough to be compelled to live in the urban deserts of this country, there will be little charity, great illusion, and perpetual fear.

The most urgent need of the moment is not only to gaze on those who are disadvantaged and to determine what can be done for them. Just as important, in my view, is to consider why this society, over so many decades, has been inhospitable to certain concrete social possibilities, including the all-important one of not allowing skin color or family circumstance to govern one's idea of what is educationally possible. In the twenty-first century, where so many will carry little in the way of ancestral baggage, of the conventional kind thought by so many in the nineteenth century to be important and dignified, dignity must attach to the individual. This can neither be mandated nor compelled; it is a free gift which reasonable people, looking to the future, may wish to bestow on their fellow beings. Some very small distance has certainly been traversed since 1945, since Vannevar Bush wrote, and this has been principally in respect to providing new educational access to American women and particular ethnic and religious minorities. A much greater distance waits to be traveled.

ENDNOTES

[1]Stephan Thernstrom, ed., *Harvard Encyclopedia of American Ethnic Groups* (Cambridge: Belknap Press, 1980), 1045.

²Donald J. Brogue, *The Population of the United States: Historical Trends and Future Projections* (London: The Free Press, 1985), 39.

³Ibid.

⁴George D. Stoddard, *The Meaning of Intelligence* (New York: Macmillan, 1943), 137; Clarence S. Yoakum and Robert M. Yerkes, *Army Mental Tests* (New York: Henry Holt and Company, 1920), 194.

⁵Edward R. Lewis, *America: Nation or Confusion? A Study of Our Immigration Problems* (New York: Harper & Brothers, 1928).

⁶Richard Alonzo Schermerhorn, *These Our People: Minorities In American Culture* (Boston: D.C. Heath, 1949), 308–9, 337–38, 370–71.

⁷U.S. Bureau of the Census, *Abstract of the 15th Census of the United States* (Washington, D.C.: U.S. Government Printing Office, 1933), 142–43.

⁸Mabel M. Smythe, *The Black American Reference Book* (Englewood Cliffs, N.J.: Prentice-Hall, 1976), 172.

⁹U.S. Bureau of the Census, *Abstract of the 15th Census*, 275.

¹⁰Ibid.

¹¹U.S. Bureau of the Census, *200 Years of U.S. Census Taking: Population and Housing Questions, 1790–1990* (Washington, D.C.: U.S. Government Printing Office, 1989), 38, 45, 61.

¹²Vannevar Bush, *Science: The Endless Frontier* (Washington: U.S. Government Printing Office, 1945), 147.

¹³James H. Bedford, *Vocational Interests of Secondary School Students* (Los Angeles: Society for Occupational Research, 1938), 38, and also see study completed by the Association of University Professors in 1921, cited by Thomas Woody, *A History of Women's Education in the United States*, vol. 2 (New York: The Science Press, 1929), 329.

¹⁴Bedford, 1.

¹⁵Thorstein Veblen, *The Higher Learning in America* (New York: B. W. Huebsch, 1918).

Moving Out of Our Shadows

Emerson once said that most of the shadows in one's life are caused by standing in one's own sunshine. There is no question that the unevenness in quality as well as quantity of education in America has cast a long shadow upon the path of American children, especially upon poor and minority children. But how much have we stood in our own sunshine?

When I graduated from elementary school in the early 1940s, most of my forty-plus classmates started high school with me, but fewer than ten completed high school. Two of those ten went on to college. Most of my classmates secured manufacturing jobs and were able to do reasonably well in providing for themselves and their families. We Americans accepted this educational division.

Civil rights came to the schoolhouse during the 1960s and 1970s. Grudgingly, we became more inclusive in our schools, and "all God's children" could attend public schools, but over time we found ways to distribute education unequally. The 1980s resulted in the rich getting richer and the poor becoming poorer.

As we enter the 1990s, we are beginning to realize that even with the highly touted education reform of the 1980s, a crisis exists in the back rows of America's public school classrooms. Our economy is failing, and one-third or more of the new workers in the next decade will be the kind of persons whom we have historically undereducated or not educated.

We have neglected such large segments of the population, we now have more to do than just improve the quality of education. We must first improve the quality of life for many of our children in order to obtain better education. *U.S. News and World Report* in November 1988 stated the following facts:

In One Day
2,753	teenagers get pregnant
1,099	have abortions
367	teens miscarry
1,287	teenagers give birth
666	babies are born to women who have had inadequate prenatal care

In One Day
- 72 babies die before one month of life
- 110 babies die before their first birthday
- 8 children die from gunshot wounds
- 5 teenagers commit suicide
- 609 teenagers get gonorrhea or syphilis

In One Day
- 988 children are abused
- 3,288 children run away from home
- 49,322 children are in public juvenile correctional facilities
- 2,269 illegitimate children are born
- 2,989 children see their parents divorced

At last we adults must realize that the basic relationship between children and their elders is that adults do things to children and are also done to.

We will beat the literacy problem in America only when our nation's children start their school day healthy, fed, supported, and not violated, not drugged, and not distracted by television or the street.

What is so frustrating is that if one looks closely at the states, and at the processes and programs in place, one sees clearly that in many places progress is being made, some of it dramatic. That we know how to teach neglected youth is also clear, and this know-how augurs well for all youth.

The recent report on the Quality Education for Minorities Project is an outstanding example of how we can provide education of good quality for all God's children.

We have robbed the future for too long. We must invest in our children so that they can meet tomorrow's need. Perhaps then our children will not stand in our shadows.

Alonzo A. Crim
The Benjamin E. Mays Professor
of Urban Educational Leadership
Georgia State University

Libraries and the Attack on Illiteracy

A growing problem in all America's large cities is the illiteracy of so many of their citizens. New York City has an estimated 1.5 million people over the age of sixteen who cannot read a newspaper or the instructions on a bottle of medicine. For these adults such simple tasks mean defeat, shame, and confusion. The consequences of illiteracy—unemployment or underemployment, social ostracism, the feeling of failure as a parent—all have one thing in common: the fear of being discovered.

Most programs to help such people are based on schools, but local public libraries have an edge. Adults can come to them without embarrassment and work in areas not furnished for children. In addition, libraries can do what schools seldom can: tailor literacy training to the immediate needs and interests of the learners. Their goals can be as different as reading bedtime stories, improving job skills, getting a driver's license, or simply filling out the innumerable forms for public assistance that are so much a part of the life of the poor.

The three New York Library systems have a total of 200 branches located in every part of the city, including many in its poorest areas. The New York Public Library, for example, runs eight literacy programs involving 1,000 students, some 50 teachers, and 200 volunteers. That effort, however, is dogged by money constraints, and each of our eight centers turns away at least as many people as it is able to accept.

The political leaders of our great cities could easily mobilize their libraries in a concerted attack on illiteracy. For instance, in New York City, if each of the 200 branches dealt with 200 learners, these libraries would reach 40,000 people each year. Experience shows that once the libraries have set a pattern, other local institutions will follow their example, borrow their people, and extend their work even further.

It is easy to create a stereotype of people who are illiterate. They are by no means all unemployed; many in New York hold jobs; their intelligence and insights are those of mature and experienced adults. Volunteer teachers find them rewarding to work with and are enthusiastic about the progress many make.

The reward for the city is enormous expansion of human potential. A literacy center in the Bronx publishes an anthology of writings by its students; one of them tells how the classes he has attended "are helping people like me not just to read but to feel good about themselves." Libraries know that one of their principal tasks is the enablement of citizens. In each of our great cities, that enablement lies ready to hand, if only we have the urban will and the budget commitment to make it work.

Timothy S. Healy, S.J.
Director
The New York Public Library

Business and the Schools

Collaboration with schools and occasionally school systems has been the primary mode in which business has involved itself to date with elementary and secondary education. Such programs as the Boston Compact are examples of business groups working together either to provide jobs for graduates of local high schools or to provide money for school projects that improve students' education. Many companies have participated in Adopt-a-School programs, and these have been particularly helpful in alerting business to the reality of children's and teachers' lives. Other companies have provided school equipment, usually equipment they have manufactured. Employees' mentoring of schoolchildren, many of whom have too few caring and competent adults in their lives, is another useful way in which business has aided the schools. Eugene Lang's promise of college support and provision of ancillary services to junior high school students if they complete high school is yet another example of motivational and financial aid to schoolchildren.

Symbolically such local programs are extremely valuable. They will not, however, provide the fundamental change that the nation requires in its schools. These programs are either too dependent on precarious relationships between employees and school people and the children themselves, or they fail to go to the heart of the issue: changing the circumstances of children's lives as well as the expectations and effectiveness of schools. The American system of caring for our young and of educating them needs profound renovation, and these palliatives will not accomplish that. They may, however, set the stage so that fundamental reform becomes more likely.

What is most important about these business-school partnerships at the local level is that they give children new and powerful advocates for the schooling they need. This power is particularly important for children in the cities, where until the advent of such business interests, there were woefully few effective supporters for children or for education.

Schools have traditionally depended on outside forces to hold them accountable for their performance. In many wealthy suburban communities, students' acceptance to the colleges of their choice has been the litmus test of whether the schools were doing a good job. In other suburban towns, the success of the football or basketball teams has been the community index of school performance. For children attending urban public schools, most of such effective external pressures from family and community have been missing in recent years. Through its involvement with children, business may provide the kind of boost that the disadvantaged need from their school systems and that wealthy suburban children already enjoy within theirs.

Patricia Albjerg Graham
Dean
Graduate School of Education
Harvard University

Comment on Scientific Literacy: Why Is It So Difficult?

Surely there is no longer any need to add to the overwhelming evidence of the dismal general state of scientific literacy in this country. Let us make the cheerful assumption that, pushed by all these data, policymakers and taxpayers alike are becoming serious about remedying the sorry state, on a large enough scale and with sufficient resources to be effective. The more obvious obstacles to overcome range from underdemanding parents and underprepared, overworked teachers to insufficient numbers of scientists who are interested in helping to find remedies.

But there is another handicap rarely thought about. To focus on it, consider the definition of the chief task of education given by Friedrich Schleiermacher in the first decade of the nineteenth century: *The aim of education is the replacement of the child's internal intellectual chaos by a coherent world picture.* It is a daunting formulation, which seems to me to apply first of all to scientific literacy. Nevertheless, it is too limited for our time, and not only because education can no longer stop with childhood. Anyone who has the task of introducing a typically underprepared class of college students to, say, the rudiments of physics, knows that it is much more difficult than removing a preexisting internal chaos of ideas, or imprinting the right equations on a slate kept clean by previous ignorance. Inducing an acceptable scientific world picture through education is especially difficult. For as one of my students—brought up with the inalienable right to choose in everything—put it, the worldview of modern science appears to be "not optional, and therefore in a sense totalitarian." By this he meant that in a humanistic area the college catalogue gave him a wide choice of topics for what is acceptable; if one did not like to gain an understanding of literature through the *Iliad* or Shakespeare, there were many entirely different paths open. But to reach even an elementary understanding of physics, such topics as Newtonian gravity and the nuclear atom seemed inescapable.

Moreover, the process of initiation into a modern scientific world picture, coming as it usually does long past the stage of high natural curiosity in early childhood, is fundamentally invasive. After the first few years, the child's chaos has been replaced by something much worse and more permanent than mere ignorance: by a robust counterpicture, a self-generated set of ideas about nature that is quietly called on to respond to the phenomena. Such a schema deserves the term "science sauvage" (*pace* Lévi-Strauss).

That is the site of the painful struggle. Long ago I gave from time to time one of those one-year courses in physical science during which the students, initially pure Aristotelians, were to be made over into Newtonians by Thanksgiving, Einsteinians by Easter, and Heisenbergians by mid-May. Among the more honest and insightful ones, there occasionally was a student who would break into tears as the intuitions were being forcibly reshaped. (More recently, the curriculum has been "improved" by making such full-year courses give way to mere one-semester exposures; there are fewer tears, and the main advantage is that now nobody can delude himself with the belief that the job can be done at all at the college level in this manner.)

During the past decade, some good research results have come from educators and cognitive scientists exploring the content of the preexisting, naive-scientific world picture. In it, material bodies come to a stop unless they continue to be propelled; electricity flows through wires as water does through pipes, only much faster; space is a big container in which matter appeared at the beginning of time; time is everywhere the same and marches on inexorably; science and engineering are hardly distinguishable; the pattern of cause and effect works most of the time, but incomprehensible and magical things do occasionally intervene; science provides truth, but now and then everything known previously turns out to have been entirely wrong, and a revolution is needed to establish the real truth. And so forth.

The least interesting thing is that all of this is wrong. The naive world picture is a legitimate form of knowledge in the sense that it is functional. It organizes and explains, up to a point, what is going on; it is a sturdy framework for interacting with the environment. Once a "baby-talk" scientific world picture has been allowed to establish itself, the internal resistance against advancing to the more sophisticated one can be overwhelming. The modern world, in which evolution is central on many levels, from biology to cosmology; where absolutes in science have disappeared, and classical causality has been replaced by a probabilistic one; where concepts are often nonvisualizable and expressed in mathematical formulas—all this is counterintuitive to the point of being sometimes repellent. For the young person, the labor of getting from the Aristotelian to the post-Darwinian and post-Einsteinian world picture is herculean.

Moreover, there is an ever-increasing distance between the two worlds. Whereas the distance from baby language to tolerable verbal literacy has remained fairly constant from century to century, and can be overcome in principle in the first decade of life, this is of course not at all true for the case of science. Gaining scientific literacy is not merely a matter of evolving from primitive talk to a more complex language but of replacing a whole, originally functional worldview, with all its concepts, hypotheses, and metaphors—and then of amending the replacement constantly. It is really no wonder that so many become embarrassed and turn against the effort itself, and that some of the best and brightest feel pain and resentment about their disconnection from one of the accomplishments of our civilization.

The transition between the two worlds is so difficult also because of a second gap. A child learning to speak a more mature form of language gets help from adults who understand and even respect "baby talk" but who of course also experienced the transformation themselves. The learner can constantly interact with them as the early language evolves into the new one. That is not the case for a changeover from the primitive to the new scientific world picture. In that case, the adults, except for some of the teachers, are themselves usually still stranded not far from the level of baby talk. During the crucial early years, in the typical American schoolroom the hope and necessity for doing some science every day is still only a utopian dream.

Such facts have to be considered before reasonable remedies can be designed. But I take comfort in the evidence—for example, in the recently begun projects of the American Association for the Advancement of Science and the National Science Teachers Association—that this is happening.

Gerald Holton
Mallinckrodt Professor of Physics and
Professor of the History of Science
Harvard University